Lecture Notes in Computer Science 3908

Commenced Publication in 1973
Founding and Former Series Editors:
Gerhard Goos, Juris Hartmanis, and Jan van Leeuwen

Alain Bui   Marc Bui   Thomas Böhme
Herwig Unger (Eds.)

Innovative Internet Community Systems

5th International Workshop, IICS 2005
Paris, France, June 20-22, 2005
Revised Papers

 Springer

Volume Editors

Alain Bui
Université de Reims Champagne Ardenne
Departement de Mathématiques et Informatique
Campus du Moulin de la Housse, BP 1039
51687 Reims Cedex 2, France
E-mail: alain.bui@univ-reims.fr

Marc Bui
Université Paris 8
Laboratoire Recherche en Informatique avancée
c/o EPHE - Complex Modelling Systems and Cognition
41 rue G. Lussac, 75005 Paris, France
E-mail: mbui@ephe-sorbonne.org

Thomas Böhme
Technische Universität Ilmenau
Institut für Mathematik
98683 Ilmenau, Germany
E-mail: thomas.boehme@tu-ilmenau.de

Herwig Unger
Universität Rostock
Institut für Informatik
A.-Einstein-Str. 23, 18051 Rostock, Germany
E-mail: hunger@informatik.uni-rostock.de

Library of Congress Control Number: 2006924583

CR Subject Classification (1998): C.2, H.3-5, D.2, I.2.11, K.4.1

LNCS Sublibrary: SL 3 – Information Systems and Application, incl. Internet/Web
and HCI

ISSN   0302-9743
ISBN-10   3-540-33973-6 Springer Berlin Heidelberg New York
ISBN-13   978-3-540-33973-1 Springer Berlin Heidelberg New York

Springer is a part of Springer Science+Business Media

springer.com

© Springer-Verlag Berlin Heidelberg 2006
Printed in Germany

Typesetting: Camera-ready by author, data conversion by Scientific Publishing Services, Chennai, India
Printed on acid-free paper   SPIN: 11749776   06/3142   5 4 3 2 1 0

Preface

This volume of *Lecture Notes in Computer Science* contains all accepted papers of the 5th International Conference on Innovative Internet Community Systems (I[2]CS), which was held at the Sorbonne in Paris, from June 20–22, 2005.

The previous four conferences in Ilmenau, Rostock, Leipzig (Germany) and Guadalajara (Mexico) developed the profile of this event. Traditionally, there are topics discussed in three main aspects. All of them must be considered in a united manner in order to investigate and understand the emergence and evolution of communities in the Internet: knowledge about networking, content and text processing as well as theory. The goal of the I2CS workshop is to bring researchers from both industry and academic fields together to discuss current progress and future developments in these areas and to eliminate the gap between theory and application.

At this point, we want to express immense gratitude to all the authors of the submitted papers and to the members of the international Program Committee for their contribution to the success of the event and a program of high quality. In a peer-to-peer review process, 17 papers were selected out of 27 submissions. Three reviewers evaluated all the papers and sent the authors comments on their work. The three invited talks discussed the innovation process revisited by the Internet, GRID computing and aspects of learning in communities. These talks were given at the beginning of each conference day, which provided a great framework for the following presentations. Sorbonne, one of the oldest and most famous universities in this world, as well as Paris gave us an inspiring environment for intensive and fruitful discussions.

Our next conference, the I[2]CS 2006, will take place in the charming city Neuchatel in Switzerland. We hope that most of our former and present participants as well as many new colleagues will take this opportunity to continue exchanging their knowledge and experiences devoted to the development and use of Internet communities.

June 2005

Alain and Marc Bui
Thomas Böhme
Herwig Unger

Organization

Steering Committee

T. Böhme, Ilmenau, Germany
G. Heyer, Leipzig, Germany
M. Bui, Paris, France (Local Chair)
A. Mikler, Denton, TX, USA
H. Unger, Rostock, Germany (Conference Chair)

Scientific Committee

A. Anbulagan, Canberra, Australia
A. Bui, Reims, France (Local Chair)
A. Brandstädt, Rostock, Germany
J. Brooke, Manchester, UK
N. Deo, Orlando FL, USA
D. Dergint, Curitiba, Brazil
K.-P. Fähnrich, Leipzig, Germany
H. Fouchal, Guadeloupe, France
T. Haupt, Mississippi State, USA
N. Kalyaniwalla, Halifax, Canada
P. Kropf, Montreal, Canada
M. Kunde, Ilmenau, Germany
V.M. Larios-R., Guadalajara, Mexico

I. Lavallée, Paris, France
C. Lecerf, Nîmes, France
S. Lukosch, Hagen, Germany
Y. Paker, London, England
U. Quasthoff, Leipzig, Germany
M.A.R. Dantas, Florianopolis, Brazil
F. Ramos, Guadalajara, Mexico
A. Ryjov, Moscow, Russia
D. Tavangarian, Rostock, Germany
D. Tutsch, Berlin, Germany
T. Ungerer, Augsburg, Germany
P. Young-Hwan, Seoul, South Korea

Organizing Committee

A. Bui, M. Bui, F. Jouen, C. Butelle (France)

Table of Contents

Innovation Processes Revisited by Internet

Serge Soudoplatoff

Partnership & Martech Director, Co-founder and President, Almatropie
serge@soudoplatoff.org
www.soudoplatoff.com

Abstract. Internet, far from being a simple technology, is truly changing our way of life. Just as the invention of the alphabet, or the printing, Internet is a fundamental technology that we have designed, but which, in turn, is impacting our behavior, our relationship with the world and ourselves. By empowering ordinary citizens, it helps us to face a cognitive paradigm shift. This is deeply rooted in the design process of Internet, which has led a new way to perform innovation.

1 Some Internet Fundamentals

1.1 The Deep Roots of Internet

When trying to understand why Internet became so important, two very important quotes come to mind.

The first one is from a extremely well-known visionary, whose work was the great announcement of the Internet era: Marshall McLuhan.[1] Not only did he foresee the "global village", not only did he say this sentence, whose implications are very difficult to admit: "The medium is the message", not only he said that technologies are extensions of our bodies, but he positioned one of the fundamental revolution that Internet is helping us to achieve: to transform us from "passive" spectators into "hot" actors. This is to be seen not in the official web sites of standard media (press, TV, radios), simple transcriptions of the content from one medium to the Internet, but in the numerous personal web pages, blogs, web forums, peer to peer systems, where million of people are exchanging ideas, contents, passion, objects, or anything that can possibly can be exchanged.

The second quote, albeit close to McLuhan's ideas, is a more comprehensive highlight of the relationship between mankind and technology. It comes from a French paleontologist, André Leroi-Gourhan, who understood the co-design between the hand and the tool. As soon as the standing position was adopted by our ancestors, the hand became free to create tools, which, in turn, changed the people, and also prepared for the invention of speech, something quite fundamental for the evolution of mankind, and the importance of interpersonal communication.

Therefore, same as the crane is an extension of our arm, and helps leverage our physical strength, Internet can be viewed as one technology which is the extension of

---

[1] Though many high quality web sites refer to Marshall McLuhan's work, there exists an official one, which can be found at http://www.marshallmcluhan.com/.

A. Bui et al. (Eds.): IICS 2005, LNCS 3908, pp. 1–16, 2006.

our brain, and helps amplify our cognitive capacities. But Internet was not the first technology which helped us in such a way. Our knowledge, our interactions, have been impacted by many other technologies, of which some major one has accompanied a society paradigm shift.

We can propose that there have been three major cognitive paradigm shifts, all based on two innovations. The invention of writing, and 3000 years later, the invention of the alphabet, have been along with the transformation of a nomadic type of society, based on hunting and fishing, to a more sedentary type of society, with the development of agriculture and breeding. The invention of the book, and 500 years later, of printing, has been the necessary technological condition to create the Renaissance, the great discoveries, and the industrial world. The invention of the computer, not in the computational sense, but in the cognitive meaning, and 25 years later, of the Internet, is what we need to move from the industrial world to something else, which is usually called either "the knowledge society", or the "communication society". We shall propose, at the end of this paper, another definition: we are entering the "interaction" society, where the big issue which we need to address is complexity.

Table 1. The three major knowledge manipulation paradigm shifts

	Knowledge representation shift	**Knowledge broadcast shift**
Farming societies	Writing	Alphabet
Industrial societies	Book	Print
Interaction societies	Computer	Internet

It is important to stress the fundamental innovation which is the alphabet. Without the alphabet, abstractions are more difficult to represent. It is a fact that the explosion of knowledge, in many fields such as medicine, astronomy, mathematics, physics, philosophy, that the ancient Greeks have created was based on the usage of an alphabet. More important for the creation of the Internet, without the alphabet, there is no code; the computer simply could not exist.

We may say that the deep roots of Internet shall be found in those innovations: the writing, the alphabet, the book, the printing. The same debates, as the one we experience nowadays about the real importance of Internet, existed during all those transition times. The most famous one is probably the denegation of writing by Socrates, who used to say that "writing does not convey knowledge, but the illusion of knowledge". A sentence that we have heard so many times about Internet…

1.2 Three Industries

It is important to recall how the Internet was built, from an industrial perspective. Its very innovative building mechanism had many consequences on the usage of Internet, of its rapid acceptance among people, and was the basis for its tremendous power of transformation.

It is usual to present the Internet as a result of a question about how to design a network which could resist a nuclear attack. This issue was raised at DARPA, the US defense agency, but it is only a minor element on the construction of the network, and brings no real clue about the fast acceptance of this network.

It must be kept in mind that the two founding papers, as quoted on the Hobbes Internet timeline[2], were the Kleinrock article [1] written in 1961 which describes packet switching communication and the Licklider & Clarck paper written in 1962 about a network encompassing social interaction [2].

The explanation of the fast growth of Internet can be found in the remark that is the result of a confrontation between three major industries: Information technologies, Telecommunication, and Media.

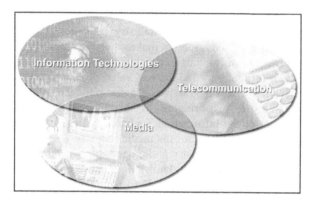

Fig. 1. The three industries which have prepared the path to the emergence of Internet

Those three industries have their own characteristics, their own culture, and they have all brought to the construction of the Internet a unique know-how.

The Information Technologies industry is composed of hardware manufacturers, software vendors, developers. It is a recent and very fast changing industry. Companies who were leaders, or well-known, have died in a few years, such as Digital, bought by Compaq, itself almost absorbed by Hewlett-Packard. IBM was on the edge of dying, and recovered by abandoning part of its hardware manufacturing. On the other hand, Microsoft and Intel have been for ever flourishing, to such a point that it is difficult to imagine what could happen to them, even though it is clear that companies die one day or another. Others, like Apple, are still searching for their market. It is an industry very much based on trial and error culture for defining its champions. The digital world is the basis for this industry.

The Telecommunication industry is made of telecommunication operators, incumbent or newly born, and the companies which they have generated, such as Lucent, Alcatel, Nortel, Siemens, Nokia, and Ericsson. It was built owing to the tax payer money, and faced the difficult technological challenge to create a network. Its

---

[2] http://www.zakon.org/robert/internet/timeline/

culture is very military oriented, traditionally composed of big corporate players, with an engineer type of management: a strong belief in the technology as superior, and a product based marketing rather than a service based one. All players in this industry have recently suffered, but their cash flow is so big that they have been able to survive, at least up to now. The digital world is just a technology like another for the telecommunication industry, which has not always been good to promote it into social values. A good example of this is the ISDN invention[3], which never found its market.

The media industry includes press, radio, TV, music, movie industry. It is composed of big major players, such as Sony, Time Warner, Universal, Murdoch, and Hollywood. It has a trend to always absorb little players to create big empires, at the image of William Randolph Hearst, whose life is beautifully told by Orson Welles in the movie "Citizen Kane". It has a real power, the one which is called the fourth power. In 1898, the Maine battleship was blown-up. One theory was that the Spanish did it, to start a war with the US. Hearst sends two photographers, who, seeing nothing serious, mailed a message to Hearst quoting this. The answer from Hearst was "You furnish the pictures, I'll furnish the war." The culture of this industry is based on the assumption that possessing the content is a unique asset that makes it above all others. The digital world is considered as the Devil for this industry, which is not able right now to understand the value beneath it. Their difficulty to find the real value of peer to peer systems was unfortunately transferred into a very aggressive behavior in the face of this phenomenon.

Each of these industries is bringing to the Internet world a unique value proposition: interaction for the Information Technology Industry, peer to peer for the telecommunication industry, content for the media industry.

The Information Technology industry is the one which has the done most research and explored a lot of new ideas in knowledge management and man machine interfaces. From Database manipulation tools to natural language query, from XML standards to hypertext ones, from keyboard to mouse, the constant quest for better interaction led to a huge richness in the interaction between human and the machine. The other two industries have not so far achieved such a level of interaction; plain old telephones, as well as TV remote controls, are probably amongst the worst machines in terms of interaction.

The Telecommunication industry has invented the peer to peer, this extraordinary facility to hang up your phone, to dial in a number, and to be connected with another person even on the other side of the planet is so usual that we forget the beauty of it. The funny thing is that, when the telephone was invented, one of the main purposes was "to listen to the music from home without the need to physically go to the concert hall". It is a constant in the telecommunication industry to invent beautiful technologies without guessing the extraordinary social impact it may have. Telephone was one, SMS another one. On the opposite, it took a long time before networking was introduced in our personal computers, and in our homes. And we shall even not mention how the media industry is considering peer to peer…

The Media industry is bringing content: meaning, beauty, pleasure, which is unique. This is not to be found in the other two industries. Internet is bringing a lot to the media Industry: content archiving, content retrieval, CD indexation systems such as cddb, Imdb, etc…

---

[3] "Innovation Subscribers Don't Need", as it was quoted.

Interactions between the industries have occurred in the past. In the years 1980s, Bulletin Board Systems (BBS) were combining interaction and some limited local peer to peer capacities. In the years 1990s, CD-Rom was combining content and interaction. But we had to wait until 1995 for the real combination of the three Industries into the expansion of Internet into wide audience.

The past 10 years have been extraordinarily rich, in terms of the explosion of Internet usages, as we all experienced it. As an example, considering recent major political issues, such as the war in Iraq, or the European constitution, it became obvious that all traditional media companies were biased, and that Internet was the only media where debate took place, where different ideas could be expressed, and confronted, seen by millions of people, with their participation.

Before moving along, we should not forget one point: there is still one huge part of our world which is not connected to the Internet; there is a huge part of mankind which does even not have access to electricity. The following figure, which it is the submarine bandwidth capacity, is a good illustration of where the interactions are located. It is one of the most efficient lessons of geopolitics that we can dream of.

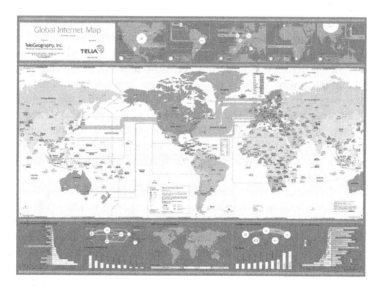

Fig. 2. The global Internet map, from Telegeography, http://www.telegeography.com/maps/

2   Four Major Disruptions

We propose that the construction, and the expansion of Internet, is based on four paradigm shifts. One is about the technology, which was designed with the idea of going totally reverse from what the telecommunication operators were promoting at that time. The second one is about funding, and how the entrepreneurial spirit of the Silicon Valley has played a key role. The third one is about Business Model, and how moving to an intangible economy is important. The last one is about the usage, and is the key point to understanding why Internet is more than a technology, and has a real sociological impact.

2.1 Technology Disruption

It is always difficult to define what really an innovation is. However, we may say that Internet, both in its construction process, and its technological choices, is a real breakthrough. We must understand Internet as a complex system based on three pillars: a network of networks, a set of protocols, and a bunch of different services, of which many of them have not been invented yet.

The fast growth of the network is explained by the founding choice to go for a packet switch network rather than a traditional commutated network. The best analogy to explain this is to compare train versus road. A commuted telephony network is a little like a train network: the bandwidth is allocated for the phone call, same as the tracks are allocated for the train. If there is congestion, the phone call cannot be placed, such as trains don't leave if the track is not open. On the opposite, in a packet network, content are placed in packets which can go through different routes to reach their destination; just like a car drivers who wants to go from one place to another has the choice of the road. Just like if the road traffic is heavy, the journey can be very long, if the network is busy, transmission time is high.

The first innovation that packet circuit brings is that it allows for an exponential growth of the global network. Connecting one more network to the Internet is simply done by building a gateway, whether it is a corporate network, a metropolitan network a university network, or simply a home network. This explains the explosion of the number of computer connected. The other advantage is a global cost reduction: the same architecture applies everywhere. The last advantage is independence between the protocol and the transport layer, whether it is copper, cable, fiber optic, or wireless. The astronauts in the space shuttle are connected to the Internet and can read their email sent by their relatives.

Along with the packet-switch network, the other big innovation was the RFC mechanism for the definition of standards. Few managers, even in 2005, believe that something intelligent can possibly emerge from a decision process based on voting. But this is how all Internet norms were designed: published "Request for Comments", followed by a discussion, then a vote, with the only constraint that there must exist a first implementation of the norm. How can this have produced such a complex object which is the Internet, without any major bug, is fascinating. But it worked.

The third innovation was the difficult choice to give up with total quality, but rather to rely on best effort strategy. This was the main concerns that telecommunication operator had towards voice over IP at its beginning: how a network based on best effort can possibly transport voice with the same quality as telephony. Again, in 2005, the voice over IP market is booming, and becomes more and more a standard offer, including from the incumbent operators themselves. The proof has been done that a best effort strategy was working.

The fourth innovation resides in the independence between services, and network. As long as a service respects the norms and protocol of Internet, no one cares about which type of network topology it is going through. This, combined with the usage disruption, has been key to the explosion of Internet.

2.2 Financing Disruption

At a time when there seems to be a debate about liberalism and a global economy, Internet is a perfect example of a good combination of both government, and private funding. At the very first period of time, Internet was funded by DARPA, the US Defense Advanced Research Projects Agency. This has worked for nearly 30 years, allowing the growth of the network to a "pre-commercial" status.

This funding could not be allowed for more commercial usage. The famous Al Gore white paper about a "National Information Infrastructure", published in 1993, started the beginning of the commercial Internet. It deliberately stated "a combination of public and private effort". But the true story is to be found in the history of Silicon Valley, and even further, in the Gold Rush.

In XIXth century, there were people in California, who had influence on the choice of the location of the train coming from the east coast, through the Rocky Mountains. They were buying such lands at low price, and reselling them to the government, making very high profit. They were called "the robber barons". One of them, after the tragic loss of his only child, decided to invest his money into a utopia, more precisely a University that would be totally different from East Coast Universities: women would be allowed, as an example; but also, the entrepreneurship would be encouraged. His name was Leland Stanford.

California has always been a land of utopia. The Gold Rush was more than just looking for riches; it was a utopia for people "disappointed by the European revolution outcome": to build a different type of society, more global. This utopia is also in the principle that were introduced in building Stanford University, the idea that technologies should not remain pure laboratory ideas, but that they should be made useful for the people. This was the basis for the creation of a system to finance the inventors. Among the first ones, the most famous where two engineers who, in their garage in Palo Alto, designed a brand new oscilloscope, two people by the name of Bill Hewlett and Dave Packard. And, later, the personal computer industry happened, which created and popularized the name of the "Silicon Valley".

However, back in the 1990s, the Silicon Valley was in a bad mood. Innovation seemed to have vanished, issues were mostly industrial, and Venture Capitalists were seeking for new fields of opportunity. And there was Internet, already widely deployed, which had successfully passed its technological proof, and offering one killer application that was just invented, the word wide web. Moreover, all our three major industries had not understood the Internet. The telecommunication industry simply ignored it, the computer industry did not understand it, and the media industry did not care. AOL and CompuServe were supposed to be the only model for interconnecting people. This situation was a dream for the Venture Capitalists. With the help of Al Gore, the network was opened, and Internet phase II could start, with the success that we know.

Just a look at those two following figures is quite illustrating. The European Commission, which had launched multi-annual R&D framework programs, was spending 16 billion Euros over a 5 year program. At the peak of the venture capital, US ventures were spending over 25 billion dollars per quarter. The Internet is truly a modern venture story.

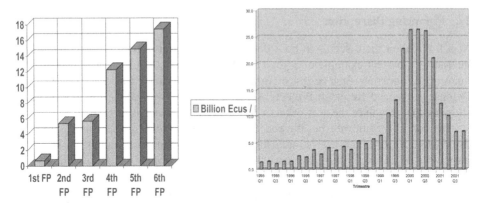

Fig. 3. Comparison between European R&D Framework Programs and US Venture investment

2.3 Business Model Disruption

Funding a company is not sufficient. It has to gain money, and for this to attract customers, and to sell them product and services.

Here comes one of the most intriguing paradoxes for many people: how come the Internet can be even more than a business, a real industry, but carrying ideas of "free" access to content or services. Of course, users need to pay for their access, but news is free, weather is free, telephony is free with VoIP, content is free with peer to peer systems. On the other side, many companies have tried to transform the value carried by Internet into profit. Some have been successful, like the three major Internet companies, often quoted for their success: Amazon, Ebay, and Google. Some others have failed, and have not survived the bubble explosion, like Altavista, who was the very first plain text search engine, many years before Google.

In fact, Internet is not a free system; it relies on the business model of an intangible economy, while many people still think of the economy of a tangible one. Internet was not the first industry to make this move: the airline industry has shown the path, some 20 years ago. Let us describe those two models.

An intangible economy is an economy of scarcity. It was the post-war economy, when everything was ruined and had to be rebuilt. It is also the economy of luxury. In an intangible economy, there are more potential buyers than products. The first consequence is that the buyer has to prove the feasibility of the transaction, and he has to compete with other buyers. The transaction is based on tangible criterions: people were opening the hood of a car to check the engine. People were buying things that would first of all last a long time. In this economy, *the value is in production.*

Then people, at least in occidental world, became richer. And slightly, the economy shifted to another model. An intangible economy is an economy of abundance. There are more products than buyers, and therefore the proof of the transaction is now on the seller side. As products tend to more and more look alike, the seller has to attract customers through intangible criterion: when buying a car, the financing scheme is now more important than the engine. In this economy, *the value resides in transactions.*

It has two impacts: first the information, and the knowledge, becomes the fundamental for the transaction to happen; second business models become instable, but it is structural, and we have to live with this.

Moreover, the rules that govern the tangible economy are not the same as the ones which govern the intangible economy. This can be illustrated through four different aspects: the price computation, the value distribution, the payer determination, and the transaction roll-out frequency. It is important to mention that all those rules are not independent one another; they altogether create the conditions to switch to a intangible world. Let us focus on each of them.

Price Computation: We have learned at school the supposed fundamental rule of economy, "price is equal to a cost plus margin". This is quite true in a tangible economy, but we are now facing a lot of cases where this rule is no longer valid, where there is no longer relation between the manufacturing cost, which becomes more and more difficult to determine, and the final price. Two examples can illustrated this: airlines seats can be very cheap at the day of the departure if the plane is not full, so the price is much lower than the marginal production cost; but people can pay more than one euro for a SMS whose production cost is virtually zero. The rule in an intangible economy becomes: "price is what people are willing to pay at the time of the consumption". Is it not what Shakespeare foresaw, when King Richard III begs "my kingdom for a horse"? Surely, the production cost of a horse is not at the same level as the value of a kingdom; in this precise case, we may suggest that the value was probably in the transaction.

Value Distribution: There was a single relationship between a buyer and a seller. Airline tickets were bought directly from Air France, Lufthansa, British Airways, KLM, etc; telephony systems were bought directly from the telecommunication operator. In a service world, what is wanted is an aggregation of services: people who want to spend a week-end in a European city do not want to bother about aggregation of services. They want a single place to get the air ticket, the airport transfer, the hotel, the restaurant, the museum entry, etc. Companies must therefore partner together, and create business eco-systems, a much more sophisticated answer than linear value chains, in order to meet the customer needs. As an example, a single ring tone download may need an eco-system of up to 8 companies dealing together, with money flows circulating sometimes both ways between them. Those complex eco-systems will be increasing in the future.

Payer Determination: Normally, the consumer should be the payer. Again, this becomes less and less true. People can watch TV, or listen to radio, for free. One of the greatest shifts when GSM was invented was to make incoming calls free for the GSM owner, and charging a lot the caller. Basically, this means that all people calling someone were in fact paying for his GSM phone. In an intangible world, the consumer is no longer the only payer. Sometimes he does not pay at all. At the beginning of Internet, Yahoo let us believe that third-party payer (mostly advertisement) was the unique model of the Internet. In fact, it was a very good model at the beginning of the Internet, when Venture Capitalists did not care about revenues, and when yahoo's main competitor was AOL. The situation is now somehow different, though we could still argue that people will never pay for content. The most profitable newspapers nowadays are free ones, such as Metro.

Transaction Roll-Out Frequency: Financial compensation were done "later", people would not count their working hours. At the beginning of airline code sharing, compensation was done once a month, and, as tickets were not at all electronic, using a very simple protocol: tickets from each airlines were physically weighed, and compensation was done according to the respective number of kilograms... Now, compensation must be done in real time and for each transaction. This is not easy to do, as not all information systems are able to provide the proper information in real time. As an example, many web sites use an overcharged number, or a SMS, to have people paying for some content. But the relationship between the content and the payment is not always done, and the revenue comes globally at the end of the month. In the music industry, as an example, this global repartition prevents from paying back the right amount to the proper artist.

In the Internet world, the key success is to position the company in an intangible economy. Internet has grown because it has positioned itself at the articulation between free and charged [3]. The Information Technology industry traditionally prices per license. The media industry uses widely third party (mostly advertisement) business model, and the telecommunication industry is very good at pay per use. But, in the Internet world, dynamic business model becomes the rule. Business models are structurally instable, and we may argue that, in the Internet world, the "killer app", which everyone is looking after, is the business model. And, in order to determine the proper business model, the best way, as there are no rules, is constant trial and error. Above all, it is important to constantly keep an eye on the business model and to be able to change it rapidly when necessary.

The best example of this structural instability of business models may be found in the very high potential threats that each of the three major industries is facing: WiFi and free IP telephony for the telecommunication sector, open sources for the IT industry, and Creative commons for the media industry...

2.4 Usage Disruption

Telecommunication operators were providing very simple and basic services. The first one, by far, is to simply make a phone call. It still remains a very fundamental usage of telecommunication.

Internet, on the opposite, offers a wide range of services. Web surfing, email, chat, radio, TV, search engines, messages board, telephony integrated with other services, e-commerce, airplane train and bus schedules, hotel reservation world-wide, parcel shipping monitoring, price comparison, meteorology, access to databases, satellite images, etc. Even the simple content offering is huge: Google is proud to announce more than 8 billion indexed web pages, but the invisible web, those pages that have never been indexed by any search engines, is much larger. A recent survey[4] showed that the 60 largest databases on the internet contain a total of more than 40 times the known web.

---

[4] http://www.brightplanet.com/infocenter/largest_deepweb_sites.asp

Telecommunication services were designed using what is called a "techno-push" attitude. This method is characteristic of the early stages of a technology. Managers are engineers; the value propositions are purely technological. The customer has no other choice than buying, and if he does not buy, the conclusion was that "the sales people are not good to explain him why he should buy" (sic).

In this techno-push world, services are very long to create. It is a linear process, which begins at the R&D center, where engineers develop ideas. Next is a prototype, then it goes to production, and, the service is delivered.

This life cycle has a strong drawback: it is very long, many years in practice. In a competitive world, customers are more rapidly changing their mood. Techno-push is a method which is insensitive to users. It has produced good results in the past, but it is no longer adequate.

Many years ago, marketing has invented another life cycle: market-pull. Marketing people listen to customers; they conduct polls, user studies, and from this, define the product that people need. They go to engineering department, and ask technicians to create the solution.

Market-pull has strong advantages: cycles are shorter, stickiness to the demand is much better, customers are happy, and tend to buy more. However, it has also drawbacks: what if no technology exists to answer the demands? As an example, there is a huge market, almost 6 billion potential customers, for a teleportation system, but no answer yet... Another drawback is that it is insensitive to innovation. Technical inventions have no way to find a market unless there is a demand for it, which is barely the case. People don't always express their demand, just because they don't know it. The project manager of the Twingo, a very innovative car made by Renault, privileged "an instinctive design rather than an extinctive marketing".

Internet could not have been done in techno-push mode, because very few would have accepted a purely technological invention without a social support. Internet would never have been invented in a market-pull world, because nobody was able, except for a few visionaries, to describe and ask for the world into which we are living right now.

It is in the development methods of Internet that we may find main reasons for it's widely spread social acceptance.

3 Innovation: The Internet Lessons

People who have created Internet have not invented original methods from scratch, because they knew somehow that innovation starts by observation. They rather have taken some good ideas coming from other industries, and have adapted them to fit their own construction needs and assembled them to make a coherent system. It is in the field of system analysis that we may grasp the keys to understand Internet innovation. It is based on two strong systemic ideas: codesign methods, and putting the power in the network.

3.1 Codesign

It is the computer industry that has popularized the ideas of codesign, although some other industries like automobile have also used such techniques. Originally, the term codesign was used by engineers who were doing both hardware chips and software to run on those chips at the same time. But the term has extended to cover other types of development where people from many different disciplines participate together to the design of an object or a service.

The basic idea behind codesign is to reduce design time, by getting away from linear processes and rather move into constant systemic loops, where all aspects of the problem are processed simultaneously. It started as concurrent engineering. This method is the exact opposite from Taylorism, and has therefore a lot of implications, including in the way companies are structured, processes are defined, and hierarchies are implicated. This does not ease the introduction of this innovation into corporate companies.

We shall present all the aspects of a codesign method, based on five different ideas.

Start with a Question. In traditional methods, a document is created, which contains all the specifications of the product, or the service. Then a call for tender is perform in order to find contractors to do the job, and the customer gives orders to a main contractor, with purely contractual relationships between the two parties. This is heavy in terms of manpower, and has a propensity to blur the picture at an early stage. On the opposite, Innovative projects tend to begin with a question, rather than heavy specification. The invention of the World Wide Web was done by Tim Bernard Lee from the basic question: "how can group of scientist remotely located share joint documents".

Create a Multi-disciplinary Team. Once the question is defined, the project is created to answer this question. The team which is set-up therefore must include all possible profiles: R&D, technology, marketing, finance, and also, more and more, customers. The concepts, the technology, the business model must be done jointly. When Internet norms were voted, it was mandatory to have a first technical implementation. In a traditional world, norms would be defined first, and then industrial companies would create. By solving all issues at the same time, many bad paths, i.e. technical solution that don't work, or choices of a wrong market, are avoided at a very early stage of a project. Therefore, there are no dead-ends, which are always time and money consuming.

Take People Away from their Hierarchies. Companies organizations trend to be vertical, thus creating more and more useless conflicts of power between various departments, which in turn leads to less and less innovation. Hierarchies are good in a top down military organization, when orders come from the top, and must be executed without any discussion. This is opposite to the idea of a customer centric company, where decision power must be as close as possible to the customer. People working on the project are taken away from their hierarchies, for the time of the project, just as the people who created the Internet were free to design the best object, with a feedback loop coming from the user, not from their hierarchies.

Run a Constant Loop Between Technology and Usage. Next characteristic, also popularized by the Internet world: instead of linear processes and planned design, the object emerges from a constant loop between technological proposition, and user acceptance, thus avoiding the shift between the two. We can even propose that a key success factor is to go through intuition phases, and rationalization phases, such as "dream", "observe", "dare", "create", "try", "learn". Obviously, the very first browser invented at CERN has nothing to compare with the actual ones, owing to such loops.

Put the User in the Loop. Traditionally, users or customers are either at the end of the process, in techno-push mode, or at the beginning, in market-pull mode, but nowhere else. Planning was mandatory, and important decisions were taken by managers internal to a project. But building a product without a market is not a very good thing to do. Introducing users at all important stages of the project insures a better stickiness between the technology, the product or the service, and the usability. In that case, decision must be based on trial and error, not purely on management meetings. This is a not a neutral revolution, because it assumes that the user is as important as the designer...

As a summary, product or services definition is more and more a joint learning experience between designers and users. People having various profiles, and various functions, can cross-fertilize each others. Information technology industry has grown by developing such methods.

But what Internet brings is two-fold: first of all, Internet has shown that something planetary, which unites millions of people (the one who are lucky to be connected), can be designed and build in only 40 years. Secondly, Internet becomes the vector which allows this method to spread and amplify. Internet, by its power of connecting people, is the key to facilitate the creation of this common learning experience.

Internet creates the condition for a brand new experience: power is now moving into the network.

3.2 Power in the Network

Although there is indubitably a focus on the blogosphere, which is fast growing, we must remember that it all started with personal web pages, and, long before this, with communities of interest.

Even before the Internet was wide open, communities were using BBS (Bulletin Board System) as an electronic tool to communicate. The very first one, the Well, was due to the vision of Howard Rheingold.[5] Among the scientist community who created the Internet, newsgroups were widely used for discussions about Request for Comments. But they were not only used for this, one of the very first discussion groups, at the early stage of the Internet, was about science fiction.

When the Internet was democratized, discussion groups became very important, giving ordinary citizen a power which they never had before. We shall give two examples of this.

The first example is about people who had AIDS. They started a discussion forum on the Internet, where they were exchanging their experiences with the illness. It had an incredible effect: it totally changed the relationships they had with their doctors.

---

[5] http://www.rheingold.com

Doctors had obviously a deep knowledge about AIDS, but patients had a real-time view of everything that was happening: how other patients were experiencing medicine, how efficient they were, who was surviving; a knowledge that doctors did not have, because they were exchanging experiences through magazine or conventions, at a much slower pace than newsgroups. Patients had a learning experience, which made them at level of knowledge equivalent to the doctor's knowledge.

The second example is quite famous, and is about the Pentium Bug. In 1994, Intel introduces the Pentium, and very rapidly, a mathematician noticed a slight error in an excel spreadsheet, and concluded, by comparing with a previous processor, that the Pentium was not computing properly. He sent an email to Intel, who denied there was a bug. The mathematician reported his experiment on an Internet newsgroup. Of course, many other people repeated it, and confirmed that there was a problem. Intel ended up admitting there was a flaw, and offered to replace the processors.

There are many other examples of such power that Internet newsgroups bring to people, but those two were early ones, and quite characteristic.

The reason for this power is to be found in knowledge and logic. People who need to synchronize clocks know about the Byzantine agreement: how to I send the other half of the army the message that contains the time of attack, and be sure they have properly received it. To solve this issue, knowledge has to be divided in three levels: local knowledge (I have the information), common knowledge (everyone has the information) and global knowledge (everybody knows that everybody has the information). The strength of ordinary Medias is to bring knowledge from local to common. Everybody who reads the same newspaper has the same level of information. The power that Internet brings is to ease the move from common to global knowledge. Intel had to face not only thousands of people who knew that there was an issue, but thousands of people who knew that other people knew that there was an issue. Doctors were facing patients who knew what other patients knew. With the discussion forums, and now the blogs, trends in the opinions are easily created, and perfectly noticeable.

By its capacity of interconnecting people, Internet is a real disruption. It allows for a mechanism well know in biology: pattern emergence. What Internet creates are information patterns.

This extraordinary power starts now being used by companies themselves. The strength of eBay is not to be an auction site; it is to have structured a community of people, by providing the notation mechanism. Each person on eBay has its own profile, but this profile does not come from a government, a company or an expert; each person votes for the other, so it is a result of the way the transaction happened. Amazon not only allowed consumer to write reviews about the products Amazon was selling, but it allowed other people to vote for or against the review.

This trend is increasing. On-going research performed by Dominique Cardon and his team at France Telecom R&D, show that innovation is more and more coming from the network. Amongst all examples they have analyzed, we may quote IMDB, the largest database on movies, which started from a newsgroup of movies fans[6],

---

[6] http://www.imdb.com/help/show_leaf?history

Wikipedia, an on-line encyclopedia done by anybody who want to contribute, the impact of Internet on social movements [4]. Interestingly, they showed that this innovation is not unstructured. Various forms of regulation, based on strong governance rules, exist within those groups. One good example is the Wikipedia policy on "neutral point of view"[7], which, along with the "no original research" and "Verifiability", forms the core of Wikipedia regulation[8].

4 Society of Interaction and Complexity

Memory is, generally speaking, very short. People tend to think that what they experience is unique, and never happened in the past. Life is always less unique that what people think, but more unique than what people would like. Internet obeys to this rule: it is on one side very deeply rooted in the past, and on the other, it supports a real disruption.

Just like books, or alphabet, Internet is more than a technology; it is something that helps mankind to switch from one model of society to another. Just like books were the basis for the creation of industrial world, just like alphabet was the basis to create the science and philosophy, Internet is the tool to create a new type of society.

It is usual to name it "communication society", or "knowledge society". But this is not a disruption: people have always been communicating with each others; they have always created and exchanged knowledge. In Alexandria, in -280, a Greek mathematician names Aristophanes had computed the diameter of the earth, with an error of less than 5%. More sophisticated, the precession of equinox was determined and measured on the basis of 150 years of observation of vernal point. This was done without optical instrument, without computers. So, what is new?

If we want to summarize what disruption brings Internet, we may consider the following table.

Table 2. The power of the Network

	Hierarchy	Network
Information	Vertical	Horizontal
Meaning	Carried by hierarchy	Carried by interactions
Leader	Manager	Moderator
Decisions	Imposed	Voted
Structure	Designed	Auto-organized

---

[7] http://en.wikipedia.org/wiki/Wikipedia:Neutral_point_of_view
[8] http://en.wikipedia.org/wiki/Wikipedia:Policies_and_guidelines

Network is the key to understand the power of Internet. However, what is unique, in this beginning of third millennium, is a network of 6 billion people, many of them interconnected, who are also connected to millions of machines. Along those connections, we have airplanes that can bring us at the other side of the planet within one day; we have real-time communication that help us being connected to many people in the same conferences; we have news which are seen by all people at the same time, and we share our feelings, our knowledge, in an interactive manner, above the physical distances.

What we need to create a new society is a network to carry knowledge, feelings, information, sense and sensibility, and everything which has not been discovered yet. But this network needs regulation mechanisms in order to work; it needs protocols to be able to grow rapidly, it needs computers to interact, it needs services, knowledge management tools, peer to peer, databases, etc.

The important issues that we face now are global: Economy, social, industry, learning, politics, are no longer isolated, and are all part of a single planet.

It is not by chance that Internet is arriving right now. Internet is the tool that we have constructed, and chosen, to help us manage this new type of society, based on network and learning. It is a global system, were knowledge appears in the interactions, and whose main characteristic is complexity.

This is why we propose to call this new society: "Interaction and Complexity" society. Complexity should be understood as the property of a global system with many potential interactions. Complexity must not be reduced; we just need to learn how to deal with it, in a learning experience equivalent to the people who were the first to learn an alphabet, 3500 years ago. Information technologies, and Internet, help us to manage this complexity.

Internet, by its constant knowledge experience, will help us understand that, in the new society, the value is in the network.

References

1. Leonard Kleinrock, MIT: "Information Flow in Large Communication Nets", 1961, downloadable on http://www.lk.cs.ucla.edu/LK/Bib/REPORT/PhD/
2. J.C.R. Licklider & W. Clark, MIT: "On-Line Man Computer Communication", 1962.
3. Michel Gensollen, Sup Telecom: "Creation of Value on the Internet", downloadable on www.gensollen.net
4. Christophe Aguiton, France Telecom R&D: "Mapping the Movement", Development, 2005, 48(2)

Lightweight Causal Cluster Consistency

Anders Gidenstam[1], Boris Koldehofe[2], Marina Papatriantafilou[1],
and Philippas Tsigas[1]

[1] Department of Computer Science and Engineering,
Chalmers University of Technology
{andersg, ptrianta, tsigas}@cs.chalmers.se
[2] School of Computer and Communication Science, EPFL
boris.koldehofe@epfl.ch

Abstract. Within an effort for providing a layered architecture of services supporting multi-peer collaborative applications, this paper proposes a new type of consistency management aimed for applications where a large number of processes share a large set of replicated objects. Many such applications, like peer-to-peer collaborative environments for training or entertaining purposes, platforms for distributed monitoring and tuning of networks, rely on a fast propagation of updates on objects, however they also require a notion of consistent state update. To cope with these requirements and also ensure scalability, we propose the *cluster consistency* model. We also propose a two-layered architecture for providing cluster consistency. This is a general architecture that can be applied on top of the standard Internet communication layers and offers a modular, layered set of services to the applications that need them. Further, we present a *fault-tolerant protocol* implementing causal cluster consistency with predictable reliability, running on top of decentralised probabilistic protocols supporting group communication. Our experimental study, conducted by implementing and evaluating the two-layered architecture on top of standard Internet transport services, shows that the approach scales well, imposes an even load on the system, and provides high-probability reliability guarantees.

1 Introduction

Many applications like collaborative environments (e.g. [1, 2, 3]) allow a possibly large set of concurrently joining and leaving processes to share and interact on a set of common replicated objects. State changes on the objects are distributed among the processes by update messages (a.k.a. *events*). Providing the infrastructure to support such applications and systems places demands for multi-peer communication, with guarantees on reliability, latency, consistency and scalability, even in the presence of failures and variable connectivity of the peers in the system. Applications building on such systems would also benefit from an event delivery service that satisfies the causal order relation, i.e. satisfies the "happened before" relation as described in [4].

The main focus of earlier research in distributed computing dealing with these issues has its emphasis in proving feasible, robust solutions for achieving reliable

A. Bui et al. (Eds.): IICS 2005, LNCS 3908, pp. 17–28, 2006.

causal delivery in the occurrence of faults [5, 6, 7, 8], rather than considering the aforementioned variations in needs and behaviour. Further, since the causal order semantics require that an event is delivered only after all causally preceding events have been delivered, the need to always recover lost messages can lead to long latencies for events, while applications often need short delivery latencies. Moreover, the latency in large groups can also become large because a causal reliable delivery service needs to add timestamp information, whose size grows with the size of the group, to every event.

To improve the latency, *optimistic causal order* [9, 10] can be suitable for systems where events are associated with deadlines. In contrast to the causal order semantics, optimistic causal order only ensures that no events that causally precede an already delivered event are delivered. Events that have become obsolete do not need to be delivered and may be dropped. Nevertheless, optimistic causal order algorithms aim at minimising the number of lost events. In order to determine the precise causal relation between pairs of events in the system processes can use *vector clocks* [11], which also allow detection of missing events and their origin. However, since the size of the vector timestamps grow linearly with the number of processes in the system one may need to introduce some bound on the growing parameter to ensure scalability.

Recent approaches for information dissemination use lightweight probabilistic group communication protocols [12, 13, 14, 15, 16, 17]. These protocols allow groups to scale to many processes by providing reliability expressed with high probability. In [16] it is shown that probabilistic group communication protocols can perform well also in the context of collaborative environments. However, per se these approaches do not provide any ordering guarantees.

In this paper we propose a consistency management method denoted by *causal cluster consistency*, providing optimistic causal delivery of update messages to a large set of processes. Causal Cluster Consistency takes into account that for many applications the number of processes which are interested in performing updates can be low compared to the overall number of processes which are interested in receiving updates and maintaining replicas of the respective objects. Therefore, the number of processes that are entitled to perform updates at the same time is restricted to n, which also corresponds to the maximum size of the vector clocks used. However, the set of processes entitled to perform updates is not fixed and may change dynamically. Our proposed approach is in line with and inspired from recent approaches in multipeer information dissemination [12, 13, 14], where the aim is at what is called *predictable reliability*, guaranteeing that each event is delivered to all non-faulty destinations with a high-probability guarantee. We present a two-layer architecture implementing cluster consistency that can make use of lightweight communication algorithms which can in turn run using standard Internet transport services. Our method is also designed to tolerate a bounded number of process failures, by using a combined push-and-pull (recovery) method. We also present an implementation and experimental evaluation of the proposed method and its potential with respect to reliability and scalability, by building on recently evolved large-scale and lightweight probabilistic group communication protocols. Our implementation and evaluation have been carried out in a real network, and also in competition with concurrent network traffic by other users.

Also of relevance and inspiration to this work is the recent research on peer-to-peer systems and in particular the methods of such structures to share information in the system (cf. e.g. [18, 19, 20, 21, 22]), as well as a recent position paper for atomic data access on CAN-based data management [23].

2   Notation and Problem Statement

Let $G = \{p_1, p_2, \ldots\}$ denote a group of processes, which may dynamically join and leave, and a set of replicated objects $B = \{b_1, b_2, \ldots\}$. Processes maintain replicas of objects they are interested in. Let B be partitioned into disjoint clusters $C_1, C_2, \ldots$ with $\cup_i C_i \subseteq B$. Further, let C denote a cluster and p a process in G, then we write also $p \in C$ if p is interested in objects of C. *Causal Cluster Consistency* allows any processes in C to maintain the state of replicated objects in C by applying updates in optimistic causal order. However, at most n processes (n is assumed to be known to all processes in C) may propose updates to objects in C at the same time. Processes which may propose updates are called *coordinators* of C. Let $Core_C$ denote the set of coordinators of C. The set of coordinators can change dynamically over time. Throughout the paper we will use the term *events* when referring to update messages sent or received by processes in a cluster.

The propagation of events is done by multicast communication. It is not assumed that all processes of a cluster will receive an event which was multicast, nor does the multicast need to provide any ordering by itself. Any lightweight probabilistic group communication protocol as appears in the literature [13, 14, 15] would be suitable. We refer to such protocols as *PrCast*. PrCast is assumed to provide the following properties: (i) an event is delivered to all destinations with high probability; and, (ii) decentralised and lightweight group membership, i.e. a process can join and leave a multicast group in a decentralised way and processes do not need to know all members of the group.

Within each cluster we apply vector timestamps of the type used in [24]. Let the coordinator processes in $Core_C$ be assigned to unique identifiers in $\{1, \ldots, n\}$ (a process which is assigned to an identifier is also said to *own* this identifier). Then, a time stamp t is a vector whose entry $t[j]$ corresponds to the $t[j]$th event send by a process that *owns* index j or a process that owned index j before (this is because processes may leave and new processes may join $Core_C$). A vector time stamp t_1 is said to be smaller than vector time stamp t_2 if $\forall i \in \{1, \ldots, n\}$ $t_1[i] \leq t_2[i]$ and $\exists i \in \{1, \ldots, n\}$ such that $t_1[i] < t_2[i]$. In this case we write $t_1 < t_2$.

For any multicast event e, we write t_e for the corresponding timestamp of e. Let e_1 and e_2 denote two multicast events in C, then e_1 causally precedes e_2 if $t_{e_1} < t_{e_2}$, while e_1 and e_2 are said to be concurrent if neither $t_{e_1} < t_{e_2}$ nor $t_{e_2} < t_{e_1}$. Further we denote the index owned by the creator of event e as $index(e)$ and the event id of event e as $\langle index(e), t_e[index(e)] \rangle$.

Throughout the paper it is assumed that each process p maintains for each cluster C a *cluster-consistency-tailored logical vector clock* (for brevity also referred to as CCT-*vector clock*) denoted by $clock_p^C$. A CCT-vector clock is defined to consist of a vector time stamp and a sequence number. We write T_p^C when referring to the timestamp and seq_p^C when referring to sequence number of $clock_p^C$. T_p^C is the timestamp of the latest delivered event while seq_p^C is the sequence number of the last multicast event performed by p. In Section 3 when describing the implementation of causal cluster consistency, we explain how these values are used. Note, whenever we look at a single cluster C at a time, we write for simplicity $clock_p$, T_p, and seq_p instead of $clock_p^C$, T_p^C, and seq_p^C respectively.

3   Layered Architecture for Optimistic Causal Delivery

This section proposes a layered protocol for achieving optimistic causal delivery. Here we assume that coordinators of a cluster are assigned to vector entries and that the coordinators of a cluster know each other. To satisfy these requirements we choose a decentralised and fault-tolerant cluster-management protocol [25] which can map a process to a unique identifier in the CCT-vector clock in a decentralised way and can inform all processes in $Core_C$ about this mapping.

Protocol Description
The first of the two layers uses *PrCast* in order to multicast events inside the cluster (cf. pseudo-code description Algorithm 1). The second layer, the causality layer, implements the optimistic causal delivery service. The causal delivery protocol is inspired by the protocol by Ahamad et. al. [24] and is adapted and enhanced to provide the optimistic delivery service of the cluster consistency model and the recovery procedure for events that may be missed due to *PrCast*.

Each process in a cluster interested in observing events in optimistic causal order (which is always true for a coordinator), maintains a queue of events denoted by H_p^C. For any arriving event e one can determine from T_p^C and the event's timestamp t_e whether there exist any events which (i) causally precede e, (ii) have not been delivered, and (iii) could still be deliverable according to the optimistic causal order property. More precisely we define this set of not yet delivered deliverable events as

$$to\_deliver\_before(e) = \{e' \mid t_{e'} < t_e \wedge \neg(t_{e'} < T_p^C)\}$$

and their event ids, which can be used for recovery, can be calculated as follows

$$to\_deliver\_before\_ids(e) =$$
$$\{\langle i, j \rangle \mid (\forall i \neq index(e) . \; T_p^C[i] < j \leq t_e[i]) \vee (i = index(e) \wedge T_p^C[i] < j < t_e[i])\}.$$

If there exist any such events, e will be enqueued in H_p^C until it becomes obsolete (prior to that process p may "pull" missing events — see below). Otherwise, p delivers e to the application. When a process p delivers an event

e referring to cluster C, the CCT-vector clock $clock_p^C$ is updated by setting $\forall i\ T_p^C[i] = \max(t_e[i], T_p^C[i])$. Process p also checks whether any events in H_p or recovered events now can be dequeued and delivered. Before a coordinator p in $Core_C$, owning the jth vector entry, multicasts an event it updates $clock_p^C$ by incrementing seq_p^C by one. The event is then stamped with a vector timestamp t such that $t[i] = T_C^p[i]$ for $i \neq j$ and $t[j] = seq_p^C$.

Since PrCast delivers events with high probability, a process may need to recover some events. The recovery procedure, which is invoked when an event e in H_p is close to become obsolete, sends recovery messages for the missing events that precede e. The time before e becomes obsolete depends the amount of time since the start of the dissemination of e, and is assumed to be larger than the duration of a PrCast (which is estimated by the number of hops that an event needs to reach all destinations with w.h.p.) and the time it takes to send a recovery message and receive an acknowledgement. At the time $e \in H_p$ becomes obsolete, p delivers all recovered events and events in H_p that causally precede e and e in their causal order. A simple recovery method is to contact the sender of the missing event. For this purpose the sender has a *recovery buffer* which stores events until no more recovery messages are expected (this is e.g. the case if $\forall i\ t_e[i] < T_p^C[i]$). Below we will present and analyse a another recovery method that enhances the throughput and the fault-tolerance.

Properties of the Protocol. The PrCast protocol provides a delivery service that guarantees that an event will reach all its destinations with high probability, i.e. PrCast can achieve high message stability. When an event needs recovery, the number of processes that did not receive the event is expected to be low. Thus a process multicasting an event is expected to receive a low number of recovery messages. If there are no process, link or timing failures, reliable point to point communication succeeds in recovering all missing events, and thus provide causal order without any message loss. The following lemma is straightforward, following the analysis in [24].

Lemma 1. *An execution of the two-layer protocol guarantees causal delivery of all events disseminated to a cluster if neither processes nor links are slow or fail.*

Event Recovery Procedure, Fault-Tolerance and Throughput

The throughput and fault-tolerance of the protocol can be increased by introducing redundancy in the recovery protocol. All processes could be required to keep a history of some of the observed events, so that a process only needs to contact a fixed number of other processes to recover an event. Further, such redundancy could help the recovery of a failed process. As it is desirable to bound the size of this buffer we analyse the recovery buffer size and number of processes to contact such that the recovery succeeds with high probability.

Following [15], we describe a model suitable to determine the probability for availability of events that are deliverable and may need recovery in an arbitrary system consisting of a cluster C of n processes that communicate using the Two-Layer protocol. Let C denote this system and T denote the time determined by

---

Algorithm 1. Two-Layer protocol

VAR
  H_p: set of received events that can not be delivered yet
  R: set of recovered events that can not be delivered yet
  B: fixed size recovery buffer with FIFO replacement.

On p creates e
  $t_e := T_p^C$; $t_e[p] := seq_p^C$; $seq_p^C := seq_p^C + 1$ /* Create timestamp t_e */
  $PrCast(\langle e, t_e \rangle)$
  Insert e into recovery buffer B
On p receives $\langle e, t_e \rangle$
  Insert e into recovery buffer B
  if e can be delivered **then**
    $deliver(e)$
    for all $e' \in H_p \cup R$ that can be delivered
      $deliver(e')$
  else
    if e is not delivered or obsolete **then**
      $delay(e, time\_to\_terminate)$
On $timeout(e, time\_to\_terminate)$
  for all $eid \in to\_deliver\_before\_ids(e)$ not in $H_p \cup R$ and eid not already under recovery
    $send(\langle RECOVER, eid \rangle)$ to $source(eid)$ or to k arbitrary processes in cluster
  $delay(e, time\_to\_recover)$
On $timeout(e, time\_to\_recover)$
  for all $e' \in to\_deliver\_before(e) \cap (H_p \cup R)$ that can be delivered
    $deliver(e')$
  $deliver(e)$
  for all $e' \in H_p$ that can be delivered
    $deliver(e')$
On p receives $\langle RECOVER, source(e'), eid \rangle$
  if p has e with identifier eid in its buffer **then**
    $respond(\ \langle ACKRECOVER, e, e_t \rangle\ )$
On p receives $\langle ACKRECOVER, e, e_t \rangle$
  Insert e into recovery buffer
  if e can be delivered **then**
    $deliver(e)$
    for all $e' \in R \cup H_p$ that can be delivered
      $deliver(e')$
  else
    if e is not delivered or obsolete **then**
      $R := R \cup \{e\}$
On $deliver(e)$
  $\forall i\ T_p^C[i] := max(t_e[i], T_p^C[i])$ /* Update T_p^C */
  Remove e from R and H_p
  Deliver e to the application

---

the number of rounds an event stays at most in $\mathcal{C}$. Note the similarity of the buffer system to a single-server queueing system, where new events are admitted to the queue as a random process. However, unlike common queueing systems, the service time (time needed for all processes in C to get the event using the layered protocol) in this model depends on the arrival times of events. The service time is such that every event stays at least as long in the queue as it needs to stay in the buffer of $\mathcal{C}$ in order to guarantee delivery/recovery (i.e. whether the queue is stable is not an issue here). Below we estimate the probability that the length of the queue exceeds the choice of the length for the recovery buffer of $\mathcal{C}$. If a_i denotes the arrival time of an event e_i, the "server" processes each event at time $s_i = a_i + T$. Observe that if the length of the buffer in $\mathcal{C}$ is greater than the maximum length of the queue within the time interval $[a_i, s_i]$ then $\mathcal{C}$ can safely deliver e_i. Consider $[t_a, t_s]$ denoting an interval of length T and the random variable $X_{i,j}$ denoting the event that at time $t_a + i$ process j inserts a new event in the system. Further, assume that all $X_{i,j}$ occur independently, and that $\mathbf{Pr}[X_{i,j} = 1] = p$ and $\mathbf{Pr}[X_{i,j} = 0] = 1 - p$. The number of admitted events in the system can be represented by the random variable $X := \sum_{j=1}^{n} \sum_{i=1}^{T} X_{i,j}$, hence the random process describing the arrival rate of new events is a binomial distribution and the expected number of events in the queue in an arbitrary time interval $[t_a, t_s]$ equals $\mathbf{E}[X] = npT$. Clearly, the length of the recovery buffer must be at least as large as $\mathbf{E}[X]$, or we are expected to encounter a large number of events that cannot be recovered. Now, using the Chernoff bound [15, 26], we bound the buffer size so that the probability of an event that needs recovery not to be present in the recovery buffer of any arbitrary process becomes low.

Theorem 1. *Let e be an event admitted to a system $\mathcal{C}$ executing the two-layered protocol, where each event is required to stay in $\mathcal{C}$ for T rounds. Each of the n processes in the system admits a new event to $\mathcal{C}$ in a round with probability p. Then $\mathcal{C}$ can guarantee the availability of e in the recovery buffer of an arbitrary process with probability strictly greater than $1 - \left(\frac{e}{4}\right)^{npT}$ if the size of the buffer is chosen greater than or equal to $2npT$.*

Due to space constraints, please see our technical report [27] for the proofs. To estimate T, we can use the estimated duration of a PrCast, e.g. as in [15]. Let PrCastTime denote this time. An event e is likely to be needed in $\mathcal{C}$ for (i) PrCastTime rounds (to be delivered to all processes with high probability); (ii) plus PrCastTime rounds, if missed, to be detected as missing by the reception of a causally related event (note that this is relevant under high load, since in low loads PrCast algorithms are even more reliable); (iii) plus the time $time\_to\_terminate + time\_to\_recover$ spent before and after requesting recovery.

Further, since processes may fail, a process that needs to recover some event(s) should contact a number of other processes to guarantee recovery with high probability. Assume that processes fail independently with probability p_f and let X_f be the random variable denoting the number of faulty processes in the system. Then $\mathbf{E}[X_f] = p_f n$. By applying the Chernoff bound as in Theorem 1 we get:

Lemma 2. *If, in a system of n processes where each one may fail independently with probability p_f, we consider an arbitrary process subset of size greater than or equal to $2np_f$, with probability strictly greater than $1 - \left(\frac{e}{4}\right)^{np_f}$ there will be at least one non-failed process in the subset.*

This implies that if a process requests recovery from $R = 2p_f n$ processes then w.h.p. there will be at least one non-faulty to reply.

Theorem 2. *In a system of n processes where each one may fail independently with probability $p_f \leq k/(2n)$ for fixed k, an arbitrary process that needs to recover events according to the Two-Layer protocol, will get a reply with high probability if it requests recovery from k processes.*

Note that requesting recovery only once and not propagating the recovery messages is good because in cases of high loss due to networking problems we do not flood the network with recovery messages. Compared to recovery by asking the originator of an event, this method may need k times more recovery messages. However, the advantages are tolerance of failures and process departures, as well as distributing the load of the recovery in the system.

Regarding replacement of events in the recovery buffer, the simplest option is FIFO replacement. Another option is an aging scheme, e.g. based on the number of hops the event has made. As shown in [15], an aging scheme may improve performance from the reliability point of view. However, to employ such a scheme here we need to sacrifice the separation between the consistency layer and the underlying dissemination layer to access this information. Instead, note that using a dissemination algorithm such as the *Estimated-Time-To-Terminate-Balls-and-bins*(ETTB)-gossip algorithm [15] that uses an aging method to remove events from process buffers and guarantees very good message stability, implies that the reliability is improved since fewer processes may need to recover events.

4   Experimental Evaluation

In this section we investigate the scalability of causal cluster consistency and the reliability and throughput effects of the optimistic causality layer in the Two-Layer protocol. We refer to a message/event as lost if it was not received or could not be delivered without violating optimistic causal order.

The evaluation of the Two-Layer protocol was done on 125 networked computers at Chalmers University of Technology. The computers were Sun Ultra 10 and Blade workstations running Solaris 9 and PC's running Linux distributed over a few different subnetworks of the university network. The average round-trip-time for a 4KB IP-ping message was between 1ms and 5ms. As we did not have exclusive access to the computers and the network, other users might potentially have made intensive use of the network concurrently with the experiments.

The Two-Layer protocol is implemented in an object oriented, modular manner in C++. The implementation of the causality layer follows the description in Section 3 and can be used with several group communication objects within our framework. Our PrCast is the ETTB-dissemination algorithm described in [15] together with the membership algorithm of lpbcast [13]. TCP was used as message transport (UDP is also supported). Multi-threading allows a process to send its gossip messages in parallel and a timeout ensures that the communication round has approximately the same duration for all processes.

Our first experiment evaluates how the number of coordinators affect throughput, latency and message size. In our test application a process acts either as a coordinator, which produces a new event with probability p in each PrCast round, or as an ordinary cluster member. The product of the number of coordinators and p was kept constant (at 6). To focus on the performance of the causality layer the PrCast was configured to satisfy the goal of each event reaching 250 processes w.h.p. (the fan-out was 4 and the event termination time was 5 hops). PrCast was allowed to know all members to avoid side effects of the membership scheme. The maximum number of events transported in each gossip

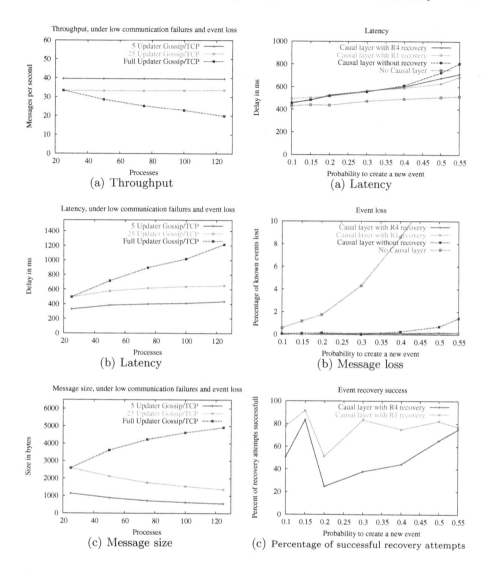

Fig. 1. Throughput and latency with increasing number of cluster members

Fig. 2. Event latency, loss and recovery behaviour under varying load with and without the causality layer

message was 20. The size of the history buffer was 40 events, which according to [15] is high enough to prevent w.h.p. PrCast from delivering the same event twice. The duration of each PrCast round was tuned so that all experiments had approximately the same rate of TCP connection failures (namely 0.2%). Fig. 1 compares three instances of the Two-Layer protocol: the full-updater instance where all processes act as coordinators, the 5-updater and the 25-updater instances with 5 and 25 coordinators, respectively. The causality layer used the

first recovery method, described in Section 3. The results show the impact of
the size of the vector clock on the overall message size and throughput. For the
protocols using a constant number of coordinators message sizes even decreased
slightly with growing group size since the dissemination distributes the load of
forwarding events better then, i.e. for large groups a smaller percentage of processes performs work on an event during the initial gossip rounds. However, for
the full updater protocol messages grow larger with the number of coordinators
which influences the observed latency and throughput. For growing group size
the protocols with a fixed number of coordinators experience only a logarithmic increase in message delay and throughput remains constant while for the
full-updater protocol latency increases linearly and throughput decreases.

The second experiment studies the effects of the causality layer and the recovery schemes in the Two-Layer protocol. Fig. 2 compares the gossip protocol and
the Two-Layer protocol with and without recovery. The recovery is done in two
ways, both described in Section 3: (i) from the originator (marked "R1 recovery") and (ii) from k arbitrary processes (marked "R4 recovery" as the recovery
fan-out k was 4). The recovery buffer size follows the analysis in Section 3, with
the timeout-periods set to the number of rounds of the PrCast. Unlike the first
experiment, the number of coordinators and processes was fixed to 25; instead
varying values of p were used, to study the behaviour of the causality layer under
varying load. Larger p values imply increased load in the system; at the right
edge of the diagrams approximately $n/2$ new events are multicast in each round.
As the load increases, more events are reordered by the dissemination layer and
message losses begin to occur due to buffer overflows, thus putting the causality
layer protocols under stress. The results in Fig. 2(b) show that the causality layer
significantly reduces the amount of lost (ordered) events, in particular when the
number of events disseminated in the system is high. With the recovery schemes
almost all events could be delivered in optimistic causal order. With increasing
load latency grows only slowly (cf. Fig. 2(a)), thus manifesting scalability. The
causality layer adds a small overhead by delaying events in order to respect the
causal order. The recovery schemes do not add much overhead with respect to
latency, while they significantly reduce the number of lost events. At higher loads
the recovery schemes even improve latency since by recovering missing events
causally subsequent events in H_p can be delivered before they time out. Fig. 2(c)
shows the success rate for the recovery attempts. The number of recovery attempts increase as the load in the system increases, when the load is low very few
events need recovery (cf. the event loss without the causality layer in Fig. 2(b)).
There are three likely causes for a recovery to fail: (i) the reply arrives too late;
(ii) the process(es) asked did not have the event; and (iii) the reply or request(s)
messages were lost. The unexpectedly low success rate during low load for the
R4 method could be because a PrCast may reach very few processes when a
gossip message is lost early in the propagation of an event. Also note that as the
load is low the number of missing events and recovery attempts is very small.
However, as load and the number of recovery attempts increase the success rate
converges towards the predicted outcome.

5   Discussion and Future Work

We have proposed lightweight causal cluster consistency, a hierarchical layer-based structure for multi-peer collaborative applications. This is a general architecture, can be applied on top of the standard Internet transport-layer services, and offers a layered set of services to the applications that need them.

We also presented a two-layer protocol for causal cluster consistency running on top of decentralised probabilistic protocols supporting group communication. Our experimental study, conducted by implementing and evaluating the proposed architecture as a two-layered protocol that uses standard Internet transport communication, shows that the approach scales well, imposes an even load on the system, and provides high-probability reliability guarantees.

Future work include complementing this service architecture with other consistency models such as total order delivery with respect to objects. Object ownership and caching are other topics that is worth studying.

References

1. Miller, D.C., Thorpe, J.A.: SIMNET:the advent of simulator networking. In: Proc. of the IEEE. Volume 8 of 83. (1995) 1114–1123
2. Greenhalgh, C., Benford, S.: A multicast network architecture for large scale collaborative virtual environments. In: Proc. of the 2nd European Conf. on Multimedia Applications, Services and Techniques. Volume 1242 of LNCS., Springer-Verlag (1997) 113–128
3. Carlsson, C., Hagsand, O.: DIVE - a multi-user virtual reality system. In: Proc. of the IEEE Annual Int. Symp. (1993) 394–400
4. Lamport, L.: Time, clocks, and the ordering of events in a distributed system. In: Communications of the ACM. Volume 7 of 21. (1978) 558–565
5. Birman, K.P., Joseph, T.A.: Reliable communication in the presence of failure. ACM Transactions on Computer Systems **5** (1987) 47–76
6. Birman, K., Schiper, A., Stephenson, P.: Lightweight causal and atomic group multicast. ACM Transactions on Computer Systems **9** (1991) 272–314
7. Raynal, M., Schiper, A., Toueg, S.: The causal ordering abstraction and a simple way to implement it. Information Processing Letters **39** (1991) 343–350
8. Kshemkalyani, A.D., Singhal, M.: Necessary and sufficient conditions on information for causal message ordering and their optimal implementation. Distributed Computing **11** (1998) 91–111
9. Baldoni, R., Prakash, R., Raynal, M., Singhal, M.: Efficient Δ-causal broadcasting. Int. Journal of Computer Systems Science and Engineering **13** (1998) 263–269
10. Rodrigues, L., Baldoni, R., Anceaume, E., Raynal, M.: Deadline-constrained causal order. In: Proc. of the 3rd IEEE Int. Symp. on Object-oriented Real-time distributed Computing. (2000)
11. Mattern, F.: Virtual time and global states of distributed systems. In: Proc. of the Int. Workshop on Parallel and Distributed Algorithms. (1989) 215–226
12. Birman, K.P., Hayden, M., Ozkasap, O., Xiao, Z., Budiu, M., Minsky, Y.: Bimodal multicast. ACM Transactions on Computer Systems **17** (1999) 41–88
13. Eugster, P.T., Guerraoui, R., Handurukande, S.B., Kermarrec, A.M., Kouznetsov, P.: Lightweight probabilistic broadcast. In: Proc. of the Int. Conf. on Dependable Systems and Networks. (2001) 443–452

14. Ganesh, A.J., Kermarrec, A.M., Massoulié, L.: Scamp: Peer-to-peer lightweight membership service for large-scale group communication. In: Proc. of the 3rd Int. COST264 Workshop. Volume 2233 of LNCS., Springer-Verlag (2001) 44–55

15. Koldehofe, B.: Buffer management in probabilistic peer-to-peer communication protocols. In: Proc. of the 22nd Symp. on Reliable Distributed Systems, IEEE (2003) 76–85

16. Pereira, J., Rodrigues, L., Monteiro, M., Kermarrec, A.M.: NEEM: Network-friendly epidemic multicast. In: Proc. of the 22nd Symp. on Reliable Distributed Systems, IEEE (2003) 15–24

17. Baehni, S., Eugster, P.T., Guerraoui, R.: Data-aware multicast. In: Proc. of the 5th IEEE Int. Conf. on Dependable Systems and Networks. (2004) 233–242

18. Stoica, I., Morris, R., Karger, D., Kaashoek, F., Balakrishnan, H.: Chord: A scalable Peer-To-Peer lookup service for internet applications. In: Proc. of the ACM SIGCOMM 2001 Conf., ACM Press (2001) 149–160

19. Alima, L.O., Ghodsi, A., Brand, P., Haridi, S.: Multicast in DKS(N; k; f) overlay networks. In: Proc. of the 7th Int. Conf. on Principles of Distributed Systems. Volume 3144 of LNCS., Springer-Verlag (2003) 83–95

20. Ratnasamy, S., Francis, P., Handley, M., Karp, R., Shenker, S.: A scalable content-addressable network. In: ACM SIGCOMM Computer Communication Review. Volume 31. (2001) 161–172

21. Rowstron, A., Druschel, P.: Pastry: scalable, decentralized object location and routing for large-scale peer-to-peer systems. In: Proc. of the 18th IFIP/ACM Int. Conf. on Distributed Systems Platforms (Middleware). Volume 2218 of LNCS., Springer-Verlag (2001)

22. Zhao, B.Y., Huang, L., Stribling, J., Rhea, S.C., Joseph, A.D.: Tapestry: A resilient global-scale overlay for service deployment. IEEE Journal on Selected Areas in Communications **22** (2004) 41–53

23. Lynch, N., Malkhi, D., Ratajczak, D.: Atomic data access in distributed hash tables. In: Proc. of the 1st Int. Workshop on Peer-to-Peer Systems. Volume 2429 of LNCS., Springer-Verlag (2002) 295–305

24. Ahamad, M., Neiger, G., Kohli, P., Burns, J.E., Hutto, P.W.: Casual memory: Definitions, implementation and programming. Distributed Computing **9** (1995) 37–49

25. Gidenstam, A., Koldehofe, B., Papatriantafilou, M., Tsigas, P.: Dynamic and fault-tolerant cluster management. In: Proc. of the 5th IEEE Int. Conf on Peer-to-Peer Computing, IEEE (2005)

26. Motwani, R., Raghavan, P.: Randomized Algorithms. Cambridge University Press (1995)

27. Gidenstam, A., Koldehofe, B., Papatriantafilou, M., Tsigas, P.: Lightweight causal cluster consistency. Technical Report 2005-09, Computer Science and Engineering, Chalmers University of Technology (2005)

Distributed Calculation of PageRank Using Strongly Connected Components

Michael Brinkmeier

Institute for Technical and Theoretical Computer Science,
Technical University of Ilmenau, Germany
mbrinkme@tu-ilmenau.de

Abstract. We provide an approach to distribute the calculation of PageRank, by splitting the graph into its strongly connected components. As we prove, the global ranking may be calculated componentwise, as long as the rankings of pages directly linking to the current component are already known. Depending on the structure of the WWW, this approach approach may be used to calculate the ranking on several components in parallel, and allows to split the problem intio significantly small subproblems.

1 Introduction

The World Wide Web is one of the most rapidly developing and perhaps the largest source of information. Due to its de-central nature the access to the relevant and needed information becomes increasingly difficult. Due to the pure amount of content, more and more search engines, indexes and archives try to harvest the information implicit in the link structure to improve speed and quality of search. One of the tools in this field is the ranking of web pages according to their relevance. PageRank, one of the most prominent systems, was presented by Page, Brin et al. in [4, 5]. It is an essential part of Google's ranking scheme. Together with content based measures, this purely link based value is the basis of the order of search results produced by this widely used and accepted search engine.

Since the ranking seems to be quite successful (if considering the number of users and their confidence in the results), the theoretical properties of PageRank raise some interesting questions and may allow a significant speed-up of its calculation. Usually PageRank is viewed as a Markov chain (e.g. [5, 12, 8, 10, 3]), even though its original definition does not constitute one, as pointed out by several authors. But if sinks, i.e. nodes without outgoing edges, are removed or connected to all other nodes, one obtains a Markov chain producing the same ranking as the original definition [3]. More general, PageRank is usually calculated by iteratively multiplying a (ranking) vector to a form of *normalized adjacency matrix* of the graph. Standard results of linear algebra and numerical mathematics show, that this iteration converges to the principal eigenvector of the normalized adjacency matrix.

A. Bui et al. (Eds.): IICS 2005, LNCS 3908, pp. 29–40, 2006.

Experiments and theoretical results prove that only a small number of iterations (compared to the size of the WWW) are needed to obtain a good approximation [5, 3, 6]. But nonetheless, the size of the graph usually requires the use of external memory, significantly increasing the required time.

In the literature some approaches can be found, suggesting parallelized or distributed calculation of PageRank. In [9] T. Haveliwala suggests a way to do one step of the iteration blockwise, reducing the number of accesses to the external memory. But this approach still requires the execution of each step of the iteration on the whole graph.

In [12] Kamvar et al. suggested to use the natural structure of the WWW for a faster calculation of PageRank. The web is split into local subwebs (for example domains), which are ranked independently. Then in a second step the net of subwebs is ranked. The resulting local and global rankings are combined to obtain an approximation of PageRank, which in turn is used as a starting vector for the standard iteration, increasing the rate of convergence. A similar approach is used in [14] by Wang and DeWitt, but instead of using the combined vectors as starting vector for the iteration, they use the global rankings (or ServerRank, as they call it) to refine the local rankings.

The approach of distributing the calculation of PageRank presented in this paper is more in the tradition of [2]. There Avrachenkov and Litvak proof that the global PageRank may be calculated from the local PageRanks on the weakly connected components. This allows to iterate each component seperateley and then combine them to obtain the global PageRank. But unfortunately, as former experiments show [7], there exists one weak giant component containing about 91% of the vertices, reducing the size of the main problem by about 9%.

Similar to Arasu et al. in [1], we go a step further and prove that the iteration may be executed separately on each strong connected component, as long as we adhere to the structure of the interconnections of the strong components. In detail this means, that we have to calculate the rankings inside a strong component before the rankings inside other components, to which it links, directly or indirectly. As [7] and additional experiments indicate, this reduces the size of the largest subproblem to about 28% ([7]) or 46% (sec. 4), and the remaining 72%, resp. 54% consist of much smaller strong components.

2   PageRank and Strong Components

2.1   Notations

Let $D = (V, E)$ be a directed multigraph with vertex set V and edge set E. For each vertex v we denote the out-degree of v by $\text{out}(v)$ and the in-degree by $\text{in}(v)$. If there exists an edge from u to v we write $u \to v$, and $u \not\to v$ otherwise.

2.2   PageRank

In [4] and [5] Page, Brin et al. described an approach estimating the importance of a web page, based purely on the link structure of the world wide web. Their proposed score *PageRank* was based on the assumption, that a document spreads its relevance equally to all documents it links to.

To 'generate' rank a fixed value $e(u)$, the *personalization value*, is given for each vertex u, and $(1 - d)e(u)$ is added to the rank, resulting in:

$$\text{PageRank}(u) = d \sum_{v|v \to u} \frac{\text{PageRank}(v)}{\text{out}(v)} + (1 - d)e(u).^1 \tag{1}$$

Using the normalized link matrix of the web, i.e. the matrix $M = (m_{uv})$ with $m_{uv} = \frac{1}{\text{out}(u)}$ if there exists a link from u to v and 0 otherwise, this equation may be reformulated as the following linear system:

$$(I - dM^T)\text{PageRank} = (1 - d)e, \tag{2}$$

with I the unit matrix. Under certain circumstances[2] the equation may be solved using the iteration

$$r_{i+1} = dM^T r_i + (1 - d)e, \tag{3}$$

which corresponds to the iterative algorithm suggested by Page and Brin[3].

Translated to the underlying graph the iteration leads to the following equation and algorithm (1).

$$r_{i+1}(u) = d \sum_{v|v \to u} \frac{r_i(v)}{\text{out}(v)} + (1 - d)e(u). \tag{4}$$

The starting vector r_0 can be chosen arbitrarily.

Page and Brin suggested an interpretation of the iteration in terms of a random surfer, who occasionally jumps or teleports to another page instead of following a link, leading to a Markov model. But unfortunately the normalized adjacency matrix M is not stochastic, since *sinks*, ie. vertices without outgoing edges, have columns summing to 0. Usually this problem is solved by adding virtual edges from each sink to all other vertices (including the sink), leading to a proper Markov model (see eg. [3, 9, 10]). Results of the theory of Markov models then ensure, that the iteration converges to a unique limit.

In [6] an alternative approach is used. There, PageRank is described as a power-series over the damping factor d, whose coefficients are probabilities of walks of a random surfer. In detail, it was proved that

$$\text{PageRank}(u) = \sum_{l=0}^{\infty} d^l(1 - d) \sum_v a_l(v, u)e(v) \tag{5}$$

---

[1] In fact, in the original paper [4] the factor with which the personalization is multiplied, was given as d. But in later publications it was replaced by $(1 - d)$. As we will see this influences the absolute values, but not on the ranking.

[2] The spectral radius of the matrix $I - dM^T$ has to be less than 1.

[3] Since they normalized the ranking vector, they could describe PageRank as an eigenvector of a specific matrix.

with

$$a_0(v, u) = \begin{cases} 1 & \text{if } v = u \\ 0 & \text{otherwise} \end{cases} \quad \text{and} \quad a_{l+1}(v, u) = \sum_{w | w \to u} \frac{a_l(v, w)}{\text{out}(w)}. \quad (6)$$

Using a slightly different notation, this allows another description as a sum over paths.

$$\text{PageRank}(u) = \sum_v e(v) \sum_{\pi : \, v \overset{*}{\to} u} P(\pi)(1 - d)d^{l(\pi)}. \quad (7)$$

where $P(\pi)$ is defined inductively over the length l of the paths,

$$P(\pi) = \begin{cases} 0 & \text{if } l = 0 \text{ and } u \neq v \\ 1 & \text{if } l = 0 \text{ and } u = v \\ \frac{P(\pi')}{\text{out}(w)} & \text{if } l > 0 \text{ and } \pi : u \overset{\pi'}{\to} w \to v, \end{cases}$$

and π is the path π' from u to w followed by the edge (x, v).

This formulation of PageRank allows an alternative description in terms of a random surfer. Instead of choosing the start vertex uniformly, the personalization value $e(v)$ is used as probability for v^4. at each step the surfer decides to either continue its walk with probability d, or to stop surfing (probability $1 - d$). If she decides to continue, two situations can occur. In the first case, the current vertex has outgoing links, and the surfer randomly chooses one of them to follow. In the second case, the vertex has no outgoing link. In this situation the surfer becomes 'annoyed' and stops surfing.

In this setting $\text{PageRank}(v)$ is the probability that the surfer ends his walk *voluntarily* in vertex v. The probability that the surfer becomes annoyed causes a loss of ranking, ie. $\sum \text{PageRank}(v) < 1$, but the resulting ranking is equivalent (cmp. [6, Prop. 2.9]).

2.3   Strong Components

An obvious consequence of equation 7 is the simple and intuitive fact, that the ranking of a vertex u is only influenced by that of another vertex v, if there exists a path from v to u, ie. if $a_l(v, u) \neq 0$ for some $l \geq N$. In [6] this was already exploited for sinks and sources in the underlying graph. In this paper we go further.

A *strong component* C of a directed multigraph $D = (V, E)$ is a maximal subgraph of D, such that for two arbitrary vertices u and v of C there exists a path from u to v and vice versa. The next theorem states that the PageRank of an arbitrary vertex may be obtained by an iteration involving only the vertices of its strong component, assumed that the PageRanks of all vertices not in the component, but directly linking to vertices in the component, are known.

---

[4] We assume $e(v) \geq 0$ for each $v \in V$ and $\|e\|_1 = 1$.

Theorem 1. *Let $D = (V, E)$ be a directed multigraph, and C one of its strong components. Then for each $v \in V$ the sequence $r^{(i)}(v)$ with $r^{(0)}(v) = (1 - d)e(v)$ and*

$$r^{(i+1)}(v) = d \sum_{u \in C | u \to v} \frac{r^{(i)}(u)}{\text{out}(u)} + d \sum_{u \notin C | u \to v} \frac{\text{PageRank}(u)}{\text{out}(u)} + (1 - d)e(v)$$

converges to PageRank(v).

Proof. If the sequence converges, the limit obviously has to be PageRank(u), because it has to satisfy the fixpoint condition (1), whose solution is unique (cf. [6, Thm 2.8]). Hence it remains to prove the convergence. This is done by comparison with the partial sums

$$\text{PageRank}^{(i)}(v) = \sum_{l=0}^{i}(1 - d)d^l \sum_{u \in V} a_l(u, v)e(u) \leq \text{PageRank}(v),$$

which form an increasing sequence converging to PageRank(v).

Obviously, we have PageRank$(v) \geq r^{(0)}(v) = \text{PageRank}^{(0)}(v)$. Now assume

$$\text{PageRank}(v) \geq r^{(i)}(v) \geq \text{PageRank}^{(i)}(v)$$

for all $v \in C$ and $i \geq 0$. Then we have

$$\text{PageRank}(v) = d \sum_{u | u \to v} \frac{\text{PageRank}(u)}{\text{out}(u)} + (1 - d)e(u)$$

$$= d \sum_{u \in C | u \to v} \frac{\text{PageRank}(u)}{\text{out}(u)} + d \sum_{u \notin C | u \to v} \frac{\text{PageRank}(u)}{\text{out}(u)} + (1 - d)e(u)$$

$$\geq d \sum_{u \in C | u \to v} \frac{r^{(i)}(u)}{\text{out}(u)} + d \sum_{u \notin C | u \to v} \frac{\text{PageRank}(u)}{\text{out}(u)} + (1 - d)e(v)$$

$$= r^{(i+1)}(v)$$

$$\geq d \sum_{u | u \to v} \frac{\text{PageRank}^{(i)}(u)}{\text{out}(u)} + (1 - d)e(v)$$

$$\geq \text{PageRank}^{(i+1)}(v).$$

Since the partial sums form an increasing sequence, converging to PageRank, the $r^{(i)}(v)$ have to have the same limit.

In the preceeding proof we neglected the question, wether the iteration is well-defined. But the answer to this question is quite simple and obvious. We iterate only on one strong component C of the graph. For each vertex v in this component, we require values for each predecessor u. But there are two types of predecessors. The first is itself a member of C and hence is included in the iteration. The second is not a member of C and hence its PageRank is assumed to be known.

At the first look, the result only allows us to iterate on a strong component C, if the exact PageRanks for the predecessors are known. But using the same estimations, one can prove the following result.

Theorem 2. *Let $D = (V, E)$ be a directed multigraph, and C one of the strong components of D and for each vertex u directly linking to at least one vertex in C, let $r(u)$ be an approximation of* PageRank(u) *satisfying*

$$\text{PageRank}(u) \geq r(u) \geq \text{PageRank}^{(j)}(u)$$

for some $j \geq 0$. For $v \in C$ define $r^{(i)}(v)$ by $r^{(0)}(v) := (1 - d)e(v)$ and

$$r^{(i+1)}(v) = d \sum_{u \in C | u \to v} \frac{r^{(i)}(u)}{\text{out}(u)} + d \sum_{u \notin C | u \to v} \frac{r(u)}{\text{out}(u)} + (1 - d)e(v).$$

Then PageRank$() \geq r^{(j)}(v) \geq$ PageRank$^{(j)}(v)$.

Proof. Use the same sequence of inequalities as for theorem 1, but replace $r(u)$ for PageRank(u), where appropriate.

This result allows us to approximate PageRank componentwise, without losing precision, as long as the number of iterations is the same for each component. In fact, we may even obtain a better approximation, than by iterating the whole graph. Unfortunately, the quality of the approximations can not be guaranteed, if the common criteria for the termination of the iteration found in the literature is used. Usually the iteration is repeated until the L_1-norm of the difference between $r^{(i)}$ and $r^{(i+1)}$, ie. the sum $\sum_{v \in V} |r^{(i)}(v) - r^{(i+1)}(v)|$, is below a given threshold. This approach does not seem to be appropriate here, if this would lead to more iterations for a given strong component, than for its preceeding components, because the usage of the earlier calculated approximations of the rankings causes a bias for the newly calculated rankings. But if the number of iterations is independently fixed, we may even guarantee the quality of the global approximation, as shown in [6]. There it was proved that

$$\|\text{PageRank} - \text{PageRank}^{(i)}\|_1 = \sum_{v \in V} |\text{PageRank}(v) - \text{PageRank}^{(i)}(v)| \leq (1 - d)d^i \|e\|_1,$$

if $(1 - d)e$ is the initial ranking. Since PageRank$(v) \geq r^{(i)}(v) \geq$ PageRank$^{(i)}(v)$, this implies

$$\|\text{PageRank} - r^{(i)}\|_1 \leq (1 - d)d^i \|e\|_1.$$

If $\|e\|_1 = 1$ this implies that the error is less than ε after more than $\frac{\varepsilon}{1-d} \ln d$ iterations.

Since the rankings for all vertices $u \notin C$ linking to vertices in the strong component C are constant, their influence may be added to the initial ranking vector e. In this way, only the edges inside the strong component and the global out degrees have to be known. The edges into the component can be neglected.

Hence we may iterate on the induced subgraph with global out degrees (not with the outdegrees in the subgraph) using the initial rankings

$$e'(v) := e(v) + \frac{1}{1-d} \sum_{u \notin C | u \to v} \frac{r(u)}{\text{out}(u)}.$$

The factor $1/(1-d)$ is required, because in the iteration the personalization vector is multiplied by $(1-d)$.

3   Distributing PageRank

The observations made above, allow us to calculate the PageRanks of all pages componentwise. Obviously, this has no effect when the graph is strongly connected. But as measurements of the Webgraph indicate, the World Wide Web consists of a lot of strong components, whose size follows a so-called Power-Law [7]. We will go further into detail about this in section 4.

Since the ranks of predecessors of a strong component C are required for the iteration, we have to ensure that these are known if we start the iteration on C. Hence we have to order the strong components appropriately. This step is discussed in the following.

Let $D = (V, E)$ be a directed multigraph. For each vertex v of D we denote the strong component of D containing v by $[v]$. The *strong component graph* $SC(D)$ of D is obtained by contracting each strong component into one vertex, deleting self-loops and merging parallel edges obtained by this procedure. In other words, the set of vertices of $SC(D)$ is the set $\{[v] \mid v \in V\}$ of strong components of D, and there exists an edge from component $[u]$ to $[v]$, if there exists an edge from u to v in D.

Obviously, the strong component graph $SC(D)$ is acyclic, since otherwise one strong component of D is distributed over several vertices of $SC(D)$ (at least the ones on the cycle). As a consequence, the calculation of PageRank can be distributed componentwise. We simply have to make sure, that before the rankings inside a strong component $[v]$ are calculated, the rankings in all preceeding strong components are already known.

First, the strong components may be computed using an algorithm of Tarjan [13], requiring $O(|V|+|M|)$ time, up to a constant the same time as an iteration step requires.

Following that, the rankings may be computed componentwise. We require a queue Q and one integer counter $c([v])$ for each strong component $[v]$. This counter is initially set to the indegree of $[v]$ in $SC(D)$, and counts the number of preceeding strong components not completed yet. If we guarantee, that $c([v]) = 0$ for every $[v]$ in the queue, we may simply extract one strong component from Q and calculate its rankings.

Obviously all *source components*, ie. those without incoming links, have $c([v])$ initially set to 0 and may be inserted into Q. If later, a strong component $[v]$ is fetched from the queue and its rankings are computed, the counters of all

---

Algorithm 1. Componentwise calculation of PageRank

---

forall $[v] \in SC(D)$ **do**
    $c([v]) \leftarrow in([v]);$
    · **if** $in([v]) = 0$ **then** Q.append($[v]$);
end
while Q *is not empty* **do**
    $[v] \leftarrow Q.get();$
    Calculate the Rankings of vertices in $[v]$;
    forall $[u]$ *with* $[v] \rightarrow [u]$ **do**
        $c([v]) \leftarrow c([v]) - 1;$
        if $c([v]) = 0$ **then** Q.append($[v]$);
    end
end

---

successors can be decreased by one, and if one counter reaches 0 the strong component is inserted into Q. This leads to algorithm 1.

3.1 The System

If Algorithm 1 is executed on a single machine, the main gain is the reduction of the size of the graphs on which the iteration has to be done. This may enable the calculation in local memory, if the strong components are small enough. Fortunately, the topology of the WWW allows a more efficient calculation, as discussed in section 4, using more machines.

If a strong component is extracted from the queue, its rankings may be calculated completely independent from all other components in the queue at the same moment. Hence we may extract as many components as we have free machines, if possible. This allows us to speed up the complete calculation, if the topology of the strong component graph is good enough.

We assume that there exists a data storage system D storing the graph, the strong component graph and the rankings. Furthermore we assume, that this depot can be accessed by several clients $C_1, \ldots, C_n$ in parallel, without a significant loss of performance. In addition there exists a server S, storing the strong component graph and handling the queue.

The clients $C_1, \ldots, C_n$ may request an id of a strong component from the server, ready for calculation. The client retrieves the necessary data from D, ie. the strong component and the rankings of all vertices linking into this component, executes the calculation, stores the results in D and sends s message to S, indicating the completion of the calculation for the component. Following that, the server updates the queue and, if it is empty, stops the whole process.

4 Measurements

The measurements and experiments described in this section were conducted on the WebBase dataset from [16] constructed from the WebBase crawl of 2001 [15].

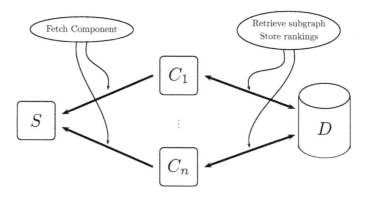

Fig. 1. A schematic sketch of the system for the distributed calculation of PageRank

Table 1. Basic numbers about the WebBase Dataset

Number of vertices	118 142 115
Number of edges	1 019 903 190
Number of strong components	41 126 852
Average size of strong components	~ 2.8726
Largest strong component	53 891 939
Second largest strong component	9 428
Third largest strong component	5 925
Number of strong components of size 1	39 843 421
Number of strong components of size 2	323 994
Number of strong components of size 3	154 786
Ratio of vertices in largest component	~ 0.456
Ratio of vertices in components of size ≤ 3	~ 0.341

Some basic numbers regarding the structure of the dataset are given in table 1. The distribution of the sizes clearly follows a power law (cmp. fig. 2).

As we can see, about 46% of the vertices form one giant strong component, while the second and third largest strong components contain 9428 and 5925 vertices. Furthermore about 34% are contained in tiny strong components of at most 3 vertices, resulting in an average size of strong components about 3.

These numbers indicate that the componentwise calculation of PageRank may significantly decrease the required time. Except for the giant component, every component may be held in the main memory of a standard computer, allowing a fast iteration. Due to the large number of very small components (≤ 3 vertices), PageRank of at least a third of the vertices may even be calculated without iteration, using a direct solution of a system of linear equations with at most 3 variables.

Assume that there exists a path of components in $SC(D)$ and that the iteration and the access to server and database for a component with n vertices

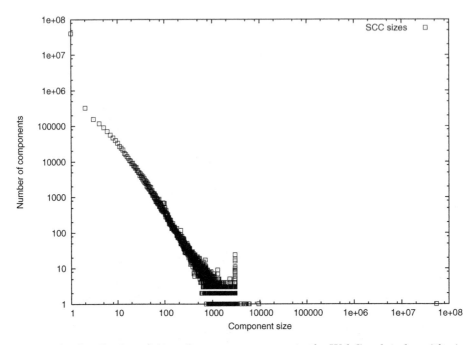

Fig. 2. The distribution of sizes of strong components in the WebGraph in logarithmic scale

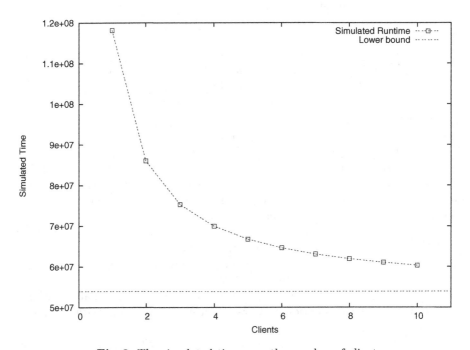

Fig. 3. The simulated time over the number of clients

takes about $O(n)$ time[5]. Since the components on this path has to be calculated subsequently, the time to calculate PageRank is bounded below by $\Omega(n)$. Hence we may use the maximal number of vertices in components on a path in $SC(D)$ from a source to a sink, as a lower bound for the time required for the calculation. This lower bound proved to be 53 903 795 vertices, which is only slightly more than the giant SCC of 53 891 939 vertices.

Using the above assumption, that the iteration takes linear time, the distributed calculation of PageRank was simulated to obtain estimations of the speedup. The server was implemented as a simple queue. The results for 1 to 10 clients are shown in figure 3. As the simulation demonstrates, the use of a small number of clients may reduce the required time significantly (2 clients to ca. 73%, 3 to ca. 64% and 4 to ca. 59%). But the speedup decreases with more clients.

4.1 Future Work

The results of the experiment seem promising, even though they indicate that only small number of clients are effective. But the conducted experiments have a major drawback. The measured "times" are not times used by real calculations of PageRank. They are estimations based solely on the topology of the strong component graph. Additional factors, like limited resources are not taken into account. These may be included in subsequent experiments.

In addition further extensions of the described system are possible. First of all, the rankings may easily be dynamically updated. As soon as a strong component changes, is split or several are composed, it may be inserted into the queue again and cause the recalculation of all succeeding components. Secondly, the calculation of the giant strong component may be distributed among several clients, reducing the resources required by single clients (but increasing the number of necessary communication and/or iterations). And last but not least, the clients may be weighted by their performance, restricting the size of the assigned components, and the extraction strategy of the queue may be varied to obtain better results.

References

[1] A. Arasu, J. Novak, A. Tomkins, and J. Tomlin. Pagerank computation and the structure of the web: Experiments and algorithms, 2001. citeseer.ist.psu.edu/arasu02pagerank.html.

[2] Konstantin Avrachenkov and Nelly Litvak. Decomposition of the google pagerank and optimal linking strategy. Technical Report RR-5101, Institut National de Recherche en Informatique et en Automatique, 2004.

[3] M. Bianchini, M. Gori, and F. Scarselli. Inside PageRank. *ACM Trans. Internet Tech.*, 5:92–128, 2005.

---

[5] In fact the required time for a constant number of iterations is about $O(n + m)$, where m is the number of edges. But since the average degree is small and can assumed to be constant, this bound can be viewed as $O(n)$.

[4] Sergey Brin and Lawrence Page. The anatomy of a large-scale hypertextual web-search engine. In *Proc. of the 7th World Wide Web Conference (WWW7)*, 1998.

[5] Sergey Brin, Lawrence Page, Rajeev Motwani, and Terry Winograd. The Page-Rank citation ranking: Bringing order to the web. Technical Report 1999-66, Stanford Digital Library Technologies Project, 1999. http://dbpubs.stanford.edu:8090/pub/1999-66.

[6] Michael Brinkmeier. Pagerank revisited. Technical report, Technical University Ilmenau, 2005. to appear.

[7] Andrei Z. Broder, Ravi Kumar, Farzin Maghoul, Prabhakar Raghavan, Sridhar Rajagopalan, Raymie Stata, Andrew Tomkins, and Janet L. Wiener. Graph structure in the web. *Computer Networks*, 33(1-6):309–320, 2000.

[8] T. Haveliwala and S. Kamvar. The second eigenvalue of the google matrix. Technical Report 2003-20, Stanford University, 2003. http://dbpubs.stanford.edu/pub/2003-20.

[9] Taher H. Haveliwala. Efficient computation of pagerank. Technical Report 1999-31, Stanford University, 1999. http://dbpubs.stanford.edu:8090/pub/1999-31.

[10] Taher H. Haveliwala. Topic-sensitive pagerank. In *Proc. of the 11th WWW Conference (WWW11)*, pages 517–526, 2002.

[11] Glen Jeh and Jennifer Widom. SimRank: A measure of structural-context similarity. In *Proc. 8th ACM SIGKDD Intl. Conf. on Knowledge Discovery and Data Mining*, July 2002.

[12] Sepandar D. Kamvar, Taher H. Haveliwala, Christopher D. Manning, and Gene H. Golub. Exploiting the block structure of the web for computing pagerank. Technical Report 2003-17, Stanford University, 2003. http://dbpubs.stanford.edu:8090/pub/2003-17.

[13] Robert Endre Tarjan. Depth-first search and linear graph algorithms. *SIAM J. Comput.*, 1(2):146–160, 1972.

[14] Yuan Wang and David J. DeWitt. Computing pagerank in a distributed internet search engine system. In *VLDB*, pages 420–431, 2004.

[15] Webbase project. Stanford University, http://www-diglib.stanford.edu/~testbed/doc2/WebBase/.

[16] Webgraph. University of Milano, http://webgraph.dsi.unimi.it/.

A Structured Peer-to-Peer System with Integrated Index and Storage Load Balancing

Viet-Dung Le[1], Gilbert Babin[2], and Peter Kropf[3]

[1] Department of Computer Science and Operations Research, University of Montreal,
C.P. 6128, Succursale Centre-Ville, Montréal (Québec), Canada H3C 3J7
levietdu@iro.umontreal.ca
[2] Information Technologies, HEC Montréal,
3000, ch. de la Côte-Sainte-Catherine, Montréal (Québec), Canada H3T 2A7
Gilbert.Babin@hec.ca
[3] Institute of Computer Science, University of Neuchâtel,
Rue Emile Argand 11, CH 2000 Neuchâtel, Switzerland
Peter.Kropf@unine.ch

Abstract. Load balancing emerges as an important problem that affects the performance of structured peer-to-peer systems. This paper presents a peer-to-peer system relying on the partitionning of a de Bruijn graph. The proposed system integrates mechanisms that perform index and storage load balancing. Index load refers to the network traffic incurred by a peer in managing an object index, while storage load refers to the storage space and network traffic required to store objects. The proposed mechanisms allow to effectively distribute both index load and storage load according to the peers' capacities.

1 Introduction

A peer-to-peer (P2P) system comprises multiple parties (called *peers*) that can request and provide services at the same time. This decentralized characteristic furthers spreading of workload among all participating peers and thus contributes to solutions for scalability issues in distributed systems. However, in comparison to a centralized system, managing shared objects becomes difficult because of the lack of a central or hierarchical control. Structured P2P systems, such as [3, 4, 7, 9, 11, 12, 14, 17], introduce efficient mechanisms to store and access these distributed objects. The principle inherent to such systems consists in mapping every object onto a key space or index (e.g., by hashing the object identifier), distributing this key space over the available peers, and maintaining a structured connection among the peers according to the keys each peer holds. The connection structure ensures to guide the search for an object to the peer responsible for the object's key in a small number of hops, often $O(\log n)$ in an n-peer system.

The system performance of a P2P network is critically affected by its overload. Indeed, the storage or processing load of the peers, the communication load and the system management load must be carefully handled to obtain satisfactory system performances which may be regarded as the fastest possible response time to user/application requests. Workload distribution and balancing mechanisms contribute to achieve good system performance. However, they may induce expensive restructuring processes, i.e.,

A. Bui et al. (Eds.): IICS 2005, LNCS 3908, pp. 41–52, 2006.

maintenance costs. Our approach aims to balance workload in P2P systems while keeping maintenance costs low. We are interested in two workload aspects: index load and storage load. In P2P systems, finding an object usually requires routing requests through intermediate peers before arriving at destination. The bandwidth used for this task makes up the index load on each peer. The storage load, on the other hand, denotes the usage of each peer's resources in object accommodation. Many load balancing approaches have been proposed. However, to our knowledge, none takes into account these two aspects of load simultaneously.

The present paper introduces a solution that simultaneously handles both index and storage load balancing by separating the concerns of peer identifiers (addresses), key management, and object storage locations. In particular, the proposed P2P structure is based on partitioning a de Bruijn graph where the node identifier space is identical to the key space. Therefore, we will use key and de Bruijn node exchangeably. Each peer holds a non-empty interval of de Bruijn nodes and maintains connections to other peers that hold neighbouring de Bruijn nodes. Based on this structure, looking for a specific key in the P2P system follows appropriate routing paths in the de Bruijn graph.

The **index load balancing** method takes into account the network capacity of the peers. It aims to minimize the network overload that may occur while routing requests in the system. This goal is different from that of most other methods which permanently adjust the load to a target. Since the decrease of the overload reacts only when an overload exists, our method saves on the costs of rebalancing. The balancing method involves two tasks: (1) locally calculating the index load on every peer and (2) dynamically transferring index load from peer to peer by modifying the key interval managed by each peer. We propose efficient mechanisms to perform these two tasks.

The **storage load balancing** method is based on separating the key and the storage location of objects. It eliminates the restriction of an object's residence to its root, where the root refers to the peer responsible for the key interval which includes the object's key. Instead, the root needs only to keep pointers to the location of its objects. This separation enables and facilitates the index load balancing since the move of a key interval from peer to peer entails moving only the involved object pointers (very small in size) instead of the objects themselves. Thus, moving keys does not affect the storage load. Without restriction to the root, the accommodation of objects chooses the storage location such that the storage load on every peer does not exceed the contributed storage capacity. In addition, we take into account the capacity of the peers in serving object requests and migration. We propose a balancing algorithm that minimizes the peer's overload with regards to its capacity. Like the index load balancing, the consideration of overload in this algorithm minimizes rebalancing costs. The algorithm is based on exchanging appropriate objects among pairs of peers in order to decrease the overload whenever it occurs. Finally, a fair advantage of separating key and storage location is the replication facility. The root of an object can maintain a set of pointers to its replicas (placed on different peers). Thus, the object availability is enhanced without further replication techniques.

The rest of this paper is organized as follows. Section 2 summarizes some recent work on load balancing in structured P2P systems. Sections 3 and 4 respectively describe the methods of index load and of storage load balancing that can operate simultaneously. The last section provides some discussion.

2   Related Work

A straightforward approach to load balancing in a structured P2P system is the equalization of the key occupation among the peers (e.g., [1, 8]). The equalization in [1] stochastically makes peers with short key intervals leave and rejoin the system by splitting peers with long key intervals. The method proposed in [8], on the other hand, balances a virtual binary tree whose leaf nodes represent the participating peers. In practice, load balance depends also on the distribution of objects on the peers, the object size, and the storage, processing, and communication capacity of the peers. Equalizing key occupation does not ensure an even load distribution when taking into account all these different factors making up the load.

The application of the *power of two choices* paradigm [2] applies multiple hash functions to map each item to multiple peers. This allows to insert an item on the least loaded peer. The methods in [5, 10] achieve load balance by exchanging key responsibility among the peers. The above approaches cannot simultaneously balance the index load and the storage load because they associate the storage location and the key. Balancing one workload aspect can break the balance of the other one, and vice versa. *PAST* [13] uses a replica diversion process to balance the storage load. However, the concerns of storage location and file identifier in *PAST* are not separated. It maintains an invariant that limits the storage location of a file to the *leaf* sets (see [12] for definition) of a number k of peers. The maintenance of this invariant introduces considerable overhead in a dynamically changing P2P system, e.g., a system with index load balancing.

Expressways [16], an extension of *CAN* [11], proposes an index load balancing method. It structures the network (of size n) as a hierarchy of $\log n$ levels, each one operating like a basic *CAN*. The balancing method is based on promoting peers with higher bandwidth to higher levels in the hierarchy. However, the reaction of the system to balance the load takes place only after aggregating the loads and the capacities of all peers in the system. Moreover, keeping each peer's and the overall system's load/capacity ratio equal can constantly bring the system to restructure itself even if individual peers would not require rebalancing.

The P2P systems introduced in [6, 9, 15] employ the partition of a de Bruijn graph. Like [1, 8], they aim at equalizing key occupation. As discussed above, this equalization is not sufficient for load balancing in structured P2P systems.

3   Index Load Balancing

3.1   System Structure and Routing

Our proposed P2P network partitions a binary de Bruijn graph $G(V, A)$ of 2^m nodes. The key space is identical to the de Bruijn node identifier space $V = [0, 2^m - 1]^1$.

---

[1] $[b, e]$ denotes the interval of integers from b to e (inclusive). If $b \leq e$, $[b, e] = \{x \in \mathbb{Z} \mid b \leq x \leq e\}$, otherwise, $[b, e] = [b, 2^m - 1] \cup [0, e]$.

Obviously, with a large enough m, the number of peers in a real network does not attain 2^m. Each peer holds and is responsible for a non-empty interval of de Bruijn nodes (also called *key interval*). Every peer is identified by its network (e.g., IP) address. Given a peer p, we denote:

- $p.a$ – the address of p,
- $p.b$ and $p.e$ – respectively the beginning and ending keys of p's key interval.

Two peers p and q must connect, denoted $connect(p, q)$, if there exists at least one arc between any two de Bruijn nodes that fall within the key intervals of p and q respectively, or if their key intervals are numerically adjacent.

$$connect(p, q) = \begin{cases} \text{true} & \text{if } (\exists x, y \mid (x, y) \in A \land x \in [p.b, p.e] \land y \in [q.b, q.e]) \\ & \lor (p.e = (q.b - 1) \bmod 2^m) \lor (p.b = (q.e + 1) \bmod 2^m) \\ \text{false} & \text{otherwise} \end{cases}$$

These connections are bidirectional, i.e., if $connect(p, q)$ then $connect(q, p)$. Two connecting peers are called *neighbours*. Each peer maintains a *neighbour list* consisting of a triple $(q.a, q.b, q.e)$ for each neighbour q in the list. The separation between peer address and key means that the peers can dynamically change their key interval $[b, e]$ without affecting the address a.

Loguinov et al. [6], and Naor and Weider [9] introduced a similar structure based on the de Bruijn graph. Their goal is to balance the partitioned zone sizes through different arrival/departure mechanisms. Our focus, however, is in balancing mechanisms taking into account the storage capacity and communication capacity of peers.

The routing function consists in directing a message to the root of a given key x from anywhere in the system. The message follows appropriate de Bruijn routing paths towards x. For convenience, all expressions on the de Bruijn node identifiers are implicitly modulo 2^m, e.g., $x + y$ means $(x + y) \bmod 2^m$. We also refer to the beginning and ending values of interval I as $I.b$ and $I.e$, respectively.

Definition 1. *The distance between two keys x and y, denoted $distance(x, y)$, is the minimum among the length of the de Bruijn routing paths[2] from x to y and from y to x.*

Definition 2. *The distance between a key interval I and a key x, denoted $distance(I, x)$, is equal to $distance(v, x)$ where $v \in I$ and $\nexists v' \in I \mid distance(v', x) < distance(v, x)$.*

In the de Bruijn graph of 2^m nodes, each node x has four arcs respectively to nodes $2x$, $2x + 1$, $\lfloor x/2 \rfloor$, and $\lfloor (x + 2^m)/2 \rfloor$. Let the arcs to $2x$ and $2x + 1$ be the fore-arcs and the arcs to $\lfloor x/2 \rfloor$ and $\lfloor (x + 2^m)/2 \rfloor$ be the back-arcs. We use notation $foredistance(x, y)$ to specify the length of the routing path following only fore-arcs from x to y. Similarly, the notation $backdistance(x, y)$ specifies the length of the routing path following only back-arcs. By Definition 1,

$$distance(x, y) = min(foredistance(x, y), backdistance(x, y)).$$

---

[2] Note that the de Bruijn routing path between two nodes in an undirected de Bruijn graph is not always the shortest path.

Claim 1. *Given a node x, the set of every node y such that $foredistance(x, y) = i$ (with $0 \leq i \leq m$), denoted $F_i(x)$, is $F_i(x) = [x2^i, x2^i + 2^i - 1]$.*

Proof. If $i = 0$, it is clear that $F_0(x) = \{x\}$.

If $i > 0$, suppose that $F_{i-1}(x) = [x2^{i-1}, x2^{i-1} + 2^{i-1} - 1]$ is correct. Following the fore-arcs of all nodes in $F_{i-1}(x)$, we have

$$F_i(x) = \bigcup_{y \in F_{i-1}(x)} F_1(y) = [x2^{i-1}2, (x2^{i-1} + 2^{i-1} - 1)2 + 1] = [x2^i, x2^i + 2^i - 1] \quad \square$$

Claim 2. *Given a node x, the set of every node y such that $backdistance(x, y) = i$ (with $0 \leq i \leq m$), denoted $B_i(x)$, is $B_i(x) = \{y_0, y_1, \cdots, y_{2^i-1}\}$ where $y_j = \lfloor x/2^i \rfloor + j2^{m-i}$.*

Proof. If $i = 0$, it is clear that $B_0(x) = \{x\}$.

If $i > 0$, suppose that $B_{i-1}(x) = \{y_0, y_1, \cdots, y_{2^{i-1}-1}\}$ where $y_j = \lfloor x/2^{(i-1)} \rfloor + j2^{m-(i-1)}$ is correct. Following the back-arcs of all y_j, we have

$$B_i(x) = \bigcup_{j \in [0, 2^{i-1}-1]} B_1(y_j)$$

where

$$
\begin{aligned}
B_1(y_j) &= \{\lfloor y_j/2 \rfloor, \lfloor (y_j + 2^m)/2 \rfloor\} \\
&= \{\lfloor (\lfloor x/2^{(i-1)} \rfloor + j2^{m-(i-1)})/2 \rfloor, \lfloor (\lfloor x/2^{(i-1)} \rfloor + j2^{m-(i-1)} + 2^m)/2 \rfloor\} \\
&= \{\lfloor x/2^i \rfloor + j2^{m-i}, \lfloor x/2^i \rfloor + (j + 2^{i-1})2^{m-i}\}
\end{aligned}
$$

For all $j \in [0, 2^{i-1} - 1]$, the pair $(j, j + 2^{i-1})$ gives all integers in $[0, 2^i - 1]$. $\quad \square$

Given a key interval I and a key x, the $distance(I, x)$ algorithm calculates $F_i(x)$ and $B_i(x)$ for i from 0 to m. If at an iteration d, $F_d(x)$ or $B_d(x)$ has common keys with I, it returns d. This algorithm is efficient because it iterates testing $F_i(x)$ and $B_i(x)$ for at most $m + 1$ times before finding the distance.

Definition 3. *The de Bruijn neighbourhood set of a key interval I, denoted $dbneighbour(I)$, is the set $([I.b \times 2, (I.e \times 2) + 1] \cup [\lfloor I.b/2 \rfloor, \lfloor I.e/2 \rfloor] \cup [\lfloor (I.b + 2^m)/2 \rfloor, \lfloor (I.e + 2^m)/2 \rfloor]) \setminus I$.*

Routing: the following algorithm routes a message from the current peer p to the peer holding key x.

1. if $x \in [p.b, p.e]$, peer p is the destination. Otherwise, continue with step 2;
2. calculate the set $U = dbneighbour([p.b, p.e])$. Find $t \in U$ such that $distance(t, x) = distance(U, x)$. Select neighbour q such that $t \in [q.b, q.e]$. Then continue routing to x from q.

The set U may contain several key intervals. We use here the notation $distance(U, x)$ to refer to the minimal distance from the intervals in U to x. The key t satisfying the equality $distance(t, x) = distance(U, x)$ is easily found: we select the key from the intersection of $F_i(x)$ or $B_i(x)$ and the interval (in U) the nearest to x while calculating the distance. This algorithm ensures to reduce the distance from the current position t to x by at least 1 after each hop. The number of routing hops is therefore bound by m.

3.2   Index Load Calculation

The index load of a peer is defined as the sum of routing message sizes passing through the peer in a unit of time. The idea of index load balancing is to transfer key intervals between peers to minimize the overload. It requires to calculate the routing traffic on different subsets (which we call zones) of each peer's key interval. For large key intervals, registering the routing traffic through all keys is inefficient or even unrealizable. To make this monitoring efficient, we restrict key interval movements. First, a peer p will only transfer keys to the peers holding $p.b - 1$ or $p.e + 1$. Second, the size of the interval transferred should range from 1 to $s - 1$ where s is the whole key interval's size. We further simplify the monitoring by dividing each peer p's key interval into k levels, where $k = \lfloor \log_2(p.e - p.b + 1) \rfloor$. Levels are further broken down into 3 zones. Figure 1 depicts this division.

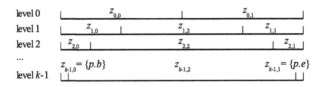

Fig. 1. Zone division at k levels on a peer p

At each level i ($0 \le i < k$), l_i, the length of zone $z_{i,0}$, is given by:

$$l_i = \begin{cases} \lfloor (p.e - p.b + 1)/2 \rfloor & \text{if } i = 0 \\ \lfloor l_{i-1}/2 \rfloor & \text{if } 0 < i < k \end{cases}$$

Then, we have the zones: $z_{i,0} = [p.b, p.b + l_i - 1]$, $z_{i,1} = [p.e - l_i + 1, p.e]$, and $z_{i,2} = [p.b, p.e] \setminus (z_{i,0} \cup z_{i,1})$. It follows that $z_{k-1,0} = \{p.b\}$ and $z_{k-1,1} = \{p.e\}$. In the special case where $p.b = p.e$, there exists only one level with $z_{0,0} = \{p.b\}$ and $z_{0,1} = z_{0,2} = \emptyset$.

Each peer p constructs a table $G_p[k][3]$ [3]. $G_p[i, j]$ registers the routing traffic through zone $z_{i,j}$. This table does not consume much memory space since $k < m$. According to the routing algorithm, when a message λ passes through peer p, λ is oriented via a de Bruijn node $t \in [p.b, p.e]$. For every level i, if $t \in z_{i,j}$ then $G_p[i, j] = G_p[i, j] + |\lambda|$ (where $|\lambda|$ denotes the size of λ). Obviously, the total routing traffic on peer p is $Tr_p = \sum_{j \in [0,2]} G_p[i, j]$, for any i.

Each peer p has a routing traffic capacity C_p. It verifies the index load periodically. We denote the period duration as δt, the beginning time of the current period as t_0, and the current time as t_c. Then, the current index load is $T_p = Tr_p/(t_c - t_0)$. In case $t_c - t_0$ is too small and may produce $Tr_p/(t_c - t_0)$ reflecting an incorrect index load of p, we calculate the load as $T_p = (Tr'_p + Tr_p)/(t_c - t'_0)$ where Tr'_p and t'_0 are, respectively, the routing traffic and the beginning time of the previous period. If $T_p > C_p$, peer p is overloaded. At the end of each verification period, if p is overloaded, it executes the index load balancing algorithm and starts a new period. Any change of $p.b$ or $p.e$ involves also a new period. The beginning of every period resets k and table G_p.

3.3 Index Load Balancing Algorithm

When a peer p discovers that it is overloaded ($T_p > C_p$), it should transfer an appropriate key interval $z_{i,0}$, $z_{i,1}$, $z_{i,0} \cup z_{i,2}$, or $z_{i,1} \cup z_{i,2}$ to the corresponding adjacent neighbour (the peer holding $p.b - 1$ or $p.e + 1$). The transfer must: (1) reduce as much as possible the cumulative overload of the two peers involved, and (2) be as small as possible. These criteria maximize the reduction of the cumulative overload while entailing the least changes. Since peer p only has local information, it does not know which key interval the destination peer can receive. Asking the destination peer for its load information before transferring would slow down the procedure. Furthermore, this may entail an incorrect decision since the status of the destination peer evolves continuously. Our solution allows peer p to propose a set of candidate key intervals to the neighbour. The transfer is completed when the destination peer chooses the most appropriate interval. Such transfer requires only one ask-answer communication between the two peers. Let $w_{h,j}$ (for integers $0 \le h < 2k$ and $0 \le j \le 1$) represent the candidate key intervals to transfer. We determine $w_{h,j}$ using the following rule:

$$w_{h,j} = \begin{cases} z_{k-h-1,j} & \text{if } 0 \le h < k \\ z_{h-k,j} \cup z_{h-k,2} & \text{if } k \le h < 2k \end{cases}$$

Thus, the routing traffic load on $w_{h,j}$, denoted $T(w_{h,j})$, is given as:

$$T(w_{h,j}) = \begin{cases} \dfrac{G_p[k - h - 1, j]}{t_c - t_0} & \text{if } 0 \le h < k \\ \dfrac{G_p[h - k, j] + G_p[h - k, 2]}{t_c - t_0} & \text{if } k \le h < 2k \end{cases}$$

Index Load Balancing Algorithm: The index load balancing algorithm (applying the key interval transfer protocol below) on peer p is as follows:

Let $n_0(p)$ denote the adjacent neighbour of p that holds $p.b - 1$ and $n_1(p)$ denote the adjacent neighbour of p that holds $p.e + 1$.

1. select the smallest h such that $\exists j \in \{0, 1\}$ and $T_p - T(w_{h,j}) \le C_p$. Then, execute the key interval transfer protocol for $w_{h,j}$ from p to $n_j(p)$. If the transfer succeeds, the load balancing stops. Otherwise, continue with step 2;
2. set $l = (j + 1) \bmod 2$. Select the smallest h such that $T_p - T(w_{h,l}) \le C_p$. Then, execute the key interval transfer protocol for $w_{h,l}$ from p to $n_l(p)$. After this step, the load balancing stops even if the key interval transfer does not succeed.

Key Interval Transfer Protocol: The transfer protocol for the key interval $w_{h,j}$ from peer p to peer $n_j(p)$ tries to move one of the key intervals $w_{0,j}$, $w_{1,j}$,..., $w_{h,j}$ from p to $n_j(p)$ such that the combined overload of p and $n_j(p)$ is minimized. Formally, the overload of p is $O_p = (T_p - C_p + |T_p - C_p|)/2$ and that of $n_j(p)$ is $O_{n_j(p)} = (T_{n_j(p)} - C_{n_j(p)} + |T_{n_j(p)} - C_{n_j(p)}|)/2$. Thus, the transfer must reduce as much as possible $O_p + O_{n_j(p)}$. The key interval transfert protocol involves the following steps:

1. p sends to $n_j(p)$ a key interval transfer proposal including the list $(w_{0,j}, w_{1,j},..., w_{h,j})$, the list $(T(w_{0,j}), T(w_{1,j}),..., T(w_{h,j}))$, and O_p;
2. if $n_j(p)$ is not able to receive a key interval or $T_{n_j(p)} \ge C_{n_j(p)}$, it refuses the transfer. Otherwise,

(a) it searches for the greatest $g \in [0, h]$ such that $T_{n_j(p)} + T(w_{g,j}) \leq C_{n_j(p)}$;

(b) if no such g exists, $n_j(p)$ searches for the smallest $g \in [0, h]$ satisfying

$$|T(w_{g,j}) - O_p| + T(w_{g,j}) - O_p + 2(T_{n_j(p)} - C_{n_j(p)}) < 0 \qquad (1)$$

      i. if no such g is found, $n_j(p)$ refuses the transfer because $O_p + O_{n_j(p)}$ cannot decrease;

      ii. if such a g is found, $n_j(p)$ sets the chosen index as g;

3. if an index g is chosen (by step 2a or 2(b)ii), $n_j(p)$ changes its key interval by $[n_j(p).b, n_j(p).e] \cup w_{g,j}$ and establishes connections to the new neighbours. Then, it sends to p an acceptance message specifying the chosen index g;

4. upon receiving the acceptance message with the chosen index g, peer p updates its key interval to $[p.b, p.e] \setminus w_{g,j}$ and releases the unnecessary connections to other peers. The transfer then succeeds;

5. in case $n_j(p)$ refuses the proposal of p, the transfer fails.

Theorem 1. *Given $w_{h,j}$ the interval to be transferred from peer p to peer $n_j(p)$ using the key interval transfer protocol. If $n_j(p)$ chooses an index $g \in [0, h]$, then transferring $w_{g,j}$ will maximize the reduction of the combined overload of p and $n_j(p)$.*

Proof. Peer $n_j(p)$ chooses an index $g \in [0, h]$ in step 2a or 2(b)ii of the protocol to accept the transfer of $w_{g,j}$. Recall that at each peer on the routing path, the routing algorithm limits the choice of the next de Bruijn node t (to direct the message to) in the de Bruijn neighbourhood set of the current peer's key interval. Therefore, if $w_{g,j}$ moves from p to $n_j(p)$, $T(w_{g,j})$ is transferred from p to $n_j(p)$ with high probability[3]. The overloads of p and $n_j(p)$ after the transfer are estimated as:

$$O'_p = (T_p - T(w_{g,j}) - C_p + |T_p - T(w_{g,j}) - C_p|)/2$$
$$O'_{n_j(p)} = (T_{n_j(p)} + T(w_{g,j}) - C_{n_j(p)} + |T_{n_j(p)} + T(w_{g,j}) - C_{n_j(p)}|)/2$$

The condition for reducing the total overload of p and $n_j(p)$ is:

$$\Delta O = O'_p + O'_{n_j(p)} - O_p - O_{n_j(p)} < 0 \qquad (2)$$

If g is set by step 2a, $T_{n_j(p)} + T(w_{g,j}) \leq C_{n_j(p)}$. Thus, $O'_{n_j(p)} = 0$. Since $O'_p < O_p$ and $O_{n_j(p)} = 0$, (2) holds.

If g is set by step 2(b)ii, (1) holds and $O'_{n_j(p)} = T_{n_j(p)} + T(w_{g,j}) - C_{n_j(p)}$. It is easy to prove that the left hand side of (1) is equal to $2\Delta O$ and that the smallest chosen index g induces the largest $|\Delta O|$. $\qquad \square$

In the key interval transfer protocol, step 2b is mandatory. Study the case where p is overloaded, $n_j(p)$ is underloaded, and there exists no $g \in [0, h]$ such that $T_{n_j(p)} + T(w_{g,j}) \leq C_{n_j(p)}$. Without step 2b, p cannot transfer any key interval to $n_j(p)$. Since $n_j(p)$ is underloaded, it does not intend to take off any part of its key interval. This situation blocks the transfer of load from p. The presence of step 2b allows peer p, in this case, to transfer the least loaded zone $w_{g,j}$ when it reduces the combined overload of p and $n_j(p)$. The load transfer thereby continues until some steady state.

---

[3] Because of the de Bruijn graph structure, it cannot be guaranteed that all trafic "transferred" will effectively be transferred.

4   Storage Load Balancing

We define the storage load of a peer as the total of size of the objects it stores. Each peer has a limited capacity available for storage which might be used for object migration. The system's management to store objects requires network bandwidth for object distribution, re-distribution, and associated index management (i.e., routing requests to the network). Consequently, the storage load balancing method has three goals: (1) keeping the storage load under the storage capacity on every peer, (2) adjusting bandwith consumption requirements to bandwidth availability, and (3) minimizing its impact on index load balancing (Sect. 3). To achieve these three goals, we propose to separate the location of the key of an object from the location of the object itself. In this way, objects can reside on arbitrary peers. Therefore, roots are only required to keep pointers to the objects under their responsibility. This approach simplifies the mechanisms required to achieve the first two goals. Finally, the independence of object and key locations enables us to achieve the third goal. Indeed, the key interval transfer remains efficient since only object pointers (very small in size) are required to move when a key interval transfer occurs.

A consequence of this approach is that replication of objects is simplified, hence enhancing object availability, without the need for multiple mapping hash functions (such as e.g. in [2]) or for maintaining invariants that constrain replication to nearby peers (e.g., [13]). A root simply needs to keep pointers to the peers that store the replicas of an object. In this paper, we consider that up to d ($d \geq 1$) replicas of an object may be stored. When a peer departs the network, it must guarantee the objects' availability. By allowing replication, we facilitate this task, since the departing peer only has to wait for objects with unique replicas to be copied elsewhere.

4.1   Object Pointer and Object Insertion

Every peer maintains two tables: *indices* and *storage*. Each entry of table *indices* contains the index of an object under the peer's responsibility. The index includes the object identifier (oid), and a list of pointers to the replicas ($replicas$). A replica pointer consists in the replica identifier (rid - a number in $[0, d-1]$), the storing peer address ($location$), and the replica's storage counter ($counter$). This counter is initially set to 0 and incremented after each change of location. Its use will be explained below. The *storage* table contains the list of objects stored on the peer. For each object, it records the object identifier (oid), the replica identifier (rid), the size ($size$), the address of the root ($root$), and the storage counter ($counter$). In order to maintain *indices* and *storage*, we propose two protocols, namely the storage notification protocol and the root notification protocol.

Whenever a peer receives an object, it sends to the root of the object a storage notification which contains its address and ($oid, rid, counter$) of the object. The *counter* field lets the root know whether the notification is newer than the corresponding pointer it holds. If the notification is new, the root updates the pointer. In the notification, the sending peer attaches the *root* field of the object header, asking whether it keeps the correct root address or not. If the information is incorrect, the root sends back a root notification.

When a peer receives a key interval, it sends root notifications to the storing peer of the objects involved. A root notification contains the root address, (*oid*, *rid*, *counter*) of the object, and the storing peer's address (*location*), as known by the root. On receiving the root notification, the storing peer updates the corresponding object's header. If *counter* or *location* are incorrect, the storing peer sends a storage notification back.

The maintenance of pointer consistency may seem complicated. However, in comparison to traditional systems which associate storage location and key, the key interval transfer used in our structure requires little effort. It involves the move of a number of pointers and some notifications but does not require any object transfer. The size of an object pointer and of a notification is much smaller than the size of the object.

The object insertion algorithm must ensure that $S_p \leq D_p$ for every peer p, where S_p and D_p are the storage load and capacity of p, respectively. In addition, it tries to store the object on up to d different peers. An insertion request contains the object identifier (*oid*) and size (*size*). The request is routed to the root of the object. If an index for the object already exists, the insertion algorithm stops. Otherwise, it starts diffusing replicas, with *rid* from 0 to $d - 1$. The diffusion process tries the root first.

A replica diffusion message λ_r contains *oid*, *size*, and *ridlist*, where *ridlist* is the list of *rids* remaining to be assigned. The message traverses multiple peers. A *ttl* (time-to-live) field limits the number of peers visited. At each peer q, if $S_q + size \leq D_q$ and q does not store any replica of the same object, q extracts a *rid* from *ridlist*, loads the corresponding replica to the local storage, and sends a storage notification to the root. If *ridlist* is not empty and $ttl > 0$, q decrements ttl and forwards λ_r to a neighbour not visited. Message λ_r maintains the list of visited peers to perform this verification. If ttl reaches 0 but no replica was stored, the insertion fails. If the number of stored replicas is between 1 and $d - 1$, the root starts a new diffusion for the remaining *rids*.

Object deletion is not considered here since it does not increase the storage load.

4.2   Storage Load Balancing Algorithm

Recall that the first two goals of the storage load balancing are to avoid storage overload and to take into account the bandwidth required respectively available to do so. Implicitly, the storage capacity of a peer D_p corresponds to the real storage available for objects. However, for the system to work properly, another boundary must be defined, which we refer to as the desired capacity on a peer $\overline{D}_p$, with $\overline{D}_p < D_p$. When inserting objects into the system, we ensure that $S_p \leq D_p$, hence allowing S_p to temporarily exceed $\overline{D}_p$ but always limiting it to D_p. Consequently, the storage load balancing problem can be specified as the minimization of the storage overload with regards to $\overline{D}_p$ while keeping $S_p \leq D_p$.

Given $A_p = \overline{D}_p - S_p$ the available space on peer p, a peer is overloaded when the overload $O_p = (-A_p + |A_p|)/2$ is positive, otherwise $O_p = 0$. The storage load balancing algorithm aims at minimizing the overload of all system components. It consists in the decentralized exchange of objects between pairs of peers. Suppose that an overloaded peer p exchanges objects with a peer q. In general, p sends to q a set of objects R_{pq} and q sends back to p a set of objects R_{qp}. Given that S_{pq} and S_{qp} are the storage loads of R_{pq} and R_{qp}, respectively, the combined overload of p and q decreases only if $A_q > 0$ and $0 \leq S_{qp} < S_{pq}$.

Definition 4. *Given that peer q receives a storage load S_{pq} from a peer p and selects a storage load S_{qp} to send back to p, the optimal exchange must (1) reduce the combined overload of p and q the most, and (2) minimize S_{qp}.*

Condition (1) guarantees the fastest reduction of the combined overload, while condition (2) minimizes the data volume sent. Hence, this approach not only reduces the storage overload, but also the bandwidth required to perform storage load balancing.

Theorem 2. *Given two peers p, q, with $A_p < 0$ and $A_q > 0$, and S_{pq}, the optimal exchange occurs when*

$$
S_{qp} = \begin{cases} 0 & \text{if } S_{pq} \le A_q \text{ or } A_q < S_{pq} \le -A_p \\ \text{closest to } \min(A_p, -A_q) + S_{pq} & \\ \text{such that } 0 \le S_{qp} < S_{pq} & \text{if } S_{pq} > \max(-A_p, A_q) \\ \text{and } S_{qp} > A_p - A_q + S_{pq} & \end{cases}
$$

Because of the limitation of space, we do not present the proof of this theorem. However, it can be found in the full version of this paper.

Storage Load Balancing Algorithm: Each peer p periodically verifies the storage load. If p is overloaded, it starts a balancing session:

1. p diffuses an available space interrogation ϕ, with a limited *ttl* (time-to-live) field, to its neighbourhood. Each peer q that receives ϕ the first time, processes ϕ, decrements *ttl*, and forwards ϕ to its neighbours excluding p and the peer from which ϕ comes. q responds to ϕ by sending $A_q = \overline{D}_q - S_q$ to p if $A_q > 0$;
2. for each reply A_q received, if p is still overloaded, p and q exchange objects such that the combined overload of p and q will decrease the most while the object migration is minimized:
   (a) p selects a set of objects R_{pq} to send to q satisfying one of the following conditions: (1) R_{pq} is the smallest that can underload p without overloading q; (2) if (1) cannot be satisfied, R_{pq} is the largest that cannot overload q; and (3) if both (1) and (2) cannot be satisfied, R_{pq} contains only the smallest object;
   (b) q selects a set of objects R_{qp} to send back to p. The selection is based on the optimal exchange condition stated in Theorem 2.

5   Conclusion

We have introduced balancing methods for index load and storage load that can simultaneously operate. The index load balancing is based on the exchange of key intervals among the peers. Unlike the *Expressways* [16] method, which must collect the load information of all peers before redistributing load, our method relies only on local information. We thus avoid the overhead of the load information communication.

The storage load balancing method manipulates the system structure at the object level, instead of the key level (such as the *Virtual servers* [10] method). The manipulation at the key level exhibits less flexibility since the all objects belonging to one key must move together with the key. Moreover, a move of keys in balancing the storage load also affects index load.

The load balancing methods presented operate on the overload instead of the load itself. Most other methods aim to adjust the load or the load/capacity ratio of every peer with a global objective function. This requires to globally calculate the targeted optimization and to continuously reorganize the system. By relying on the local examination of the overload, we need to react only when the overload exists and when it can be reduced. Experiments to evaluate the proposed load balancing methods are currently being conducted. So far, preliminary results have confirmed their anticipated efficiency. These experimentation results will be presented and discussed elsewhere.

References

1. M. Bienkowski, M. Korzeniowski, and F. M. auf der Heide. Dynamic load balancing in distributed hash tables. In *IPTPS'05*, February 2005.
2. J. Byers, J. Considine, and M. Mitzenmacher. Simple load balancing for distributed hash table. In *IPTPS'03*, February 2003.
3. P. Fraigniaud and P. Gauron. Brief announcement: An overview of the content-addressable network d2b. In *ACM PODC'03*, page 151, July 2003.
4. M. F. Kaashoek and D. R. Karger. Koorde: A simple degree-optimal distributed hash table. In *IPTPS'03*, February 2003.
5. D. R. Karger and M. Ruhl. Simple efficient load balancing algorithms for peer-to-peer systems. In *ACM SPAA'04*, pages 36–43, June 2004.
6. D. Loguinov, A. Kumar, V. Rai, and S. Ganesh. Graph-theoretic analysis of structured peer-to-peer systems: Routing distance and fault resilience. In *ACM SIGCOMM'03*, August 2003.
7. D. Malkhi, M. Naor, and D. Ratajczak. Viceroy: A scalable and dynamic emulation of the butterfly. In *ACM PODC'02*, pages 183–192, July 2002.
8. G. S. Manku. Balanced binary trees for id management and load balance in distributed hash tables. In *ACM PODC'04*, pages 197–205, July 2004.
9. M. Naor and U. Weider. Novel architectures for p2p application: the continuous-discrete approach. In *ACM SPAA'03*, June 2003.
10. A. Rao, K. Lakshminarayanan, S. Surana, R. Karp, and I. Stoica. Load balancing in structured p2p systems. In *IPTPS'03*, February 2003.
11. S. Ratnasamy, P. Francis, M. Handley, R. Karp, and S. Shenker. A scalabale content-addressable network. In *ACM SIGCOMM'01*, pages 161–172, August 2001.
12. A. Rowstron and P. Druschel. Pastry: Scalable, decentralized object location and routing for large-scale peer-to-peer systems. In *IFIP/ACM Middleware'01*, November 2001.
13. A. Rowstron and P. Druschel. Storage management and caching in past, a large-scale, persistent peer-to-peer storage utility. In *ACM SOSP'01*, October 2001.
14. I. Stoica, R. Moris, D. Karger, M. F. Kaashoek, and H. Balakrishnan. Chord: A scalable peer-to-peer lookup service for internet applications. In *ACM SIGCOMM'01*, pages 149–160, August 2001.
15. X. Wang, Y. Zhang, X. Li, and D. Loguinov. On zone-balancing of peer-to-peer networks: Analysis of random node join. In *ACM SIGMETRICS'04*, June 2004.
16. Z. Zhang, S.-M. Shi, and J. Zhu. Self-balanced p2p expressways: When marxism meets confucian. Technical Report MSR-TR-2002-72, Microsoft Research, 2002.
17. B. Y. Zhao, J. Kubiatowicz, and A. D. Joseph. Tapestry: An infrastructure for fault-tolerance wide-area location and routing. Technical Report UCB/CSD-01-1141, University of California Berkeley, April 2002.

Grid-Based Vehicle Locating System

Dhaval Shah, Dhawal Patel, and Sanjay Chaudhary

Dhirubhai Ambani Institute of Information and Communication Technology (DA-IICT),
Gandhinagar, 382009, India
{dhaval_shah, dhawal_patel, sanjay_chaudhary}@da-iict.org

Abstract. Advances in Information Technology have led to development of various Automatic Vehicle Location (AVL) systems. The automotive industry quickly adopted this system as it provides location services for vehicles through wireless technologies. But these systems are not explicitly optimized to take advantage of grid computing. Grid computing offers the infrastructure for developing coordinated, scalable resource sharing in a dynamic environment to maximize the utilization of the available resources in the network. Resources can be microprocessors, storage media, files, bandwidth, sensors etc. The problems like dynamic nature of resources, single point of failures, scalability, real time delivery of vehicle location information are mostly ignored in the design of such systems. The data grid concept, which addresses the above issues, can be used to improve the performance of Automatic Vehicle Location systems. We propose the architectural model for the vehicle transport system to be operated in grid environment to address the above mentioned problems, discuss implementation related issues, and benefits of our proposed model.

Keywords: AVL, Grid Computing, GPS, GIS, Data-grid, Web Services, Peer-to-Peer, Overlay networks.

1 Introduction

Heading towards the Information Technology age, more and more people and their vehicles will depend on wireless technologies to keep them connected with others and to facilitate safe, and efficient travel. To realize this concept, the present system of public transport has to be modified to exploit the IT infrastructure. There are several problems in the present transport infrastructure employed by the Government, which does not use the IT very effectively. Problems like traffic congestion, delays, accidents, inability to track the vehicle, inability to get route and schedule information, theft vehicle tracking, obstacle awareness etc, can be addressed.

Many transportation applications can be supported by centralized location and navigation systems, which utilize the wireless communication networks, host facilities, and other infrastructure together with the on-board vehicle equipment to locate and navigate. These applications include public transit system supported by wireless communications network [1][2][3][4][5]. Among numerous benefits of an automatic vehicle location systems are:

A. Bui et al. (Eds.): IICS 2005, LNCS 3908, pp. 53–67, 2006.
© Springer-Verlag Berlin Heidelberg 2006

Schedule Adherence: One major reason for reluctance among the customers is to use a public transport service is the uncertainty of the arrival time of bus at origin, destination and in-between points. Information regarding arrival of public transport vehicles can alleviate these problems and citizens will rely on the schedules of public transport system.

Safety and Security: Knowing the location of the buses ensures the safety and security of operators and customers, in case of normal and emergency situations.

Public Information: A high level of public information can be provided to general public on devices like mobile phones, PCs (Personal Computers) and other smart devices.

Improve Fleet Management: To respond to the spotty demands created by special circumstances.

We need to have accurate vehicle location services to address these issues.

2   Location Technologies

Most automatic vehicle location systems uses Global Positioning Systems (GPS) and Geographical Information System (GIS) data to locate the vehicle and get additional information about the location and features of the place. There are basically several location technologies [6]:

2.1   Dead Reckoning and Map-Matching

Dead-reckoning systems monitor the vehicle's internal compass and odometer and calculate its position by measuring its distance and direction from a known central starting point. Dead-reckoning systems frequently get off track and can be corrected using a technique called map matching. Map-matching systems store a map of the vehicle's coverage area in a database and assume that when a vehicle changes direction, it must have turned from one road on to another. When a vehicle does make a turn, map-matching systems alter the vehicle's record location to the nearest possible point at which the turn could have taken place. Because of the low degree of positional accuracy of dead reckoning and map matching, most AVL systems use more advanced technology options.

2.2   Signpost

When vehicles, such as transit buses, regularly travel a fixed route, many fleet operators have found that sign-post-based positioning systems offer an alternative to more advanced AVL technologies. Antennas are placed at locations throughout the vehicle's route and record the time when the vehicle passes nearby. Probe-based surveillance using toll tags and readers constitute a form of signpost-based AVL system. With some transit-based systems, the "signpost" also transmits the location of the signpost (and, therefore, the bus itself) to the bus; and the bus then transmits this information to center via radio communications.

2.3 Ground-Based Radio Navigation

In "terrestrial" or "ground-based" radio navigation, the AVL vendor sets up several receiving antennas in a metropolitan area. Each appropriately equipped vehicle broadcasts a radio frequency (RF) signal to all nearby receiving antennas. By measuring the time it takes for the signal to travel to the antenna, the distance from the vehicle to the antennas can be determined. When three or more antennas receive the vehicle's signal, the vehicle's position can be uniquely determined. A recent approach to radio navigation involves cellular telephones – determining a vehicle's location by measuring signals resulting from cellular phone usage within the vehicle. A disadvantage of radio-navigation is that RF signals have difficulty in transmitting through large obstructions, such as mountains, tunnels, parking garages, and metropolitan canyons formed by the large buildings that line many downtown city streets.

2.4 Global Positioning Systems (GPS)

Global positioning systems (GPS) use a network of satellites that are continuously orbiting the Earth to locate any object anywhere on the planet. The satellites are available free-of-charge to anyone with a device capable of receiving the satellite signals. The position of the objects is determined measuring how long a radio signal takes to reach the object from multiple satellites. GPS is by far the most accurate global navigation system ever devised, with accuracies in the range of 5 to 30 feet. Similar to radio-navigation, GPS signals have difficulty transmitting through large objects. The signals also have trouble transmitting through opaque objects, such as leaves on trees.

3 Automatic Vehicle Locating System: Present Status

Europeans identified a term for automatic vehicle locating system, in terms of "telematics" [7]. Telematics is the use of computers to receive, store, and distribute information about any mobile objects including vehicles over telecommunications system.

Large amount of work has been done to develop automatic vehicle locating system, but the present architecture has certain limitations. The Metadata about the resources (sensors, processors etc.) are stored on the central directory server, which makes the server less scalable. Another problem is the inability to maximize the utilization of the useful and critical resources like sensors, processors, memory, and storage media, which remain idle for most of the time. These resources could be utilized to perform certain computation intensive tasks [8][9] like:

- Prediction of wear and tear of roads.
- Prediction regarding the usage of vehicles during festival time and to plan for management of vehicle route accordingly.
- Data mining on traffic data, vehicle data etc gathered from the AVL systems.

- Traffic analysis to predict severity of injury, incident management, identification of a driver and vehicle characteristics through data mining the highway crash data.

The present architecture is to be reformed to provide support for these applications, by including the support of Grid Computing.

4 Distributed Computing Technologies

Several distributed computing technologies exist to address the said problem. Some of these technologies are compared and use of grid computing is justified below.

4.1 Client Server Technology

It is a network architecture in which server node(s) serves the various client requests. The processing is done on the server nodes only. It uses 2-tier architecture and suffer from several problems like scalability, server overloading, inability to utilize the client processors, which normally remains idle for most of the time, centralized control (security etc), single point of failure, transparency to users, lack of co-ordination among servers to solve a particular problem. Client/server technology is not suitable to solve the above mentioned problems for AVL systems.

4.2 Cluster Computing

It is a network architecture, which uses a group of connected processors that work together as a parallel computer to solve a given problem. They revolutionized the parallel computing technology. A cluster may consist of multiple nodes; each node is consisting of one or more processors. The memory, disk and devices of a node may be shared among all the processors in a cluster. Cluster computing is primarily concerned with computational resources and clusters usually contain a single type of processor and operating system. Clusters typically contain a static number of processors and resources. Clusters are physically housed in a same complex in a single location. The technology to interconnect nodes in a cluster delivers extremely low network latency, when nodes in a cluster are not physically close.

4.3 Peer-to-Peer (P2P) Computing

Computing paradigm in which each peer i.e. each participating computer can act both as a client and as a server in the context of some application. P2P system lacks a central point of management, which makes it ideal for providing anonymity and offers some protection from being traced. The lack of centralization in P2P environments carries two important consequences:

1. P2P systems are generally far more scalable than grid computing systems.
2. P2P systems are generally more tolerant of single-point failures than grid computing systems.

This means that the key to build grid-computing systems is finding a balance between decentralization and manageability. Also, while an important characteristic of grid computing is that resources are dynamic, in P2P systems the resources are much more dynamic in nature and generally are more fleeting than resources on a grid. Utilization of the distributed resources is a primary objective for P2P and Grid Computing. A final distinction between the two systems is standards. The general lack of standards in the P2P world contrasts with the host of standards in the grid universe. Based on the mutual benefits that grid and P2P systems seem to offer to each other, we will use both approaches to design the AVL system [10][11].

4.4 Grid Computing

A system in which there are shareable coordinated resources that are not subject to centralized control that uses standard, open, general-purpose protocols and interfaces to deliver non-trivial quality of service [12][13][14]. Grid computing will provide seamless, transparent, secure access to IT resources such as hardware, software, scientific instruments, and services etc. We will use the resource discovery mechanisms of peer-to-peer and resource sharing mechanisms from grid computing to include the advantages of both peer-to-peer and grid computing technologies.

5 Co-operative Distributed Web Services

Traditional techniques for a distributed web server design rely on manipulation of central resources, such as routers or DNS services, to distribute requests designated for a single IP address to multiple web servers. The goal of the Distributed Cooperative Web Server (DCWS) system development is to explore application-level techniques for distributing web content. The techniques to implement DCWS are discussed in [15], which are listed below:

- Hyperlink Graph
- Entry-Points Hypotheses
- Lazy Migration

Any of the techniques can be applied to our vehicle locating system since there are certain cases where the use of Distributed Cooperative Web servers is required. The information kiosks and PCs will connect to a central web server on which a default portal of vehicle locating system will be hosted and is responsible for distributing the requests to other web servers with whom, the data requested by the end users, will be stored. This technology will not be useful when only mobile units are incorporated into the system since the location of the end-user is available through which the request may be directed to their respective web servers.

6 Computational and Data Grid for Vehicle Locating System

A computational grid is a hardware and software infrastructure that provides the dependable, consistent, pervasive, and inexpensive access to high-end computational capabilities. We suggest the development of computational grid to yield several advantages in vehicle locating system, like increase in demand-driven access to computational power for data mining applications, which are described in section 13.

In addition to computational grid, we also suggest to develop the data grid infrastructure on the computational grid infrastructure. Data grid is the architecture for distributed data management [16]. In vehicle locating systems, the vehicle transit data acquired through the telematics installed in each vehicle, are distributed at various locations. Depending on the number of vehicles in each region, this volume of the data will increase to terabytes. To support the analysis of this data and figure out the trends, data needs to be accessed and analyzed. This combination of large dataset size, geographic distribution of users and resources, and computationally intensive analysis results in complex and stringent performance demands that are not satisfied by existing data management architectures. Thus, there is a need for data grid to overcome these limitations.

7 Functionalities in Proposed System

7.1 Assumptions

- We have assumed that Geographical Information System (GIS) is installed at each regional vehicle control center and GIS database is distributed to each regional vehicle control center.
- A satellite is available to transmit the data.
- We use the existing mobile network framework to route the data.

We propose the architecture of grid-based vehicle locating system in which following functionalities are envisioned:

1. End Users/citizens should be able to locate the vehicle/bus by giving appropriate selection parameters like source, destination, bus identification, route etc. through mobile handsets/ PCs/ Information kiosks.
2. Passengers/bus driver is able to send information regarding the status of the vehicle, e.g. information about accident, route, passengers through the telematics installed in the vehicle to the respective regional vehicle control center.
3. The regional vehicle control centers are able to poll the status of the vehicle, able to reprogram the interval of the status information to be sent to the vehicles.
4. All regional vehicle control centers are able to utilize the existing processing power and storage media present in the organization created by inter-connection of all regional vehicle control centers for several computational and data intensive analysis.
5. Vehicle control centers of various states are able to retrieve and store the knowledgebase gathered from several regional servers connected to it and share it with other state vehicle control centers.

8 Proposed Architecture

The architecture of the proposed system is shown in figure 1. The components of the telematics to be installed in the vehicle are described below:

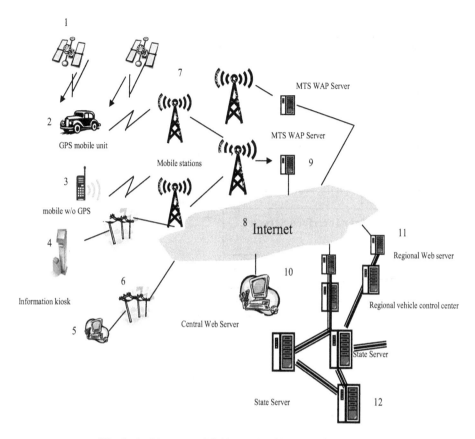

Fig. 1. Architecture of Grid-based vehicle locating system

1. **GPS Satellites:** The Satellites continuously transmit the signals, which would be useful to locate the device. There are several techniques to locate the mobile devices [6]. To receive the signals from satellites, special GPS receiver is installed in the telematics.

2. **GPS mobile unit (telematics):** This component actually receives the GPS data from satellites, and processes it and again transmits in the form of mobile radio signals through special mobile radio transceiver installed in it to the regional mobile base stations of mobile service provider. See Fig. 2.

3. **Mobile handset without GPS unit:** This component is meant to browse through the information about bus/vehicle location and other details. This device does not transmit any kind of location information to regional vehicle control center. It transmits requests to the nearest mobile base station of the mobile service provider.

4. **Information kiosks:** This device is installed at particular predefined locations, which are not nomadic. These devices are meant for browsing the vehicle information for the citizens, who are not able to use the mobile phones to access the vehicle information.

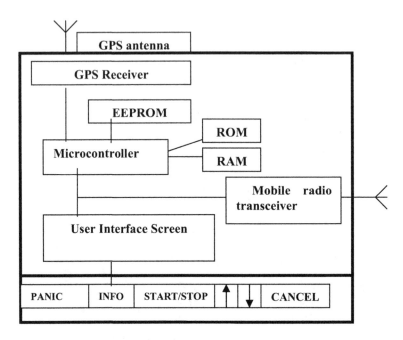

Fig. 2. Components of 'telematics'

5. **Personal computer:** End user can access the vehicle information through the personal computer connected to Internet. It uses a modem to convert the digital data to analog and analog to digital so as to render suitable for transmission through PSTN.

6. **PSTN (Public Switched Telephone Network):** This network basically carries the information about the end user's requests to regional servers and vehicle information from regional servers to the end users. This network will be useful when requests comes from any of the devices.

7. **Mobile stations:** The tower basically routes the vehicle information, location information etc from mobile vehicles to other mobile station (if not in same region) or to nearest mobile switching office, where data is intercepted by WAP (Wireless Application Protocol) server to convert it into TCP/IP (Transmission Control Protocol/Internet Protocol) format so as to make suitable to transmit in internet to the nearest regional vehicle control center.

8. **Internet:** We assume that Internet infrastructure exists for routing the requests for vehicle information. Information kiosks as well as PCs are connected to Internet.

9. **Mobile Telephone Switching Office (MTSO) WAP server:** This server basically converts the wireless data, which is in the format of 802.11 wireless protocols standard into the HTTP protocol so as to connect to regional vehicle control centers via web servers. This data/information generated by mobile devices basically are routed to the respective regional vehicle control center for

their requests to be served. This functionality is due to the fact that the mobile system has the capability to locate the mobile device. Thus, by taking advent-age of the mobile network infrastructure, the data are routed to their respective regional servers in which they are originated.

10. **Central web servers:** It is a central web server to resolve various queries of the end users. The requests are transferred to the respective regional vehicle control center web server. The web servers in this architecture are distributed co-operative web servers for which various strategies for routing the requests exists.

11. **Regional vehicle control center:** It consists of web services, database server, grid middleware to carry out various functionalities. Each center hosts the distributed GIS database used to provide information about the location features. The bus information, route and schedule information of the bus belonging to the respective region is also hosted by these servers. The data grid is developed on the basis of computational grids. It is consisting the resources of regional vehicle control center. We suggest to install grid middleware at each regional vehicle control center. These centers also host the distributed web services for which the requests may come from central web server or directly from end users. The data mining services to be executed periodically to perform traffic analysis.

12. **State control center:** It stores the knowledgebase about traffic that is useful in various applications. All regional servers are connected to one state server with leased line employing fibre optics technology. It consists of database servers where the knowledgebase is stored and all the servers are interconnected.

9 Grid Components in Vehicle Locating System

Essential grid components for the grid infrastructure are suggested to develop the grid of processors and storage media available in all regional vehicle control centers. The major services to be provided as a part of grid infrastructure are described below:

9.1 Grid Information Services for Vehicle Locating System

The major components of this service are information providers and information subscribers [17][18]. The information providers are those whose resource has to be utilized to carry out the task. The information subscribers are those who wish to be informed about the availability of a resource. The protocols for querying about resources include GRIP (Grid Resource Information Protocol) and GRRP (Grid Resource Registration Protocol) [18]. The vehicle locating system will include the aggregate directory servers located at each region that will keep information about the resources provided by the information providers. Each regional vehicle control center will include the aggregate directory services, which will keep information about the resources available in that particular regional center. The information subscribers of a particular regional control center will request the local aggregate directory services to provide the information about the resource availability to fulfill the processing or data demands for a job to be completed. Information providers in the similar manner will provide the information about the status of the resources to their local aggregate directory services. The directory server may not be a separate server, it can run as a service also. The clients (information subscribers) needs to register itself in the grid and notify its availability through GRRP to their local aggregate directory server and access information about the resources through GRIP.

9.2 Grid Resource Management Services

Several architectural models have been proposed for grid resource management [19][20][23] in which hierarchical, abstract owner and computational market/economy model are proposed. The hierarchical model is well-established model to realize the resource management in grid. We suggest to select hierarchical model. Each regional center in our system must include the resource broker, which handles the discovery of resources, selection of best resources from the discovered resources, mapping of tasks to the resources, staging the applications and data for processing and gathering the results.

9.3 Grid Data Management Services

The data grid established over the computational grid infrastructure, requires several additional services like replica management, replica selection and metadata services as high-level components that use the underlying grid infrastructure. Core services that must be provided to enable data grid support for vehicle-locating system includes storage systems, data access services, and metadata access services. Metadata access service includes application metadata, replica metadata and system configuration metadata [21].

9.4 Grid Security Services

We assume that grid middleware includes the GSI (Grid Security Infrastructure) Implementation [22].

```
while(true)
    {
     // process incoming message
          receive_message(X)
    if(validate_message(X))
          //update the data structures that keep the awareness information
          //in node
          {
                  if(X is status message of particular resource)
                          {       get the list of local subscribers Z

                                  if( X was subscribed by any of the local
                          subscribers in list Z)
```

```
                                        {
                                        send the status message to the
                                        respective node in the list z
                                        return from the funtion
                                         }
                        }
             }
    else
            {       timeout(n)
            }

    if(currenttime>lastsenttime + n)
           {        lastsenttime=currenttime
                    //send to logical neighbor aggregate directories
                    get the list of neighboring nodes (aggregate directories) y
                         for each node in y
                            send status update message
           }

}
```

10   Information Dissemination in the Grid

The data to be processed and information of the resources available in the grid needs to be disseminated to the relevant information subscribers. Several methods exist for information dissemination in grid and peer-to-peer computing [24][25]. Below are the models:

Polling Model: Information subscriber will query at specific period of interval, to the known servers for the resource availability or information.

Event Based Model: Information providers will notify the clients, who need the information about the resources or data as and when they are free or available respectively. This model is further refined into Publisher/Subscriber Model.

Publisher/Subscriber Model: The publishers are information providers or producers of events/notifications. The subscribers have the ability to express their interests in an event or a pattern of events, and the system provides them with every event fired by a publisher matching their registered interest. This model can further be classified into:

1. Topic/Subject-based model.
2. Content-based model.

11   Logical Model

Main objects are identified in the systems and the design is clarified by developing the class diagram of this system. The class diagram is shown in Fig. 3.

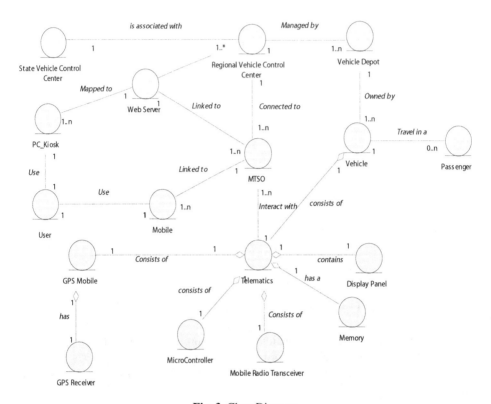

Fig. 3. Class Diagram

12 Algorithm for Information Dissemination in a Grid-Based Vehicle Locating System

This algorithm is written to disseminate the information about the computational resources to the respective subscribers.

12.1 Assumptions

1. The information/data dissemination occurs between the regional servers that will be used for various data intensive application, e.g. traffic analysis.
2. Information provider is a service, which provides the information about the resources.
3. Information subscriber is a service, which subscribes itself for a particular event/information.
4. The regional servers are interconnected through the private network.

12.2 Algorithm

1. Information provider registers with the local aggregate directory service to provide the information about the resource(s).

2. The aggregate directories are organized in a hierarchical manner (see Fig. 4.) to avoid single point of failure and to provide easy location services.
3. Subscribers subscribe to their local aggregate directory for the particular event to be delivered via GRRP.
4. The providers also dynamically register themselves to their local aggregate directories.
5. The local aggregate directories will disseminate the subscriber's interests to the neighbor aggregate directories depending on neighborhood size.
6. The algorithm uses neighborhood awareness [26]. It checks the distance from source to the current node and discards the message, if it exceeds the pre-defined limit (as described below). The below code runs in each aggregate directory.

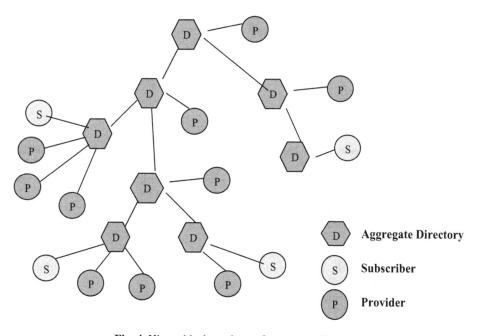

Fig. 4. Hierarchical topology of aggregate directories

13 Applications

Grid-based Vehicle Locating System will be able to provide the support for various critical functionalities:

1) The data that is collected at regional servers can be mined to extract the useful information.
2) Traffic analysis can be performed. The prediction of severity of the injury with the help of accident data can be made to take the effective rescue operations.
3) Incident management system can be developed to estimate the number of vehicles required, predict travel time, and provide the logistics.

4) Identification of driver and vehicle characteristics through data mining the highway crash data.
5) To predict wear and tear of roads during a season.

14 Conclusion and Future Scope

In this paper we have proposed the architecture of Grid-based vehicle locating system. It will utilize the wireless technology, internetworking and grid computing technology to maximize the utilization of resources distributed over the network to improve efficiency, pervasiveness, enable more data and processor intensive applications. Various grid-components that are critical in the functioning of this system are identified to justify the usage.

The system can be modified to provide the useful information to the government regarding the usage of the vehicles during festival time to plan in an effective manner. Route adjustment mechanisms to be developed to plan for alternative routes in case of emergency situations. Appropriate algorithms can be developed for route adjustment mechanisms.

References

[1] Greenfeld, J., "Automatic vehicle location (AVL) for transit operation," *Electro technical Conference, 2000*. MELECON 2000. 10th Mediterranean, Volume: 2, 29-31 May 2000.
[2] Burch, R.C; "Automatic Vehicle Location System Implementation" *Position Location and Navigation Symposium,* 1996, IEEE 1996, 22-26 April 1996.
[3] Sankar, R.; Civil, L, Southeastcon '97, "Intelligent traffic Monitoring system using wireless cellular communications," *Engineering New Century, Proceedings.* IEEE, 12-14 April 1997.
[4] Bonora, S.; Engels, D., "Guidelines for the use of GPS-based AVL systems in public transport fleets," *Public Transport Electronic Systems, 1996, International Conference on (Conf. Publ. No. 425)*, 21-22 May 1996.
[5] Taylor, S., "Developing automatic vehicle location systems," *Computing & Control Engineering Journal*, Volume: 14, Issue: 1, Feb. 2003.
[6] Yilin Zhao, Senior Member, IEEE, "Mobile Phone Location Determination and Its Impact on Intelligent Transportation Systems," *IEEE Transactions on intelligent transportation systems*, vol. 1, No. 1,March 2000.
[7] Yilin Zhao, "Telematics: Safe and Fun Driving", *IEEE Intelligent Systems*, January-February 2002, p.10-14.
[8] Miao M. Chong, Ajith Abraham, Marcin Paprzycki, "Traffic accident analysis using decision trees and neural networks."
[9] Der-Horng Lee1, Shin-Ting Jeng and P. Chandrasekar, "Applying data mining techniques for traffic incident analysis," *Journal of The Institution of Engineers, Singapore*, Vol. 44 Issue 2 2004
[10] Karl Aberer, Manfred Hauswirth, "Peer-to-peer information systems: concepts and models, state-of-the-art, and future systems."
[11] I. Foster, Adriana Iamnitchi, "On Death, Taxes, and the Convergence of Peer-to-Peer and Grid Computing."
[12] S Foster, I., "Internet Computing and the Emerging Grid," Nature Web Matters, 2000.

[13] Foster, I. and Kesselman, C. (eds.). "The Grid: Blueprint for a New Computing." Infrastructure." Morgan Kaufmann, 1999.

[14] J. Blythe, E. Deelman, Y. Gil, C. Kesselman, A. Agarwal, G. Mehta, K. Vahi, "The Role of Planning in Grid Computing," *ICAPS 2003*, 2003.

[15] Scott M. Baker and Bongki Moon, "Distributed Cooperative Web Servers."

[16] A. Chervenak, I. Foster, C. Kesselman, C. Salisbury, S. Tuecke, "The Data Grid: Towards an Architecture for the Distributed Management and Analysis of Large Scientific Datasets." *Journal of Network and Computer Applications*, 23:187-200, 2001 (based on conference publication from Proceedings of NetStore Conference 1999).

[17] Kerschberg, L.; Gomaa, H., "Data and information architectures for large-scale distributed data intensive information systems," Menasce, D.; Jong Pil Yoon; Scientific and Statistical Database Systems, 1996. *Proceedings, Eighth International Conference on*, 18-20 June 1996.

[18] K. Czajkowski, S. Fitzgerald, I. Foster, C. Kesselman, "Grid Information Services for Distributed Resource Sharing," *Proceedings of the Tenth IEEE International Symposium on High-Performance Distributed Computing (HPDC-10)*, IEEE Press, August 2001.

[19] G. Singh, S. Bharathi, A. Chervenak, E. Deelman, C. Kesselman, M. Mahohar, S. Pail, L. Pearlman, "A Metadata Catalog Service for Data Intensive Applications," G. Singh, S. Bharathi, A. Chervenak, E. Deelman, C. Kesselman, M. Mahohar, S. Pail, L. Pearlman. *Proceedings of Supercomputing 2003 (SC2003)*, November 2003.

[20] K. Czajkowski, I. Foster, N. Karonis, C. Kesselman, S. Martin, W. Smith, S. Tuecke, "A Resource Management Architecture for Metacomputing Systems," *Proc. IPPS/SPDP '98 Workshop on Job Scheduling Strategies for Parallel Processing*, pg. 62-82, 1998.

[21] Bill Allcock1 Joe Bester, John Bresnahan, Ann L. Chervenak, Ian Foster1, Carl Kesselman, Sam Meder, Veronika Nefedova1 Darcy Quesnell Steven Tuecke, "Data Management and Transfer in High -Performance."

[22] Foster, I., Kesselman, C., Tsudik, G. and Tuecke, S., "Security Architecture for Computational Grids." *In ACM Conference on Computers and Security*, 1998, 83-91.

[23] Buyya R., Chapin S., DiNucci D., "Architectural Models for Resource Management in the Grid."

[24] Datta, A.K.; Gradinariu, M.; Raynal, M.; Simon, G, "Anonymous publish/subscribe in P2P networks", *Parallel and Distributed Processing Symposium.*

[25] Peter R. Pietzuch, Jean Bacon, "Peer-to-Peer Overlay Broker Networks in an Event-Based Middleware."

[26] Maheswaran M.; Krauter K.; Lecture Notes In Computer Science, *Proceedings of the First IEEE/ACM International Workshop on Grid Computing,* Pages: 181 - 190 Year of Publication: 2000

The Guadalajara Urban Traffic Control
Project – An Overview About Features and Needs
for Tomorrow's Mobile City Communities

Helena Unger

Departamento de Sistema de Información,
Centro Universitario de Ciencias Economicas y Administrativas (CUCEA),
Universidad de Guadalajara (UdeG),
Anillo Periférico Nte. No. 799, Núcleo Los Belenes, Zapopan
helena@cucea.udg.mx

Abstract. The current contribution gives an overview on the different complex
and concatenated aspects and problems of traffic control in large urban
environments with a high population and traffic density. It intends to show that
without innovative, Internet based technologies no suitable simulation, analysis
and control of the urban traffic situation in a big city can be realized, especially
under the conditions of third world countries.

Beside the introduction of a new, GRID based simulation it will be
conceptually discussed, how existing infrastructural and other low cost concepts
may be used to achieve significant improvements for every member of the local
population community.

1   Introduction

Congestion in urban transportation systems has reached unprecedented levels.
Transport problems have become more wide-spread and severe than ever in both
industrialized and developing countries alike. Accidents kill tens of thousands of
individuals each year, and pollution from vehicle emissions degrades the quality of
life of every citizen. Transportation systems have broad, far-reaching economic and
social impacts in our modern society. Travel delays are a constant source of stress,
frustration, and dissatisfaction to the commuting public every day [1].

In particular, Guadalajara, the capital of the Mexican state of Jalisco shall be
considered. The metropolitan area of Guadalajara is mainly formed by Guadalajara,
Zapopan, Tlaquepaque, and Tonala. In addition, there are suburban areas which signi-
fycantly affect Guadalajara's metropolitan area traffic conditions such as Tlajomulco,
El Salto, Juanacatlan and Ixtlahuacan.

With its today's population of more than 7 million persons, Guadalajara metropolitan area is the second biggest and important city in México. However, the
Guadalajara metropolitan area is also a very dynamic, fast developing system: in 1980
this area had a population of 2,3 millions people, while in 2000 already approximately
3,5 millions lived here.

A. Bui et al. (Eds.): IICS 2005, LNCS 3908, pp. 68–78, 2006.
© Springer-Verlag Berlin Heidelberg 2006

The amount of private cars per one thousand of population grew from 111, 4 at 1980 until 217.9 at 2000 and Guadalajara's population still increases 2.3% every year [2, 3, 4]. Nevertheless, the Guadalajara area has not so such a dramatic congestion situation like most large cites of Europe or USA because 68% of all trips are still realized with public transport, 30% are private cars and 2% others transport media. Buses compose 30% of traffic flow [2].

Consequently, there is currently an ongoing controversy discussion especially in the area of improving public transport operations, e.g. what routes should be realized, with which capacity of buses and with which schedules [5].

The work consists of two parts which also give the structure of the present paper. At first, the real sources of traffic problems must be analyzed and suitable alternatives must be developed. Due to the danger of experimenting with operational systems and the limitations of purely analytic techniques, effective modeling and simulation tools are essential to solve these problems. The respective concepts and the used distributed GRID based simulation architecture is described in the following section 2 of the article.

On the basis of the achieved results, the respective traffic control and communication systems may be realized. The used innovative architectural concepts are the subject of the considerations in section 3. A summary of the currently done work and an outlook on the next steps conclude this presentation.

2 Simulating Large Urban Traffic Systems

2.1 Main Concepts

Urban planning is not easy: People simultaneously want to have access to transportation and not be bothered by it. This is a contradiction which is not easily resolved, in particular not in densely populated areas. Urban and transportation planning are the disciplines which deal with this contradiction.

In addition, any software package designed to help with these questions needs to address the fact that humans are "intelligent" and are able to adapt and to learn and to react on any available situation. One example in the realm of transportation planning is called induced traffic, i.e. the fact that better streets or better train connections leads to more traffic. That is why transportation planning is not an exercise of how to best deal with a given and fixed demand, but it has to balance the interests of people using the transportation system with the interests of people suffering from it [6].

More than 80% of the users use traffic simulation for design and testing of control strategies. The second most common application for traffic simulation is the evaluation of large scale schemes (45%) for. 20% of the users use traffic simulation for on-line traffic management or for evaluation of product performance. Other areas of application are research and education [7].

So, the optimization of the Guadalajara Urban Transport System can be realized solving the following main tasks:

1. *Analysis and Design of Transportation Systems.*
   Simulation is used extensively to evaluate the needed changes in the entire transportation system. This includes e.g. the addition or modification of road-ways, the

control algorithms of traffic lights, changes in the schedule of the public transport as well as the introduction of an Intelligent Transport System (ITS).

The typical goals of these simulative studies are to assess the impact of the proposed change on efficiency, safety and pollution.

2. *Traffic Management.*

Basing on the made simulations, later the transportation system must be changed. This includes changes in the road network as well as infrastructural changes (i.e. all systems which influence the traffic flow like traffic lights, sensors, signposts as well as communication possibilities between participants). Hereby, the simulation is used as a tool to evaluate different approaches before their realization.

A good approach to such complex problems is multi-agent simulations. For a multiagent simulation all entities, in particular the travelers, are resolved individually and carry all the information about the simulated system. Consequently, they have internal rules according to which they make decisions and move inside of a synthetic, simulated environment.

The most advantage of this agent-based, microscopic approach is that it can be easily improved by locally limited changes if it is mentioned that it is not realistic enough in certain aspects. This is the most difference to all other methods, which eventually reach a level where more details can not included any more. In addition, if once one has accepted the microscopic or agent-based paradigm, one can start very fast and with rather simple models a good simulation.

Roughly considered, microscopic models consist basically of two main components:

- an accurate description of the road network geometry including traffic facilities as traffic lights, traffic detectors,
- a very detailed modeling of the traffic behavior, which reproduces the dynamics of each individual vehicle, distinguishing between different types of vehicles and offering the possibility to take behavioral aspects of (classes of) vehicle's drivers into account.

In detail, any multi-agent package have not only to contain the traffic micro-simulation, which moves vehicles and travelers through the system, but also modules for route planning, for activity generation, and, most importantly, for human learning. It is not claimed that the resulting transportation simulation package is calibrated and validated [8] in advance and thus useful for any policy questions. However, it is certainly complete enough to do computational research with respect to methodological and computational questions and it will be the definite starting point for our project. In particular, it is possible to replace the modules one by one by more realistic ones and still keep the structure of the whole system intact.

Finally can be figured out that microscopic simulation models are a better representation of the reality and reproduce the traffic system much better [6]. Only with this approach the wide range of traffic scenarios appearing in the Guadalajara area can be considered. Since the whole model is divided in small local and therefore easy manageable units, precise descriptions of all traffic structures and traffic management schemes can be explicitly included and validated (what is definitely impossible with all other models and the huge dimension of the considered area).

The creation of this multi-agent simulation model of our urban transport system requires having all input information which is necessary for the creation and validation of the model. Due to the activities of CEIT and OCOIT [2, 3] a complete statistics is available, which make the intended work possible. In such a manner, the Guadalajara metropolitan area is unique and one of the few possible test-beds for such a project.

Processing such models for a large number of individuals and their mutual influences normally result in huge resource requirements and long simulation times, even when powerful parallel or distributed architectures are used.

2.2 Existing, Distributed Simulators

As mentioned above, to model the huge, complex transportation system of Guadalajara with the needed exactness, only a micro-simulation approach can be used [9].

Using this method means to represent every agent, object or microscopic entity in its respective environment. In this case every car (with the special behavior of its driver), every bus, every traffic light or anything that takes part or influence the Guadalajara's traffic is an agent in a big multi-agent system. The behavior of every agent must be modeled either separately or by a subclass, from which the generation of the particular agent maybe derived. It is clear that in such a case the simulation of the Guadalajara traffic requires the generation of up to 10 million agents and their handling. That is why the simulation becomes very time consuming and needs the respective computational power which can be only obtained from a massively parallel or distributed [10] GRID architecture; the below table give an overview on existing, similar solutions [11].

Since the performance of existing tools was not sufficient, a new micro-simulator was developed within the last several years. The developed and verified simulation architecture will be introduced in the following section.

Project	Number of agents	Number of links	Number of CPU's	Speed up	RTR[1]	Hardware	Source
PARAMICS [12]	120 000		32		3	Cray T3E.	http://www.paramics-online.com/
TRANSIMS [13]	100 000	20 000	32		65	PC cluster with 100MB Ethernat	http://transims.tsasa.lanl.gov/
AIMSUM2 [14, 15]			8	3,5		Shared memory architecture	http://www.aimsun.com/aimsun.html
VISSIM		160 km freeway network	13	6		Cluster PC	http://www.ptv.de/
MATSIM [11]	162464	28 624	32		770	32 dual CPU PC+Myrinet.	http://www.matsim.org/

---

[1] **Real time ratio (RTR)** – describes how much faster than reality the simulation is. For example, an RTR of 100 means that 100 minutes of traffic are simulated in 1 minute of computing time. This number is important no matter if the simulation is parallel or not.

2.3 Structure of the Developed Simulation Tool

The software package using for modeling and simulation of Guadalajara transport system based on previous activity-based modeling projects like TRANSIM [13] and MATSIM [11]. Derived from made experiences, the developed (distributed) software package has the following modules:

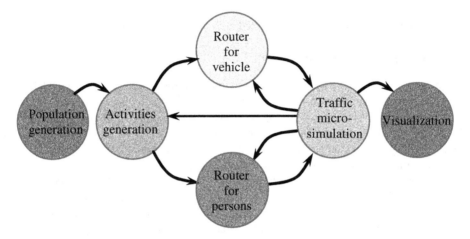

Fig. 1. The adapted MATSIM module structure for the Guadalajara's traffic project

- **Population Generation**:
  The model uses the demographic data and generates the agents representing the persons for the further simulation. This information is based in census and the typical data such as gender and age.
- **Activity Generation**:
  The Activity Generator module generates a list of activities for each member of a synthetic population [16, 17]. Each activity consists of a type and priority and this team decides based on the Synthetic population the start and ending time and currently we use an OD matrix for this task.

  A **modus sub-module** is to specify a transportation mode for each activity depending on certain values, which could be economical status, distance, comfort, etc.
- **Route generation:**
  This module generates the routes that an agent should follow depending on where he must start his activities and where he must end them. In our project we have two routers, one for vehicles (including cars and buses) and second providing routing of passengers (persons using buses).
- **Micro Simulation:**
  The input of this module is the city map and the agents with their plans. It outperforms the mobilization of each one of the agents. This module gives an output of which feeds the route generation in order to perform some re-planning.

- **Visualization:**
  This module present all results in a suitable manner on the screen. Possible are animations, diagrams and rough data within tables.

Currently, a GRID-cluster of 24 Pentium PC's connected via Internet is used, which is freely scalable. The software package was developed with Java, for communications between the nodes and the library standard RMI and the TCP/IP protocol are used. Differing to other systems, a good scalability could be achieved since simple master slave architecture was used. Therefore, a (more complex than usual) *BrainModule* controls all simulation process as master process. Differing to classical master processes, the *BrainModule* also provides the feedback for re-routing and re-planning mechanisms.

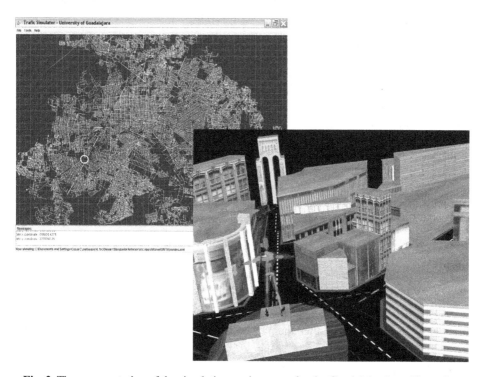

Fig. 2. The representation of the simulation environment for the Guadalajara's traffic project

3   Concepts for an Urban Community Traffic Control

3.1 Frame Conditions

From the above said become clear that a successful traffic simulation, analysis and control is more than just building a powerful simulation tool. Indeed, it needs a co-operation of a big community of scientists form different disciplines as well as a well optimized communication with the local population. In such a manner, the local community will influence the computation and vice versa.

Especially in third world countries, financial aspects may play an important role for the realization of the intended traffic control projects. While mobile phones are already well established, navigation systems and whole city covering WLAN systems may not be available to all or at least a large group of people.

Finally must be mentioned that usually used centralized computing systems have already reached their performance limits in large urban environments and the possibilities to react on a fast changing infrastructure as well as to compensate a higher number of system faults are no more satisfying. In addition, the costs for a first installation of such system are too high for most cities.

The below subsections will therefore give an overview on the new developed systems, which will now be used within our project.

3.2 Low Cost User Communication

A first important point is definitely the data collection within the system. While contemporary traffic sensors and processing units may measure most physical parameters of the traffic flow, any other communications (e.g. to obtain exact individual travel information) must be done either via existing or pretty cheap new installed communication infrastructures (since they are needed in a mass). This can be realized in the best manner on the basis of existing Internet and mobile phone connections allowing a personalized communication with the respective traffic processing and control computers. However, wireless LAN solutions and mobile ad-hoc-networks may also be used and included in that system in the future.

On the first point stands the data collection from the daily commuters in order to

- …have well qualified and personalized data for the modeling and simulation process
- …support navigation hints to the commuters basing on experience, simulation based predictions and current traffic situation as well.

Since no automated communication via navigation systems can be broadly implied, the idea is that users use either the WWW or SMS via mobile phone to send their travel plans consisting of

- its origin,
- its destination and
- the desired leaving time

to the respective traffic sub-centers (as we will later discuss, the new control system structures bases mostly on decentralized structures). Based on the current calculations, optimal routing suggestions, the travel time to be expected and some special routing information can be given back. In the case of a mobile phone [18], even on-line communication may be supported via SMS (and maybe for additional payments) in case of larger changes of the traffic situation and available routes.

3.3 Data Collection from Public Transport Systems

However, to include and optimize public transport due to its high traffic load generation within the considerations, also passenger movements must be measured (while normally pedestrians are not considered). That is why additional communication units may be placed in buses and other public transportation system [19], which allow to

- Collect reliable data about daily requirements (rides, times, frequencies)
- Adapt schedules to the changing needs
- Organize changes between different public transport systems
- Observe and compensate delays and cancellations due to technical and others problems
- Keep customers informed about the current state and traffic situation

Fulfilling these tasks means to build a flexible but also cheap data collection and communication system including every public transport medium (bus, tram etc), information systems on selected stations and the transport companies. Differing to today's only-existing radio-based communication units the information system shall be an automated one and work mostly driver independent.

One possibility therefore is the adaptation of the below shown wireless LAN based communication system of the University of Rostock (Germany), in which the moving buses and trams itself carry the information and may exchange them with other units and may be connected - via the installed network access points – with the internet and the central servers of the transport companies.

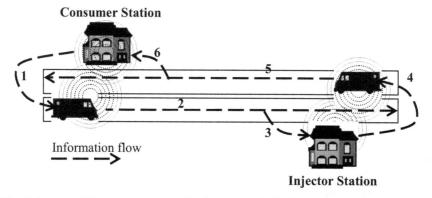

Fig. 3. A new public transport communication system (with high latency but low cost) [20]

Busses and other equipped vehicles need just to have an own embedded computer with a normal, cheap WLAN card. So they may collect data on passengers, traffic, traffic jams while moving through the urban environment. When passing one of the consumer stations along the streets (other central points) the WLAN card may contact the access point within the station and transfer therefore the collected data to the Internet where they can be used. In addition, information can be also given by injector stations to the cars (like route changes, closed streets etc). Although the latency may be in the area of minutes (depending on the distance of the injector and/or consumer station) this approach is pretty usual for the (comparable) slow moving traffic: although no city-wide WLAN cover is needed, actual data can be obtained and no large data storages are needed in the vehicles. In addition the system maybe used to transfer online information and advertisements to the passengers, what maybe an additional source of money.

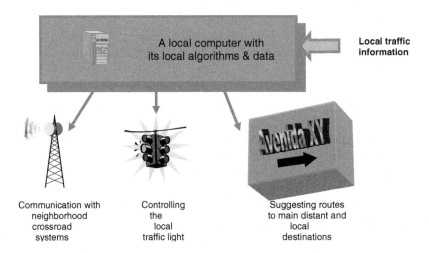

Fig. 4. A decentralized crossroad system hardware to built a self-organizing traffic control systems

3.4   A Concept for a Self-organizing Traffic Control System

Finally, Fig. 4 shows the heart component of the system – the traffic control units. The needed system must be built in such a manner that it

- Is able to do the huge amount of computation in real time,
- Is robust,
- Is easily maintainable,
- Is fault tolerant,
- Is scalable,
- Is self-organizing and adaptive and
- Causes low costs.

That is why the development of a new concept for a traffic control is the heart of the Guadalajara Urban Traffic Control Project. Such system can only base on small, autonomously working crossroad systems which are connected wireless

Every system contains a local, small computer knowing the local environment street map, measuring with local sensors the local traffic and controlling the traffic light as well as the local electronic signposts. In addition this system is equipped with a wireless LAN device, over which it may communicate with neighborhood crossroad.

4 Conclusion

The contribution gave an overview on the Guadalajara Urban Traffic Control Project. It introduces a new simulation technique to model huge urban environments in an adequate manner. The results of the made micro-simulations have shown that the traffic city in such complex systems may be analyzed and that the results may be used to improve the traffic situation significantly.

However, there are a lot of interactions between the simulated community and its activities. They require a manifold communication between technical system and people as well as system components on a low cost basis with standardized and well accepted end devices. Internet and the respective additional wireless LAN-supported technology with a new kind of self-organizing and adaptive algorithms may solve the open problems in the near future.

Acknowledgements

The authors specially thank to the National Science and Technology Council (CONACYT) and Universidad de Guadalajara for the support provided during the realization of this research.

References

1. R. Fujimoto J. Leonard II, 2002. "Grand Challenges in Modeling and Simulating Urban Transportation Systems" Proceedings of the First International Conference on Grand Challenges for Modeling and Simulation (ICGCMS 2002), January 27-31, 2002, San Antonio.
2. "Movilidad. Una visión estratégica en la zona metropolitana de Guadalajara" Report of A traffic investigation center in Guadalajara (CEIT), 2001
3. "Complicatón de resultados de las mesas de trabajo de las Jornadas de Movilidad Urbana Sustentable" (CEIT), 2002, www.jalisco.gob.mx/organismos/ceit/agenda/index.html
4. Adriana I. Olivares Gonzále, Marco F. de Paolini "Globalización y Ciudad en América Latina: debilidades y potencialidades", Memorias del V Congreso de las Asociaciones Latinoamericana Escuelas de Planeación, Urbanismo y Diseño Urbano.VI Congreso de la Asociación Nacional de Escuelas de Planeación, Urbanismo y Diseño Urbano. 2003
5. Maria Luisa García Yerena "Guadalajara: procesos de la ciudad región y la planeación urbana regional", Memorias del V Congreso de las Asociaciones Latinoamericana Escuelas de Planeación, Urbanismo y Diseño Urbano.VI Congreso de la Asociación Nacional de Escuelas de Planeación, Urbanismo y Diseño Urbano 2003
6. Nurhan Cetin, Kai Nagel, Bryan Raney, Andreas Voellmy, 2001. "Large scale multi-agent transportation simulations", *Proceedings of the Computational Physics Conference 2001 Aachen*
7. Staffan Algers, Eric Bernauer, Marco Boero, Laurent Breheret, Carlo Di Taranto, Mark Dougherty, Ken Fox and Jean-François Gabard Review of Micro-Simulation Models August 1997, http://www.its.leeds.ac.uk/projects/smartest/deliv3.html
8. Lianyu Chu, Henry X. Liu, Jun-Seok Oh and Will Recker A Calibration Procedure for Microscopic Traffic Simulation. (January 2004), CTSS WORKING PAPER SERIES 2004, http://www.its.uci.edu/its/Npub.html

9. Bryan Raney and Kai Nagel, 2004. "An Improved Framework for Large-Scale Multi-Agent Simulations of Travel Behavior", *Institute for Computational Science, ETH Zurich, May 2004*

10. Henry X. Liu, Wenteng Ma, R. Jayakrishnan, Will Recker "Large-Scale Traffic Simulation through Distributed Computing of PARAMICS " CTSS WORKING PAPER SERIES 2004, http://www.its.uci.edu/its/Npub.html

11. Nurhan Cetin, Adrian Burri, Kai Nagel, 2003 "A Large-Scale Agent-Based Traffic Microsimulation Based On Queue Model" 3rd *Swiss Transport Research Conference*

12. G. D. B. Cameron and C. I. D. Duncan. PARAMICS —Parallel microscopic simulation of road traffic. *Journal of Supercomputing*, 10(1):25, 1996.

13. K. Nagel and M. Rickert. Parallel implementation of the TRANSIMS micro-simulation *Parallel Computing*, 27(12):1611–1639, 2001.

14. J. Barceló, J. L. Ferrer, D. García, M. Florian and E. Le Saux, The Parallelization of AIMSUN2 Microscopic Simulator for ITS Applications, 3rd. World Congress on Intelligent TransportSystems, Orlando, 1996.

15. J. Barceló, J. L. Ferrer, D. García and R. Grau "Microscopic Traffic Simulation for ATT Systems Analysis a Parallel computing Version", 25th Anniversary of CRT/8/13/98, http://www.aimsun.com/crtpap1st.pdf

16. Michael G. McNally, 2000, "The Activity-Based Approach" (December 1, 2000). *Center for Activity Systems Analysis*. Paper UCI-ITS-AS-WP-00-4. http://repositories.cdlib. org/itsirvine/casa/UCI-ITS-AS-WP-00-4

17. Xu, Min, Michael AP Taylor and Steve Hamnett (2003) "A microsimulation model of travel behaviour for use in urban transport corridor analysis", paper presented at the 10th International Conference on Travel Behaviour Research, Lucerne, August 2003.

18. J.-L. Minoi, P. Green, S. Arnab, "Navigation Application with Mobile Telephony: Shortest-path", http://www.gisdevelopment.net/technology/lbs/techlbs008.htm

19. Bengsch, Andreas; Kopp, Heiko; Petry, Andre; Tavangarian, Djamshid. Evaluation of a Communication Environment for High-Speed Mobile Wireless LAN-Clients. In: Unger, Herwig, (Hrsg.), *Innovative Internet Community Systems (I2CS)*, S. 1-9, Springer Verlag, Leipzig, Juni2003.

20. D. Tavangarian "Ad-hoc mobile Wireless Local Area Networks" Piloteproject.

Towards P2P Information Systems

Magnus Kolweyh[1] and Ulrike Lechner[2]

[1] Universität Bremen, Fachbereich für Mathematik und Informatik
mag@informatik.uni-bremen.de
[2] Universität der Bundeswehr München, Fakultät für Informatik,
Institut für Angewandte Systemwissenschaften und Wirtschaftsinformatik
Ulrike.Lechner@unibw.de

Abstract. P2P systems draw large communities of users and create most of the Internet traffic. Two typical P2P myths are (1) that P2P is about sharing of audio and video content and (2) that P2P networks are only about sharing files between anonymous users. We present the results of an empirical study in the P2P network Direct Connect. We find that P2P networks are places to share all kind of data. We also find that there is a significant amount of communication going on in P2P networks.

1   Introduction

Currently, Peer-to-Peer (P2P) systems create most of the Internet traffic and we see novel P2P platforms with various P2P clients to be announced on various platforms. P2P systems are new and very popular types of distributed information systems and distributed system technology is considered to be the next step for many application areas. .NET or Grid Computing are technologies for distributed information systems. They have been developed with professional applications in mind. The main application area for P2P systems has been and currently is file sharing.

P2P systems are very popular with users. Common P2P file sharing networks seem to be the perfect prototype for distributed applications as they are popular and serve a huge number of peers. This new distributed paradigm leads to a new information system scenario with ubiquity and ad-hoc distribution of data. On the performance and cost side, decentralized networks have several advantages over traditional client-server platforms. In theory, these systems scale indefinitely in terms of peers or data size without decreasing search time and without the need for costly centralized resources [1, 2]. However, we observe selfishness of nodes [3] as well as problems with content contribution, quality and availability of content [4]. The business models of popular file sharing networks are neither legal nor sustainable [5, 6].

We analyze first the kind of contents being shared and then the degree of social interaction within P2P systems. We find that P2P networks are more than mere and anonymous audio and video sharing networks. They are multi-purpose content sharing networks in which users interact. Thus, we conclude that P2P

A. Bui et al. (Eds.): IICS 2005, LNCS 3908, pp. 79–90, 2006.
© Springer-Verlag Berlin Heidelberg 2006

have the tendency to move towards information systems and this opens up new chances for research and for applications.

This paper is organized as follows. We begin with an analysis of the state of the art with a presentation of current research topics and key aspects of P2P systems (Sect. 2); discuss their relevance and present basic challenges for P2P from an information systems point of view. We identify two P2P myths - commonly used assumptions of file sharing systems (Sect. 3) and present our research approach (Sect. 4). We explore then the kind of data being shared in P2P systems (Sect. 5) and the interaction within P2P systems (Sect. 6). The paper concludes with a discussion of our findings (Sect. 7).

2   State of the Art and Literature Review

P2P networks are driven by applications and their success. In this section, we review the state of the art, first in the development of P2P applications, then the advances in P2P technology and, finally, in P2P business models.

2.1   The P2P Paradigm and P2P Applications

The area of P2P networks became popular with P2P file sharing applications as (the original) Napster and gnutella in the year 2000. Those applications drew huge communities to share an incredible amount of audio files [7].

As of April 2005, P2P networks are far more differentiated. P2P applications are grouped to three areas: (1) File sharing, (2) Distributed Computing and (3) Communication [1]. While mass media often name Napster, Morpheus, Limewire and Kazaa as the most important file sharing systems, they are best sorted by their protocol. Popular protocols are Gnutella, Fasttrack, Edonkey and the recently developed Bittorrent [8].

Grid Computing and Seti@home belong to the P2P distributed computing category and Grid computing is gaining momentum for professional contexts [9].

P2P communication is often associated with Instant Messaging Clients like ICQ or Jabber. Skype, a P2P based telephony system, is one of the latest popular applications in that field. Groove, is an example for a P2P collaboration tool. There seems to be a new popular P2P application area Communication besides file sharing. To sum up the development of P2P applications – P2P seems to reach out for application areas beyond mere file sharing. So, what is done in research and development to enhance P2P technology?

2.2   P2P Technology

On the performance and cost side, decentralized networks have several advantages over traditional client-server platforms. In theory, these systems scale indefinitely in terms of peers or data size without decreasing search time and without the need for costly centralized resources [1, 2]. They utilize the processing and networking power of a huge amount of nodes and these resources grow proportionally to the network size. Each new node joining a network potentially adds storage capacity, processing power and bandwidth to the network. Thus, by decentralizing resources, P2P networks are able to virtually eliminate costs that are associated with a large centralized infrastructure. Also, P2P networks may have advantages concerning redundancy, robustness and performance.

Current research on technology in P2P systems tries to further expand those performance and cost advantages. It focuses on various subjects like network architectures [10,11] Distributed Systems [12,13] and scalable algorithms [14]. Improvements have been achieved on the low-level concerning efficiency, robustness and scalability. Advanced implemented services are searching, indexing dissemination, rendezvous and redundancy concepts.

While improvements in efficiency, scalability, robustness and security seem crucial for current applications, we need to deal with the emerging prospects of P2P applications. There seems to be some gap between academically drafted concepts for P2P and the design of most popular systems today. Distributed Hash Tables (DHTs) are powerful build-in data structures used by many modern distributed concepts like CHORD [10] or CAN [11]. Despite their power DHT's are rarely seen in file sharing protocols so far, solely Freenet [15] and Overnet implement DHT-like data structures. Recent file sharing applications like, e.g. Gnutella, Kazaa and Edonkey would benefit from scalable search strategies for their millions of connected peers but implement simplistic and therefore inefficient protocols [2]. Also, the lately emerged Bittorrent uses relatively basic concepts with network overhead and security slowdowns for data management compared to CHORD-systems, whose efficiency has been mathematically proven [10]. Bittorrent serves the need for a distributed file transfer service that works similar as the central, easy-to use ftp but with enormous distributed power. The Bittorrent protocol seems to be designed very plain with huge space for improvements like reducing network overhead and security slowdowns. Bittorrent is used for all kinds of file-sharing and this includes in particular the distribution of large Open Source packages, like, e.g., like full Linux Distributions (Fedora).

The technical approaches are able to solve some of the network problems of current P2P networks and enhance the special properties of P2P networks. However, the success of a P2P network often seems to be rather independent of the achieved network performance. Are there any sustainable business models for this P2P technology?

2.3 P2P Business Models

P2P gets with its potential and the various challenges a lot of attention from researchers, users and media industry [9]. Each of those groups seems has its view. Media reports nearly every day on new attacks from the media industry on P2P end users or whole networks and even researchers have to deal with the illegal content in scanning typical P2P systems [6].

Research in information systems on P2P focuses on the business models. There are several proposals for innovative business models and services as digital rights management systems for P2P networks [6,16,17,18]. Again, there seems to be a gap between academic concepts and the development of the P2P sector as the predominant applications seem to do fine without digital rights management and sustainable business models.

Research on behavior of users reveals several obstacles to built sustainable P2P business models. The imbalance between a small number of contributors vs. a large number of sharing users, the lack of quality or the concentration of queries and available contents on a small is being analyzed e.g. in [4]. Only recently, P2P applications implemented some concepts and services to manage interaction. There are virtual currencies (cf. Applejuice), concepts that force users to keep parts of downloads online as long as they are trying to download a piece of digital content (Bittorrent). Some networks are open on an invitation only basis. Some networks rely also on (human) management of the interaction (cf. Direct Connect [19]). Thus, there seem to be a problem with content and user management within P2P systems. This lack of sustainable, legal business models looks like a challenge in developing information systems as P2P systems.

We observe that the variety of P2P application increases and that novel applications in Grid Computing and communication gain momentum. We also observe that P2P technology advances. However, there are no valid business models and hardly any approaches to manage content and users in P2P networks. Thus, a reality check, what is going on in P2P networks in terms of availability of content and communication between users is necessary — to see whether P2P is still about sharing music.

3   Peer-to-Peer Myths - The Research Hypotheses

P2P gets with its potential and the various challenges a lot of attention from researchers, users and media industry [9]. Each of those groups seems to have its view. Media reports nearly every day on new attacks from the media industry on P2P end users or whole networks and even researchers have to deal with the illegal content in scanning typical P2P systems [6]. To equate P2P with illegal music sharing seems to be lowest common denominator. Is this a P2P myth? We question if that association is still that clear.

Hypothesis 1: File sharing systems are not single-purpose networks for sharing audio (mp3) files or files of some particular data format. Today, P2P networks are multi-purpose networks to share many kinds of digital content.

A second wide-spread assumption is that users try to act as anonymously as they can due to the illegal nature of P2P systems. However, interaction and social bonds are deeply rooted human needs and from research on virtual communities, it is known that interaction and the social network that emerges from interaction positively influences the quality of content and interaction [5]. To equate P2P with anonymous users whose only interest is file sharing seems to be a common perception – the second P2P myth. We would like to question whether P2P is really about file sharing between anonymous users and whether P2P is about file sharing at all.

Hypothesis 2: Users are willing to communicate and interact with other users on a topic of interest. Thus, on P2P systems that are dedicated to a particular topic we expect more communication between the users than in systems without such topics.

4   Research Design

The Direct Connect network [19] is chosen as P2P network for our research. Direct Connect has been released by Neo-Modus in November of 1999. Since then Direct Connect has developed a steady user base. Unlike other P2P networks, its user numbers have never exploded just to break down shortly after. This makes it a good basis to study a "mature" P2P network with its content and users.

Direct Connect is a hybrid P2P network. Hubs provide the connectivity to the Direct Connect network, do most of the network management and manage, in particular, queries. Peers connect to the hubs and hubs may have hub rules. I.e., peers can only connect to a hub, if they meet the hub rules. Those hub rules are, e.g., share size (the amount of content a users is willing to share) or open upload slots (the bandwidth a user is willing to sacrifice when sharing).

According to www.hublist.org, a list of registered hubs, Direct Connect has approximately 2 million users worldwide on over 20000 hubs (November 2004). Note that there is no need to register a hub.

In the first part of the study we collected and classified data from peers. We classify data with a set of commonly known data extensions that we obtain from the Internet extension data base http://filext.com. In the study, we collected data from 4800 Peers over three days in October 2004 on selected hubs. The hubs were randomly selected from a publicly available hub list of the Direct Connect Network at www.hublist.org.

5   Peer-to-Peer = Illegal Music Sharing?

The first part of the empirical study is concerned with the kind of data being offered for sharing. We connect with a modified client to the Direct Connect network to collect data from peers. From the peers, we obtain for this first part of the study the file lists. The file lists carry the file names of the files that a peer offers. We are interested in the content types of the files from the file lists and classify the files into content types according to their file extension. We collect data on (1) Total volume of a content type, i.e., the sum of the size of all files in a content type (total GB), (2) average size of files of a content type (average MB) and (3) the total number of files (number) of a content type.

We utilize a set of on average 20 file extensions for 12 chosen data types to classify the files of the peers file lists. Files without file extension are discarded. Ambiguities are resolved by grouping ambiguous extensions to one of the possible data types. E.g. a .class extension denotes a pure binary, a library of a java application, or an Internet file. Note, that this ambiguity and its arbitrary resolution are not critical, because our interest is to what extent

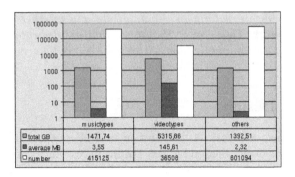

Fig. 1. Popular classes of data on Direct Connect Hubs (log scale)

file sharing still is about audio and video files and the kind data being offered in a P2P network.

Figure 1 depicts the results on the amount of data (total GB), the average size of files (average MB) and the number of files (number) for audio files, video files and files that neither belong to audio nor video types (other). We observe that audio-type content is most popular according to the number of files, but is only second position in total volume. Video content dominates in the average size of the content category. Since an audio file is much smaller than a video file (3.6 MB vs. 145.6 MB), the total amount of audio types is much smaller (1.4 TB vs. 5.3 TB). The "other" file type comprises more files in total and by number than the two popular file types audio and video together. We observe that users share huge amounts of various "other"data like text data, source files, web pages and images. That content outnumbers audio and video in terms of total number of files but is less in total size than audio or video files (cf. Fig. 1). An analysis of the other type (Fig. 2) reveals the variety of content types being offered in the network.

Figure 2 details the other type of file offered in the Direct Connect network. Users share images, office files, source code and all kinds of text files. Surprisingly high is the amount of files classified as Internet type. Internet types are mainly

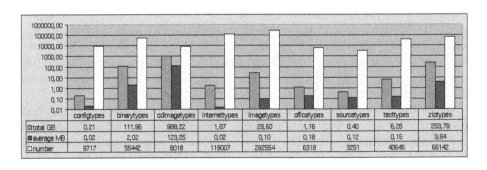

Fig. 2. Collection of 'other' data (log scale)

files with extension .html and therefore web pages. Note that the hyperlink structure of web pages often relies on location and context of a file and that html files typically are part of a collection of files and location and context eventually changes when sharing a file on a P2P network. Our study shows hat Internet type files are offered within networks despite the fact that P2P is not the right 'habitat for this kind of file.

Note that the average file size differs for the file types. This is an indicator that files, in particular audio and video files, are not disguised as other kinds of files (zip, html, files) in our data set. Note furthermore that both audio and video files can be shared as zip files. There are many zip files and zip files that can carry any kind of content, but the number of files and the overall volume of zip file does certainly not dominate the overall picture. Since we are interested in the kind of content that is distributed not the content itself, we refrain from analyzing the kind of content of the zip files.

One source for the abundance of files and file types apart from the audio and video types might be the hub rules. Some hubs require a minimum share and users might be tempted to declare any kind of collection of data as share to get permission to connect to those hubs. This is still an open question and only the measurement of traffic can determine whether files offered and actual sharing traffic match.

Let us briefly discuss the findings. Our data shows that file sharing is not about sharing audio and video types any more. All types of content are found in a P2P network. This has implications on technology and business models. While Internet service providers mainly have to be concerned with the total size of pieces of contents due to the traffic these files generate, they still can keep their view on file sharing systems as multi-media sharing. From an information system point of view, the number of information objects and the variety of information objects are of interest.

Measurement of P2P traffic becomes increasingly difficult due to the new P2P protocols. Most important factor here is the use of non-standard, dynamically changing, arbitrary ports in protocols as, e.g., Bittorrent [20]. Additionally, those systems often use package encryption nowadays which makes simple payload measurements inapplicable. Thus, measuring the offerings instead of the traffic is sensible when one is interested in content rather than P2P network issues.

In the first part of the empirical study, we observe that data supports Hypothesis 1. File sharing today is not all about audio or video sharing. This leads to the next question, whether P2P is about file sharing at all. Despite the fact that the media industry and most of the users associate P2P with file sharing, there are a significant number of P2P applications apart from pure file sharing. Examples include Freenet, Skype, FreeHaven, and Edutella [21]. These applications are about communication or about organizing content and interaction. In the second part of the empirical study, we analyze communication and the correlation between content and communication within P2P network.

6   Peers = Anonymous Users?

In this second part of the study, we try to detect social network structures within P2P networks. Our guiding hypothesis is that social networks emerge in P2P networks and that a strong social network eventually benefits the file sharing and the P2P network. We motivate this research with the analogy of P2P networks to virtual communities. As communication is a deeply rooted human need, we expect that users are willing to communicate in P2P systems. Research on Virtual Communities describes the social network of a community as the reason for users to contribute to the community, to be altruistic and to comply with rules of a community [5]. We expect that a commitment of users, i.e., tough hub rules correlates with the strength of a social network, i.e., communication between users provided that the topic is legal and users are not forced into strict anonymity. We also expect that hubs with topics are more likely to have interaction and social networks than hubs without such a topic.

As in the first part of the study, the focus lies on the hubs and the interaction on a hub. As described earlier, a peer connects to a hub to search for data and file lists of other peers simultaneously connected to the hub. Peers can connect to a hub only if they meet certain hub rules and/or confirm to data-filtering entrance rules. Those hub rules include the minimum amount of shared data (min_share) and the minimum of open upload slots (the amount of bandwidth a user sacrifices for download of contents offered by the peer). From a protocol view, all hubs can have a hub description like, e.g., 'romantic music here'. Those topics describe what content is being shared on a hub. Users that are interested in a particular topic select hubs accordingly.

We refer to hubs with a certain description and corresponding data-filtering entrance rules as topic_given hubs and to all others as 'free-form hubs'.

Let us describe how we measure the communication on a hub. The Direct Connect Protocol discriminates between query messages for files and normal P2P communication (chat). Such messages are of the form

```
$To: <othernick>
  From: <nick> $<<sendernick>> ;<message>  (chat message)
$Search <ip>:<port> <searchstring> (search message)
```

Another form is

```
$To: <<sendernick>> <message> (public message)
```

which sends a public message to the hub board. Such messages can be seen by all connected peers via a central hub message screen, depending on the implementation of the particular Direct Connect client.

It is important to notice that are are several popular Direct Connect hub servers beside the official Neo-Modus hub server. While they are all implementing the standard Direct Connect protocol there are also protocol extensions and differences in the communication with a client. For instance, some hub servers will not tolerate flooding messages and immediately kick users while other rely on hub administrators to kick flooding peers.

Because we are mainly interested in communication between the peers and interpret file requests as a special form of communication, we measure both public and private message commandos, file requests and file transfers as message units. We use the term message unit here according to its meaning as a unit of measure for charging telephone calls, based on parameters such as the length of the call. Depending on the particular server instance we are not always able to measure private messages or download requests on the hubs. In the case of download requests, we can always scan the number of requests to our particular client and compare that with similar hubs and make a projection for the total number of transfer requests. For messages we take the always available public messages as the basis to approximate all private messages when we are not able to scan them directly. We call a message msg_unit now the average sum of all chat, search and file request messages, that we measure on a hub in one second.

Besides the mentioned 'topic given'-parameter we test for a minimum share size and the minimum number of peers connected to the hub. While min_users is mainly serving as a test attribute to control how messaging units raise with the user amount we are interested whether the minimum share size has an effect on the communication.

The results of the data collections are presented in Fig. 3. We measure the message units and the attributes min share, the minimum amount of shared data on a hub, topic-given, if there is a topic given for a hub and min users, the minimum number of users connected to a hub. While min_share (0, 10, 100 Gigabyte) and min_users (1, 10, 50 peers) can take three values, topic-given (yes, no) is a binary attribute. This produces $3 * 3 * 2 = 18$ possible hub rule sets.

The result of the relation minimum share (min_share) vs. topic given in the left table of Fig. 3. Message divergence (msg_divergence) indicates how the message units diverge when the number of users is changed in the setup. There is a tendency that with a smaller number of users and for smaller shares there is relatively more communication going on. Also the percentage of communication

min share vs. topic given				
min users	topic given	min share	msg units	msg divergence
1	yes	0	0,011	0,004
10	yes	0	0,005	-0,002
50	yes	0	0,004	-0,003
1	no	0	0,003	0,000
10	no	0	0,002	-0,001
50	no	0	0,003	0,000
1	yes	10	0,040	0,013
10	yes	10	0,025	-0,002
50	yes	10	0,016	-0,011
1	no	10	0,017	-0,002
10	no	10	0,019	0,000
50	no	10	0,021	0,002
1	yes	100	0,559	0,029
10	yes	100	0,452	-0,078
50	yes	100	0,578	0,048
1	no	100	0,431	0,001
10	no	100	0,430	0,000
50	no	100	0,430	0,000

msg units vs. topic given				
min users	topic given	min share	msg units	msg ratio
1	yes	0	0,011	3,67
1	no	0	0,003	
1	yes	10	0,040	2,35
1	no	10	0,017	
1	yes	100	0,559	1,30
1	no	100	0,431	
10	yes	0	0,005	2,50
10	no	0	0,002	
10	yes	10	0,025	1,32
10	no	10	0,019	
10	yes	100	0,452	1,05
10	no	100	0,430	
50	yes	0	0,004	1,33
50	no	0	0,003	
50	yes	10	0,016	0,76
50	no	10	0,021	
50	yes	100	0,578	1,34
50	no	100	0,430	

min users vs. topic given				
min users	topic given	min share	msg units	msg increase
1	no	0	0,003	
1	no	10	0,017	5,67
1	no	100	0,431	25,35
1	yes	0	0,011	
1	yes	10	0,040	3,64
1	yes	100	0,559	13,98
10	no	0	0,002	
10	no	10	0,019	9,50
10	no	100	0,430	22,63
10	yes	0	0,005	
10	yes	10	0,025	5,00
10	yes	100	0,452	18,08
50	no	0	0,003	
50	no	10	0,021	7,00
50	no	100	0,430	20,48
50	yes	0	0,004	
50	yes	10	0,016	4,00
50	yes	100	0,578	36,13

Fig. 3. Message unit measurements

messages increases with the share size and is higher for the topic-given hubs in comparison to the free form hubs. This supports hypothesis 2.

The middle table provides the msg_ratio, i.e. the ratio between topic-given and free-form hubs. Topic-given hubs have more communication messages than free form hubs and the ratio between topic-given hubs and free-form hubs on communication messages is higher for hubs with a smaller number of users and a smaller size. I.e. interaction on hubs with less users and less minimum share seems to be more about communication whereas the big hubs with lots of content and lots of users are more about sharing and less about communication. Again, this validates hypothesis 2 that P2P is not about file sharing alone. Moreover, this is an indicator that there are hubs that exist because of interaction, since users could as well chose larger hubs with more content (and less interaction).

In the third table at the right of Fig. 3, we observe the influence of the min share parameter on the message units. The larger the minimum share, the more communication takes place. There is a tendency that this applies more to free-form hubs. So the free form hubs seems to communicate about files and in the topic given there seems to be other reasons for communication and the minimum share that is a metric of how many files are available within the network does not increase the messages in the same way as this happens in free-form hubs.

Let us briefly discuss our findings. The most obvious correlation is between the number of users and the generated message traffic on the hubs; more users simply generate more traffic. We observe a non-linear increase of msg_increase in the "min_users vs. msg_ units"-part of Fig. 3. We do not find a correlation between the minimum share size and the communication traffic. Finally, our study shows a significant correlation between a given topic and the generated traffic. This is depicted also in Fig. 4. There is a significant difference of the generated traffic when in comes to the topic-given-parameter with a quite constant differential ratio. In 8 out of the compared 9 different rule pairs, the generated communication traffic is higher on the topic-given hubs. Figure 4 illustrates this in a log-scale diagram. On topic-specific hubs users seem to be more interested

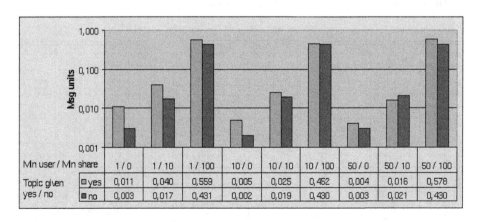

Fig. 4. Message units on topic-given and free-form hubs (topic-given no)

in interacting with other peers than on anonymous hubs. This validates our hypotheses as users are willing to connect to hubs with certain topics.

This validates our hypothesis - P2P is not all about file sharing users are willing to interact and therefore are not totally anonymous, as the myth tells.

7   Conclusions

The paper analyzes the state of the art in the area of P2P applications and the current use of P2P systems. The empirical research was done within a well established P2P network, the Direct Connect network. We conclude from the empirical research that P2P networks are about sharing all kinds of data – not only audio or video types. This opens a chance for new designs of P2P systems as general purpose information systems. We also observe that users do more than just file-sharing they are willing to interact and a focus on a topic in a network or on a hub fosters communication. More research needs to be done to validate the impact of those interactions in a P2P network. Both our hypotheses could be validated and this demystifies P2P. With the evolution of formerly huge, chaotic anonymous music-sharing networks to distributed systems with various types of content and P2P communities we expect next-generation P2P applications to provide an opportunity for powerful information systems.

Acknowledgments

We would like to thank Achim Dannecker for stimulating discussions and the anonymous reviewers for valuable comments.

References

1. Milojicic, D., Kalogeraki, V., Lukose, R., Nagaraja, K., Pruyne, J., Richard, B., Rollins, S., Xu, Z.: Peer to peer computing. Technical Report 57, HP Labs (2002)
2. Ripeanu, M., Foster, I., Iamnitchi, A.: Mapping the gnutella network: Properties of large-scale peer-to-peer systems and implications for system design. IEEE Internet Computing Journal **6** (2002)
3. Shneidman, J., Parkes, D.C.: Rationality and self-interest in peer to peer networks. In: Proc. 2nd Int. Workshop on P2P Systems (IPTPS'03). (2003)
4. Adar, E., Huberman, B.: Freeriding on gnutella. Firstmonday **5** (2000) www.firstmonday.org.
5. Lechner, U.: Peer to Peer beyond Filesharing. In Unger, H., Boehme, T., Mikler, A., eds.: 2. Conference on Innovative Internet Computing Systems. Lecture Notes in Computer Science 2346, Springer Verlag (2002) 153–162
6. MacInnes, I., Hwang, J.: Business models for peer to peer initiatives. In Gricar, J., Wigand, R., eds.: 16th Bled Electronic Commerce Conference. (2003) CD-Rom.
7. Kolweyh, M., Lechner, U.: Data Mining in Peer-to-Peer Systemen. In Engelien, M., Meiner, K., eds.: Gemeinschaften in Neuen Medien (GeNeMe 2004). Josef Eul Verlag (2004) 103–114

8. B. Cohen: Incentives build robustness in BitTorrent. In: Proceedings of the First Workshop on the Economics of P2P Systems. Berkeley (2003)
9. Schoder, D., Fischbach, K.: Peer-to-peer prospects. Communications of the ACM **46** (2003) 27–29
10. Stoica, I., Morris, R., Karger, D., Kaashoek, M., Balakrishnan, H.: Chord: A scalable peer-to-peer lookup service for internet applications. In: Proceedings of the 2001 conference on applications, technologies, architectures, and protocols for computer communications, ACM Press (2001) 149–160
11. Ratnasamy, S., Francis, P., Handley, M., Karp, R., Shenker, S.: A scalable content addressable network. In: Proceedings of ACM SIGCOMM 2001. (2001)
12. Unger, H., Unger, H., Titova, N.: Structuring of decentralized computer communities. In: High Performance Computing 2002 (HPC 2002), San Diego, CA, USA (2002) 245–250
13. Dingledine, R., Freedman, M. J., Molnar, D.: The free haven project: Distributed anonymous storage service. In: Workshop on Design Issues in Anonymity and Unobservability. (2000) 67–95
14. Kubiatowicz, J., Bindel, D., Chen, Y., Eaton, P., Geels, D., Gummadi, R., Rhea, S., Weatherspoon, H., Weimer, W., Wells, C., Zhao, B.: Oceanstore: An architecture for global-scale persistent storage. In: Proceedings of ACM ASPLOS, ACM (2000)
15. Clarke, I., Sandberg, O., Wiley, B., Hong, T.: Freenet: A Distributed Anonymous Information Storage and Retrieval System. In: ICSI Workshop on Design Issues in Anonymity and Unobservability, Berkeley, CA (2000)
16. Piotrowski, K., Langendrfer, P., Kulikowski, D.: Moneta: An anonymity providing lightweight payment system for mobile devices. In Grimm, R., N J., eds.: Virtual Goods (2004). TU Illmenau (2004)
17. Unger, H., Böhme, T.: A probabilistic money system for the use in p2p network communities. In: Virtual Goods (2003), Ilmenau, Germany (2003) 60–69
18. Clement, M., Nerjes, G., Runte, M.: Bedeutung von P2P Technologien fr die Distribution von Medienprodukten im Internet. In Schoder, D., Fischbach, K., Teichmann, R., eds.: P2P. Ökonomische, technische und juristische Perspektiven. Springer Verlag (2002) 71–80
19. NeoModus: Direct connect (2004)
20. COLLAB. NET: Project jxta (2004) Access Nov 2004.
21. Nejdl, W., Wolf, B., Staab, S., Tane, J.: Edutella: Searching and annotating resources within an RDF-based P2P network. In: Proc. Semantic Web Workshop, at the 11th Iternational World Wide Web Conference (WWW2002). (2002)

A Random Walk Topology Management Solution for Grid

Cyril Rabat, Alain Bui, and Olivier Flauzac

Université de Reims Champagne-Ardenne,
BP 1039, F-51687 Reims Cedex 2, France
{cyril.rabat, olivier.flauzac, alain.bui}@univ-reims.fr

Abstract. GRID computing is a more and more attractive approach. Its aim is to gather and to share the resources of a network like the content, the storage or CPU cycles. A computational distributed system like *SETI@home* produces a power up to 70 TFlops whereas the current best parallel supercomputer *BlueGene* produces a power of 140 TFlops. Such a supercomputer costs very much contrary to a system like *SETI@home*. But the use of many computers to increase the global computational power involves several communication problems. We must maintain the GRID communication in order to make any type of computation even though the network is volatile.

In this paper, we present a model to represent GRID applications and networks in order to show faults impacts. We present a fully distributed solution based on a random walk to manage the topology of the GRID. No virtual structure needs to be maintained and this solution works on asynchronous networks. We also present some simulations of our solution.

1   Introduction

GRID computing is used to manage resources sharing and to gather resources over a network. We can distinguish two kinds of GRID:

- *High Performance GRID Computing (HPGC)* is composed by few supercomputers gathered in a cluster. During a computation, we cannot disconnect any computer. When a fault occurs, the computation stops and we must restart it. But this kind of GRID has two main advantages: all the results are true and we do not need topology management.
- *Desktop GRID* is composed of many nodes. Connections and disconnections from the GRID can be numerous. Often, no authentication is used on nodes and results can be wrong or corrupted. So even if no failure occurs on the network, we must check all the results. There is no fixed architecture and we need to manage the GRID topology.

In this paper, we present a new GRID topology management. This solution is based on a random walk and is tolerant to nodes disconnections. To describe it, we introduce an original network and application model for GRID. We use several layers to distinguish communication graph, routing protocol, messages exchanges and GRID application.

A. Bui et al. (Eds.): IICS 2005, LNCS 3908, pp. 91–104, 2006.
© Springer-Verlag Berlin Heidelberg 2006

In the next section, we present an overview of current GRID application types and particularly we focus on their architectures. Then we present our 5-layer model with a description for each one. Finally we show our random walk based solution with fault management and in the last section, we discuss on some simulations using this solution.

2   Related Works

2.1   An Overview of Current GRID Applications Architectures

For several years, as claimed in [12], GRID computing has been the unavoidable solution for resources sharing: computation power, data, storage and applications. Demands for these kinds of resources grow exponentially but, on the other hand, many resources are unused. GRID computing enables us to federate them. Many solutions have been designed. We can gather them in three main categories:

- *Applications* designed to solve specific problems. In this category, we find the first version of the SETI@home project[1] developed to Search for Extra Terrestrial Intelligence ([3]).
- *Protocols* and *libraries* providing tools to develop GRID applications like JXTA ([14]).
- *Middlewares* offering a set of different services like resources discovery and monitoring, topology management... We find the following solutions: Xtrem-Web ([6]), Globus ([1, 11]), Diet ([5]), CONFIIT([10, 13]) or BOINC ([2]).

Whatever the category, several problems occur and particularly with the topology management. In order to provide a QoS over the GRID, to gather with its management and integration of new resources, it is necessary to define a strategy depending on the chosen centralization degree. Based on this criterion, we can classify the topology management of GRID applications into three categories: centralized, distributed and hybrid (semi-distributed).

Centralized Topology Management. This is based on pure client-server model: there is only one server on which all clients are connected. Submitters send requests to the server that distributes it to clients. Results are collected and returned to the submitter.

SETI@home ([3, 2]) for example, uses this kind of management: the data to be analyzed are centralized on the Berkeley server. Based on free cooperation, users download a client application that automatically contacts the server and downloads computation parameters. Results are collected by the server and saved into a large database. Links between clients and server are not critical: connections and disconnections are numerous (up to 4 million volatile clients) and each task is computed several times (2 to 3). The first reason is to avoid computational

---

[1] http://setiathome.ssl.berkeley.edu/

errors or malicious computation with comparison between results and the second one is to manage clients' failures.

This kind of management involves the overload of servers and a critical access: if the server crashes, the GRID fails to work.

Hybrid Topology Management. This kind of management establishes a hierarchy between nodes. Several interconnected layers of servers are substituted for the server. Nodes are managed by the lowest server and offer resources: storage, data, applications or/and computational power.

DIET [5] uses this architecture: it is composed of several interconnected servers called master agents (MA) in order to limit breakdown effects. If one of them does not respond, clients can contact another one. Under MAs, we have several layers of agents and at the bottom, the leader agents (LA) communicate directly to nodes. MAs are used to federate the GRID and to receive and diffuse requests to lower agents. LAs have a local knowledge of their associated resources. Upon job submission, the submitter contacts an MA that diffuses its request to intermediate agents and so on, down to nodes. If one of them suits this request, it reports its local agent and the response goes up to the MA and then to the submitter.

With this management, we decrease the overload of servers and we increase the breakdown tolerance. But it is difficult to establish a good hierarchy that has to suit the network topology as much as possible. Moreover, it overloads special management nodes and the breakdown of one of them involves GRID disconnection of the lower agents and their associated resources.

Distributed Topology Management. For this management, no hierarchy between nodes of the GRID is needed. There is no server: each node has the same purpose and is called a *servent*. It provides client and server tasks: computation, local resources management and communication.

For example, we find the fully distributed middleware CONFIIT ([10, 13]). Each node is set up into a virtual ring. When a neighbor crashes, nodes contact their next neighbors and so on. A token maintains the ring topology and another one manages the computation.

Although it is fully distributed, a ring structure is needed and it must always be maintained. This management uses too much computational power. Furthermore, a fixed structure like a ring or a tree involves default paths. They are more sensitive to breakdowns and each breakdown has more impacts.

2.2   Random Walk

A random walk is defined by a sequence of vertices visited by a token that starts at node i and visits other vertices according to the following rule: when the token is at node i at time t, at time $t + 1$, it is on one of the neighbors of i. This neighbor is chosen uniformly at random among all of them and probability to reach one of the neighbors is exactly $1/deg(i)$, where $deg(i)$ is the number of neighbors. In [15], the author shows us a survey on random walks.

A random walk has some quantities to evaluate its efficiency:

- the *cover time* C is the average time to visit all nodes of the graph.
- the *hitting time* denoted by $h_{i,j}$ is the average time to reach a node j for the first time starting from a given node i.
- the *return time* is the average time for a random walk to return to its original node. It is the special hitting time $h_{i,i}$.

Each quantity has a lower and upper bound as proved by U. Feige in [7, 8].

Random walks are used in several cases. In [9], the author gives an algorithm to compute routing tables of the shortest paths. But we can also find GRID applications. In [4], the authors show a method to distribute the tasks of a problem into a computational GRID in bounded time and in [16], an algorithm based on multiple random walks enables us to decrease the number of messages when querying in peer-to-peer networks.

3   Preliminaries

3.1   Model

To adapt our random solution to a network, we need to model GRID applications as represented on figure 1 and described below. The model is composed of five

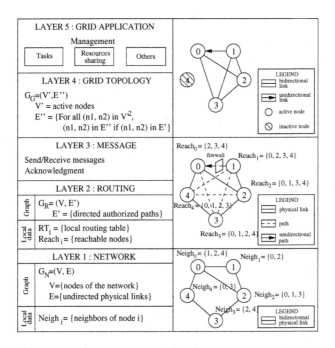

Fig. 1. On the left, figure shows layers of our model and on the right, a network and its representation through each layers

layers. The first one is a representation of a network and, in each layer, we have special mechanisms and protocols like a routing protocol, messages passing... At the top, layers are assigned to GRID management and its applications.

Layer 1: Network. A network is modeled by a graph $G_N = (V, E)$, where V is the set of nodes and E the set of edges. Each node represents a computer (we can use computers, processors or resources indifferently) of the network and each edge represents a physical link: $\forall n_1, n_2 \in V^2, (n_1, n_2) \in E$ if n_1 and n_2 are connected physically. Each node is associated with an unique identifier and communicates with its neighborhood by passing messages through communication links. We consider the network to be asynchronous. Each node owns a set $Neigh_i$ which contains its neighborhood and is automatically maintained.

Layer 2: Routing. In this layer, a routing protocol computes local routing table in each node. For example, in [9], the author shows how to build them with a random walk. But we can use classical algorithms like *distance vectors* or *link states*. We define the sets as called $Reach_i$; they contains all the network nodes that node i can reach. $Reich_i$ are automatically maintained. So, we build a new graph G_R from these sets. With restricted access rights by firewall, for example, G_R has directed links and if there are few firewalls, we can suppose that this graph is dense. We obtain $G_R = (V, E')$ with $E' = \{n_1, n_2 \in V^2, (n_1, n_2) \in E'$ if a path exists from n_1 to $n_2\}$.

Layer 3: Communications. A communication protocol works on G_T in order to exchange messages between nodes that have a route between them. This protocol supplies functions *send* and *receive* with errors and acknowledgments management: if a message is not transmitted to the destination node, the sender of the message is informed. This layer also ensures the correctness of received data and corruptions can be detected. The network is asynchronous, but we suppose we have an upper bound on communication delay.

Layer 4: GRID Topology. In this layer, we distinguish two node states. When a node enters the GRID its state is called *active*. Conversely, a node of the network that does not collaborate with the GRID is called *inactive*. Within layer 3, this node keeps relaying messages. We construct a graph $G_G = (V', E'')$ with $V' = \{n \in V/n$ is active$\}$. $V \backslash V'$ is the inactive nodes set. The set of links of G_G is $E'' = \{\forall n_1, n_2 \in V'^2, (n_1, n_2) \in E''$ if $(n_1, n_2) \in E\}$. We have the following properties: $\forall n_1, n_2 \in V'^2, \exists$ path between n_1 and n_2 and $G_G \subseteq G_R$. The $Reach_i$ sets contain active and inactive neighbors of nodes.

Layer 5: GRID Application. Applications that work on the GRID must add several kinds of management: task management, resources sharing... In this paper, we focus on computational GRID. So we only describe tasks management that has to distribute tasks into the GRID and to collect results.

We use the solution introduced by CONFIIT. Each task of a problem is tagged by a state: *uncomputed*, *computed* or *in progress*. Each node owns an array that contains the whole set of tasks with its state. A random walk circulates into the GRID containing a copy of the sender local array. It updates local arrays of each GRID node. When a node wants to compute a task, it chooses at random one of *uncomputed* tasks in its local array and tags it with the *in progress* state. At the end of the computation, the task is tagged *computed* and the node chooses another one. When all tasks are computed, the problem is finished.

In order to avoid uncomputed tasks and to accelerate the global computation, when a node has not any uncomputed task, it chooses randomly one of the *in progress* tasks. For example, we can have a node that chooses a task and crashes before terminating it. This task is considered as a *replicated task*.

3.2   Fault Impacts

In each layer of our model, we can have internal faults or impacted ones from lower layers.

Layer 1. We can only have definitive breakdowns in this layer: a node can fall down or a link can be disconnected. If a link $(i, j) \in E$ is disconnected, nodes i and j update their neighborhood. A node crash is a disconnection of all its links: $\forall j \in Neigh_i, Neigh_j \leftarrow Neigh_j \backslash \{i\}$.

Layer 2–3. When a fault is impacted from layer 1, the routing protocol has to compute new paths. If it succeeds, local routing tables are updated and higher layers do not detect any fault. Otherwise, we can have path loss and some nodes can still be unreachable. They are supposed to be disconnected.

Layer 4. This layer ensures the GRID topology management. If some nodes are disconnected, there are deleted from the GRID. We also have to manage deactivation of GRID nodes. If one of them wants to go out of the GRID (voluntarily

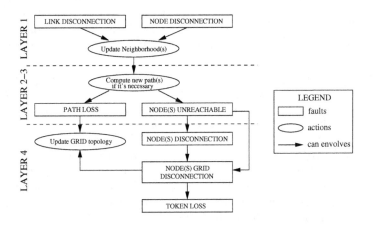

Fig. 2. Impacts of faults through layers of our model

or not), the protocol has to update the topology. In the same way, if we use a token for the protocol, it can be lost when a node crashes. So we need a recovery mechanism.

Notice that when a node crashes, the task that it is computing is deleted. It must be computed by another node.

Figure 2 shows the fault management scheme.

4   Topology Management with a Random Walk

4.1   Introduction

The GRID topology (layer 4) is updated by a token. The state of the GRID is an adjacency matrix. Each node i owns a local matrix M_i defined by:

$$\forall i, j \in V'^2, M_i(i,j) = \begin{cases} 1 \text{ if } j \in Reach_i \\ 0 \text{ if } j \notin Reach_i \end{cases}$$

The topology token contains a copy of the sender matrix M_T. It is used to update the local matrices of other nodes.

To manage tasks (layer 5), we use the solution introduced in the CONFIIT middleware described in section 3.1. We need a token containing a state tasks array A_T which is a copy of the local array of the sender node. State tasks are updated in each node.

The two tokens circulate at random in the GRID. We choose to merge them into a single token to reduce the number of messages.

4.2   Algorithm

When a node receives the token (M_T, A_T), it updates its local matrix and its local array. When it is finished, the token is sent with M_i and A_i. To update the local matrix, we can distinguish the following cases:

- $\exists n \in M_T/n \notin M_i$: a new node n has integrated the GRID. n must be inserted into matrix M_i. We use the *Add* function which adds a new row and a new column and updates neighbors.
- $\exists n \in M_i/n \notin M_T$: the token does not contain node n. Only node i knows this node. It is a new one and its entry point is node i.
- $\exists n \in M_T$ and $n \in M_i$: we update neighbors for node n into M_i with the *Update* function.

$State_i(t)$ represents the state of a task t in the array of node i. It values either uncomputed (0), or in progress (1) or computed (2). The function called *UpdateTasks* update the local array A_i by keeping the better task progression to update each task state. Algorithm 1 shows the reception of a token (M_T, A_T) by a node.

Algorithm 1. *Token reception* from a node j in node i

```
1:  // Add new nodes and update M_i
2:  for all node n_T ∈ M_T do
3:     if n_T ∈ M_i then
4:        Update M_i
5:     else
6:        Add n_T into M_i
7:     end if
8:  end for
9:  UpdateTasks
10: // Send the token
11: Send TOKEN to a random neighbor with M_T ← M_i and A_T ← A_i
```

4.3   Connection to the GRID

When a node wants to enter the GRID, it has to contact one of the GRID nodes called an *entry point*. We need a bidirectional link between the new node and the entry point. The new node sends a *connection request* message which contains its neighborhood. The entry point answers by sending its adjacency matrix and its local tasks states array. In case of success, the two nodes update their local matrix. The new node is integrated into the GRID and can compute a task. With its local knowledge, it becomes a possible entry point. The entry point also has to verify if there are only two nodes in the GRID. In this case, it has to create the GRID token and to send it to the new node.

4.4   Fault Management

On layer 4, we have to solve faults impacted from lower levels of our model. As we have shown in section 3.2, we need to manage nodes and links disconnection. A node detects it with the automatic updating of its set *Reach* by layer 2. We also have to manage the deactivation of a node and the token loss.

Link or Node Disconnection. When a node detects a neighbor disconnection, it cannot know if it is a link or a node disconnection. So, it only updates its adjacency matrix. With the latter, the node can build a spanning tree rooted on it. If it detects that some nodes are not included in this tree, these nodes are unreachable and can be deleted from the matrix: they are considered as inactive nodes.

GRID Node Deactivation. A GRID deactivation can be voluntary if a user wants to stop its collaboration. In this case, it can send messages to its neighbors to inform them about it. But if the application suddenly crashes, it cannot send any messages. It becomes an inactive node but its disconnection is not yet detected by its neighbors: it is still in the network and neighborhoods, but it cannot response to GRID messages. When one of its neighbors receives the token and tries to send it, an error occurs. So this neighbor can update its local matrix. To ease the management and to avoid any message creation, we do not distinguish these two cases. For a voluntary disconnection, nodes have not to send any messages.

Token Recovery. According to layer 3, the data into the token can not be corrupted. In the same way, the token can not be lost: when a node sends a message, it has an acknowledgment. But when a node crashes after reception of the token and before sending it to one of its neighbors, the token is lost. So each node owns a timeout T_i that allows the regeneration of a token when it ends. In this case, node i updates its local matrix with its neighborhood knowledge: M_i only contains its neighbors. For each one, the node tests its reachability in order to delete inactive ones. Then, the node chooses a random neighbor and sends the token. The initial value of the timeout depends on the GRID size. If the value is too low, many tokens will be created and, on the other hand, if the value is too high, a token loss induces a reaction time before regeneration.

After the crashing of a node or link, it is possible for the GRID to contain more than one token: the timeout ends before its incoming of the token. We have to add a new mechanism to delete additional ones. In [13], the authors chose to mark the token with a sequence number seq and the identity of node id that creates it. Each node keeps a memory of the sequence and identity of the latest token. When a node enters the GRID, its sequence number and id equal 0. When a node generates a new one, it increases this sequence number. Then at reception of a token with sequence $newSeq$ and identity $newId$, we have the three following cases to consider:

- $seq > newSeq$: the token is an old one so it can be destroyed.
- $seq < newSeq$: the token is more recent than the latest one, so seq and id can be updated.
- $seq = newSeq$: it is a normal case according to the value of id and $newId$:
  - $id = newId$: normal case.
  - $id < newId$: the token is more recent than the latest one, so seq and id can be updated.
  - $id > newId$: token is an old one so it can be destroyed.

4.5   Full Algorithm

When a node receives the token, it has to test the reachability of its neighbors. For each one, it uses the function $reachable(n)$, that returns $true$ if node n is still reachable: $n \in Reach_i$ and $n \in G_G$. It can update its local matrix. Then, from the matrix, it can build the spanning tree rooted on it in order to discover detached nodes and to delete them. Algorithm 2 shows the full process to remove all the unreachable nodes of the GRID.

Algorithm 2. Removing unreachable nodes

```
1:  // Delete inactive nodes
2:  for all node nᵢ ∈ Mᵢ do
3:      if nᵢ ∉ M_T then
4:          if reachable(n_T) == false then
5:              Delete nᵢ into Mᵢ
6:          end if
7:      end if
8:  end for
9:  // Search unreachable nodes
10: Tᵢ = tree rooted in i
11: Delete all nodes n ∈ Mᵢ / n ∉ Tᵢ
```

In algorithm 3, we describe the behavior of a node which receives the token. First, we have to test the validity of the token according to its sequence. Then, the node updates its local matrix. When it has to add a new node included in its neighborhood, it must test if this node is already active.

Algorithm 3. *TOKEN* reception from node j at node i

```
 1: if sequence of TOKEN is not valid then
 2:     Destroy TOKEN
 3: else
 4:     // Add new nodes and update Mᵢ
 5:     for all node n_T ∈ M_T do
 6:         if ∃n_T ∈ M_i then
 7:             Update M_i
 8:         else
 9:             if n_T ∈ Reach_i then
10:                 if reachable(n_T) == true then
11:                     Add n_T into M_i
12:                 end if
13:             else
14:                 Add n_T into M_i
15:             end if
16:         end if
17:     end for
18:     Removing unreachable nodes
19:     Update tasks array
20:     // Send the token
21:     Send TOKEN to a random neighbor with M_T ← M_i and A_T ← A_i
22: end if
```

---

5 Simulations

We have developed a C++ program to perform simulations based on random walk solution. We use the decomposition of a Langford problem in irregular and independent 1366 tasks. Length tasks are given thanks to a computation on the CONFIIT middleware. Thus we obtain very irregular lengths (2,000 ms to 18,432 ms). A sequential computation takes $T_s = 14,913,112\ ms$.

We launch simulations on several random networks so as to obtain an average time to finish the whole computation T_t and an average number of the replicated tasks. In order to compare the distributed solution with the sequential one, we compute an efficiency factor e that depends on the size of the network (n is the number of nodes) and is given by the following formula:

$$e = \frac{T_t * n}{T_s}$$

If a network contains n nodes, an optimal distributed solution must spend n less time to finish computation and has an efficiency factor equal to 1.

We launch a number of simulations on random networks with 10 to 100 nodes. For each series, we fix the network and we obtain the results on figure 3.

In order to show the breakdowns tolerance, we add voluntary and regular node disconnections during a fixed length. After a breakdown, the node wakes up and sends a connection request to one of its neighbors. We launch the simulations on

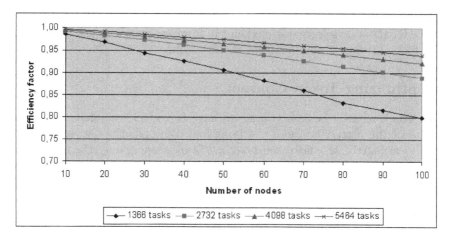

Fig. 3. Efficiency factor in function of network size

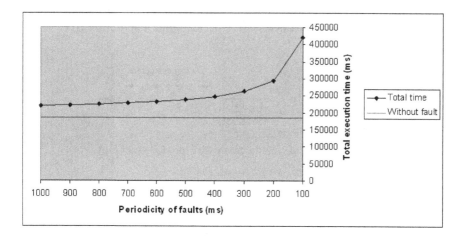

Fig. 4. Impacts of periodic breakdowns

a fixed random network with 100 nodes. We increase the frequency of breakdown and we obtain the results on figure 4.

The more the network grows, the longer the time to cover the graph. It induces a reaction time to inform other nodes and increases the likelihood of a node choosing the same task as an other node. It produces more replicated tasks and the efficiency factor decreases. For these simulations, we have 1366 tasks to compute for 100 nodes: only 14 per node.

As far as breakdowns are concerned, we notice a number of replicated tasks triggered by the tasks management. A node starts a task. It receives the token that informs the other nodes that the task is in progress. If this node crashes, the task is tagged as *in progress* but it cannot be computed. With a larger number of breakdowns, after a given time, local task arrays contain only *in progress* tasks. When a GRID node selects one of them, it supposes that it is a replicated one but in fact, this task is computed for the first time.

6   Optimizing Token Content

For an adaption to a large network, we have to consider a number of nodes. The size of the matrix becomes too large and overloads the network. We can reduce local matrix M_i and token matrix M_T by keeping only the useful data: the directed spanning tree. To build it, we introduce the *predecessor* notion: when node i receives the token from node j, j becomes its predecessor. The tree is represented in node i as an array G_i which contains the predecessor of each GRID node. When a node crashes, we allow only its predecessor to delete it from the GRID. For example, figure 5 shows a GRID with a node crash. Node 3 receives the token and detects that node 4 is disconnected. We build a spanning tree from array G_3. It shows that node 3 is the predecessor of node 4, so it can destroy it and its subtree from the GRID nodes set.

This solution reduces local data and length of the token but some problems occur. If the token produces a cycle, we can not build a spanning tree.

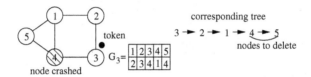

Fig. 5. Example of a node crash with predecessor solution

7   Conclusion

We show that the topology management using a random walk is an efficient solution as shown by simulations. It allows many topological changes without GRID falls and without the management of a virtual structure. But we notice that the growth of the network implies a decreasing efficiency. The size of the token and data into each node must be reduced to keep a good performance level. Some solutions can be presented. For a larger network, we are planning to use multiple random walks and clusterings in order to reduce replicated tasks by increasing the update of local task arrays.

Acknowledgments

This work was partly supported by "Romeo"[2], the high performance computing center of the University of Reims Champagne-Ardenne, the "Centre

---

[2] http://www.univ-reims.fr/Calculateur

Informatique National de l'Enseignement Superieur"[3] (CINES), France and by the project ACI GRID-ARGE funded by the French ministry of research.

References

1. W. Allcock, A. Chervenak, I. Foster, L. Pearlman, V. Welch, and M. Wilde. Globus toolkit support for distributed data-intensive science. In I. Press, editor, *Computing in High Energy Physics (CHEP'01)*, September 2001.
2. D. P. Anderson. BOINC: A System for Public-Resource Computing and Storage. In *GRID '04: Proceedings of the Fifth IEEE/ACM International Workshop on Grid Computing (GRID'04)*, pages 4–10, Washington, DC, USA, 2004. IEEE Computer Society.
3. D. P. Anderson, J. Cobb, E. Korpela, M. Lebofsky, and D. Werthimer. SETI@home: an experiment in public-resource computing. *Communications of the ACM*, 45(11):56–61, November 2002.
4. A. Bui, M. Bui, and D. Sohier. Randomly Distributed Tasks in Bounded Time. In T. Böhme, G. Heyer, and H. Unger, editors, *IICS*, volume 2877 of *Lecture Notes in Computer Science*, pages 36–47. Springer-Verlag, December 2003.
5. E. Caron, F. Desprez, F. Lombard, J.-M. Nicod, M. Quinson, and F. Suter. A Scalable Approach to Network Enabled Servers. In B. Monien and R. Feldmann, editors, *Proceedings of the 8th International EuroPar Conference*, volume 2400 of *Lecture Notes in Computer Science*, pages 907–910, Paderborn, Germany, August 2002. Springer-Verlag.
6. G. Fedak, C. Germain, V. Neri, and F. Cappello. XtremWeb: A Generic Global Computing System. In *IEEE/ACM - CCGRID'2001 Special Session Global Computing on Personal Devices*. IEEE Press, May 2001.
7. U. Feige. A tight lower bound on the cover time for random walks on graphs. *Random Structures & Algorithms*, 6(4):433–438, 1995.
8. U. Feige. A tight upper bound on the cover time for random walks on graphs. *Random Structures & Algorithms*, 6(1):51–54, 1995.
9. O. Flauzac. Random Circulating Word Information Management for Tree Construction and a Shortest Path Routing Tables Computation. In R. G. Cardenas, editor, *OPODIS*, Studia Informatica Universalis, pages 17–32. Suger, Saint-Denis, rue Catulienne, France, 2001.
10. O. Flauzac, M. Krajecki, and J. Fugère. CONFIIT : a middleware for peer to peer computing. In C. T. M. Gravilova and P. L'Ecuyer, editors, *The 2003 International Conference on Computational Science and its Applications (ICCSA 2003)*, volume 2669 (III) of Lecture Notes in Computer Science, pages 69–78, Montréal, Québec, June 2003. Springer-Verlag.
11. I. Foster and C. Kesselman. Globus : a metacomputing infrastructure toolkit. In I. Press, editor, *Supercomputer Applications*, volume 11 (2), pages 115–128, 1997.
12. I. Foster and C. Kesselman, editors. *The Grid: Blueprint for a Future Computing Infrastructure*. MORGAN-KAUFMANN, September 1999.
13. M. Krajecki, O. Flauzac, and P.-P. Mérel. Focus on the communication scheme in the middleware confiit using xml-rpc. In *18th International Workshop on Java for Parallel Distributed Computing (IW-JPDC'04)*, volume 6, page 160b, Santa Fe, New Mexico, April 2004. IEEE Computer Society.

---

[3] http://www.cines.fr

14. S. Li. JXTA 2: A high-performance, massively scalable p2p network. Technical report, IBM developerWorks, November 2003.
15. L. Lovász. Random walks on graphs : A Survey. In T. S. ed., D. Miklos, and V. T. Sos, editors, *Combinatorics: Paul Erdos is Eighty*, volume 2, pages 353–398. Janos Bolyai Mathematical Society, 1993.
16. Q. Lv, P. Cao, E. Cohen, K. Li, and S. Shenker. Search and replication in unstructured peer-to-peer networks. In *ICS '02: Proceedings of the 16th international conference on Supercomputing*, pages 84–95. ACM Press, 2002.

Content-Oriented Self-organization in Unstructured P2P Data Sharing Systems. An Approach to Improve Resource Discovery

German Sakaryan and Herwig Unger

Computer Science Dept., University of Rostock,
18051 Rostock, Germany
{gs137, hunger}@informatik.uni-rostock.de

Abstract. The flooding-based search is a major problem in unstructured peer-to-peer file sharing systems like Gnutella or KaZaa since it results in a significant portion of Internet traffic. This article intended to demonstrate that flooding can be avoided by using a content-oriented self-organization mechanism. In contrast to connections that are usually made randomly between peers in unstructured systems, each peer set up its connections based on content interests represented by offered and downloaded files. Through the simulation, it was shown that these local activities resulted in a global content-related network topology even under highly dynamic conditions. It was demonstrated that the content-oriented topology could be used to organize focused search in order to avoid flooding.

1 Introduction

Peer-to-peer (P2P) file sharing systems like Gnutella or KaZaa are large scale distributed networks built at the application level. These systems utilize the resources of end-user machines (bandwidth, computer power, and storage capacity) for file sharing. Accordingly, these applications can survive without employing expensive server infrastructure since the costs of file sharing are distributed among a large number of individual hosts. These networks suffer from high network dynamics caused by a transient peer population. To be part of a network, each peer keeps a certain number of connections with a set of other peers typically called neighbors. These connections are mostly formed randomly; thus, the respective networks are unstructured. If some connections die, a peer sets up new connections using pre–cached addresses of other peers. In order to maintain a cache of addresses, peers use a network discovery ping-pong protocol [1] that returns addresses of available peers within a certain radius. Therefore, the most available powerful peers with good bandwidth are the most frequently pre-cached. This simple behavior results in topology self-organization. The resulting topology exhibits strong small-world properties represented by small graph diameter, a high clustering coefficient and various power-law relationships [2, 3].

A. Bui et al. (Eds.): IICS 2005, LNCS 3908, pp. 105–116, 2006.

Because of self-organization, P2P networks demonstrate self-maintenance, self-repairing and adaptation properties [4]. Accordingly, they cope with dynamics and deliver high fault tolerance.

Since the connections between peers are mainly made randomly, the resulting network topology is not related to data placement. Accordingly, unstructured applications use mainly flooding-based search [1] to locate files when a user query is propagated among network peers. As a result, P2P applications are the main source of Internet traffic [5], which causes a major problem.

In contrast to unstructured Gnutella-like systems, the systems like CAN [6], Chord [7], Pastry [8] etc. are based on the Distributed Hash Tables (DHT) paradigm. Every file in these systems is associated with a key which is produced by hashing the name or content of the file. The range of the output values of the hashing function forms an ID space. Every peer is responsible for the part of the ID space by storing files (or the information about files) with respective keys. DHTs are highly structured with well defined content-related overlay topologies (e.g., grids, rings, etc.). Peers are linked to each other depending on the parts of the ID space, for which peers are responsible. In order to achieve a scalable search with small search traffic, fixed structures are required for correctness of operations. Therefore, DHTs are considered less reliable in the face of transient peer populations.

This paper shows that network flooding can be avoided due to content-oriented self-organization. At the same time, the good properties of unstructured systems can be preserved. For this purpose, a new content-oriented approach to the organization of unstructured systems was discussed. Each peer arranged its connections in accordance with its content interests represented by locally offered or downloaded files. Through simulations, it was proved that a content-oriented network topology emerged even under highly dynamic conditions. It was demonstrated that the resulting network organization had a positive influence on the search operations. The respective focused search algorithm is discussed.

The remainder of this article is organized as follows. Section 2 discusses the concepts of content-oriented self-organization and search. Section 3 describes the simulation environment. The simulation results are discussed in Section 4. This section is followed by a conclusion.

2   Network Organization and Search

2.1   Content-Oriented Self-organization

The users of P2P systems have common interests in file sharing. They form a virtual community where the relations between users can be defined based on files which are shared and/or searched. In social communities, such joint interests lead to self-organization. People self-organize in groups depending on their particular interests (e.g., group of people which are interested in the songs of a "XYZ" artist). Such an organization has a positive influence on information searches. In this case, the rule "I know somebody who has the same interests as I do" might decrease the search time and improve the quality of the search results.

In the current unstructured P2P file sharing networks, this self-organization effect is ignored because the connections between peers are mostly formed randomly. Accordingly, the P2P topology is unrelated to content interests of the respective users and cannot be effectively used for the search.

To bring the structure of the user community onto the network level, the connections between peers should be made according to user interests. Each peer set up its connections in accordance with following strategies:

- Social. Neighbors offered content most similar to the content offered locally. It was called social restructuring (SR).
- Egoistic. Neighbors offered content most similar to the content a user was interested in (downloaded files) (ER).
- Intergroup. Neighbors offered content least similar to the content offered locally (IR).

In order to support content-oriented organization, the content of peers was indexed (see Section 3.2). The respective index (description) of a peers' content can be transfered across a network; it is also used to determine whether different peers offer similar content or not.

For network discovery, a special search message structure was developed. In addition to traditional parameters like TTL (Time To Live), a message has contained a Log, which included the addresses of visited peers and a description of their content. In this way, additional messages for the network discovery were avoided. The discovered information was cached locally by peers and was used to set up appropriate outgoing P2P connections in accordance with a chosen strategy.

2.2 Content-Oriented Message Forwarding

To organize an informed search, each peer stored content descriptions of its neighbors. A forwarding algorithm consulted these descriptions every time a search message has been forwarded. To make decisions, the forwarding algorithm dynamically created a *routing table* for each of the search queries. A routing table included a list of peers locally known. Every table's record also contained a calculated similarity of the respective peer's content description to the user query. The peer for the next hop was randomly chosen from the peers that had equivalent highest similarity to a query. In this way, a query was always forwarded as closely as possible to the peers offering content similar to the content a query was looking for. To increase efficiency of the search, messages were not forwarded to the peers which had already been visited. The TTL was used to limit the life time of the message and prevent extra, useless network loads. If a TTL has reached zero, the message would be directly sent to its starting peer where it was analyzed and sent into the network again. If the required data was found, a message would be directly sent back to the starting peer informing it about the address of the found peer.

3   Simulation Setup

The presented approach was extensively evaluated. Network dynamics and content description and distribution, as well as modeling of the user queries (popularity of files and frequencies – how often a user places a query) play a very important role for the realistic evaluation of a content-oriented approach. At the same time, the effect of heterogeneous peer capabilities (bandwidth and computer power)was eliminated for simplicity.

3.1   Network Dynamics

It was shown [9, 10, 11], that P2P systems have transient peer populations. Only a small part of peers is available for a long time, while the majority of peers tend to be available only for short times.

To model the availability of a peer, two main states were distinguished: on-line state (peer is available) and off-line state. An on-line peer was active and could communicate with other peers. Accordingly, the peer performed all network operations (e.g., data search). An off-line peer was unavailable.

The on-line peers formed a P2P network and off-line peers formed a pool of candidates. In this article, the dynamics of the peer population were limited only to transitions from on-line state to off-line (from P2P network to pool) and vice versa. After joining a P2P network, a peer stayed connected until a certain time had expired and then disconnected. An off-line peer behaved also in the same way.

To model peers' availability, two parameters were used for each peer. The first one was the length of the continuous time interval a peer stayed on-line, the so-called "on-line time". The second parameter described the time interval a peer stayed off-line. These two parameters formed a time profile, which characterized a peer's user.

Empirical studies demonstrate that the on-line time of peers can be modeled by an exponential distribution with the assumption that only a limited number of peers (3–5%) is available during the entire observation time [9]. The respective on-line time was obtained for each peer in the network by mapping randomly generated values in the range of [0–100] to the corresponding time by using the exponential distribution [12] below:

$$y = 100 \cdot e^{(-k \cdot t)} \qquad (1)$$

where y-is a probability that the peer has the respective on-line time t.

In order to have dynamics during the simulations similar to the those discovered in [9], it was assumed that $y_e = 5\%$ was the probability to have an on-line time bigger than the time of simulation. Accordingly, the constant k was calculated by using the following formula:

$$k = \frac{ln(\frac{100}{y_e})}{t_e} \qquad (2)$$

where t_e was total time of simulation.

The size of real networks oscillates with 24-hour and 7-day periods [10, 13], which is caused by users' locality. Since these fluctuations are not so big in comparison with average network size, they were not considered in the presented model.

According to many estimations, the size of real P2P networks is estimated to be less than 10% [14] of a total number of potential peers (on- and off-line). Modeling this ratio is prohibitively expensive for simulation purposes, e.g., having 2,000 peers on-line requires simulating at least 20,000 peers. Therefore, it was assumed that the size of the on-line network is at the level of 50% of total number of simulated peers. To achieve this level, the exponential distribution laws used to generate on-line and off-line time are set to be equal.

3.2   Modeling Shared Content

For network organization and search purposes, the content should have a unified representation across a network, which includes a unified representation of offered files, a unified representation of peers' content (peer's content summary/descriptions), unified representation of a search query and a unified representation of users' interests (summary of the downloaded files). In addition, it is necessary to have the possibility to measure similarity between different files, peers and so on.

For simplicity, each file was represented in vector form, where each dimension was associated with a distinct term (e.g., keyword). The weight of a term reflected the importance of this term for this file. The collection of shared files formed a peer's content. For convenience, similar files were grouped in categories. A category was represented in the same vector form as files. The set of categories, with numbers of the respective files stored in the each of them, formed the content summary of the peer.

The search query and summary of the users' interests were described in the same way, i.e., by using vectors to represent search queries and a set of categories with the number of files to represent downloaded content.

The similarity between files, categories, queries and files were measured generally as a cosine of the angle between corresponding vectors [15]. The similarity between a query and a particular peer was the largest similarity between a query and all categories kept on the peer. The similarity of a peer n_j to a peer n_i considered not only presence of similar categories but also the absolute number of documents kept in them. To do so, the similarity was measured as a size of the intersection vector (which includes common categories for both n_i and n_j) divided by the size of n_i. The weight for a common category in an intersection vector was chosen as a minimum of the weights of that category on peers n_i and n_j respectively. The developed approach helped to compare not only the content of the peers but also to consider the size of the peer from a number of offered files perspective.

The important terms and their weights used to describe files can be obtained in different ways. If a P2P application is devoted to text documents sharing, a term can be a keyword used in the document body and the weight can represent its frequency/importance. If content of the file cannot be analyzed (e.g., mp3) than terms are simply keywords used in the name of the file.

The content plays an important role in influencing the operations of P2P file sharing networks. Files are usually replicated. The shared content replication can be approximated by Zipf's law [10]. The most popular 10% of files account for about 50% of the total number of stored files. An average replication rate is 1.3717 [16]. Because the size of the simulated network was not so big, it was assumed that files were not replicated in order to test the worst case. In addition, the pessimistic assumption that only 2% of peers offered similar content (similarity bigger than zero) was used.

3.3 Simulating User Request Structure

The two aspects of the user request structure, which influence network operations, were modeled for the simulation purpose:

– Popularity of requested files. Results obtained from the analysis of the file transfer statistics in Gnutella [10] and KaZaa networks [17] show the strong correspondence between a particular file and its popularity among users. The file popularity is significantly skewed. A limited number of files are requested very often (65% of downloads go to the 20% most popular files for KaZaa network), while most of files are requested rarely. This skewness in user requests influences the query flow in the network, which may lead to traffic concentration around peers which store popular items.
– User query frequency, i.e., how often a user requests files. This important characteristic influences the traffic in the network.

The skewness in file popularity among users does not exactly follow Zipf's power law distribution in contrast, for example, to Web statistics [18]. In spite of this fact, the usual power-law distribution can be used for simulation purposes. Since the files have different popularities in real networks, one might expect that a peer storing popular content suffers from a significantly bigger load. This problem is partly solved by file replication, where the most replicated files are mainly the most popular among users. Therefore, such replication improves load balancing.

It was assumed (see Section 3.2) that files were not replicated. In this way, the usage of the power-law distribution to model file popularity among users would result in a very limited number of permanently overloaded peers, which will negatively influence the operations of the simulated network. Accordingly, such bad simulation conditions would be unrealistic. Therefore, to improve simulation conditions, it was assumed that the popularity distribution is linear. This resulted in less skewed peer loads. On the other hand, the content popularity still influenced the message flow.

To model the popularity of the documents among users and to simplify simulations, all documents in the simulated network were split into 4 groups of equal size. Documents of group A were requested 40% of the time, while documents of group B were requested 30% of the time, C-20%, and D-10% accordingly. Even though the most popular 25% of documents were requested 40% of the time in contrast to 20%–65% (for KaZaa network), the peers storing the most popular content were expected to receive more requests due to lack of replication than in real networks.

For simulation purposes, each peer was assigned a summary of users' queries. Each summary consisted of descriptions of the documents to be requested during a simulation.

During a simulation run, it was assumed that the summary of the user's queries was not changing. To create this summary, each document (its description) was randomly selected from the set of documents available in the network taking different popularity into consideration.

The search request was generated in two cases:

- A peer joined a network. When a peer entered an on-line state, it generated a query by random selection of the document description from the assigned summary of user's queries.
- The previous query successfully proceeded. To test the worst conditions, a peer generated a new query only after a previous query had successfully proceeded, i.e., a required file was found.

These simple rules corresponded to a measurement study done for KaZaa network [18]. It was discovered that the biggest query activity is generated by newcomers which have joined a network recently. It was also shown, the longer P2P clients stay on-line, the less they demand from the system. In our case, peers will generate less queries with time since some part of queries will not be satisfied (e.g., discarded queries).

3.4   Network Settings and Algorithms

The previous results [19], obtained in *networks with static membership*, demonstrated that the best system performance was achieved when a peer had both social and egoistic-type neighbors (SER- was used). Accordingly, the SER was chosen for the experiments under dynamic conditions.

To get reliable results, the size of the network must be large enough. On the other hand, simulating large networks becomes a problem since simulation time rapidly increases with growth of a network. Considering both arguments, the size of a network was 2048. In this way, 10 neighborhood entries were equally divided between egoistic and social parts. The results presented below were obtained for a network with 2048 peers (the size of the neighborhood 10). Similar results were demonstrated in networks with 1024, 4098, and 8196 peers; the size of the neighborhoods was 10 and 20 accordingly.

The initial network was generated as a random graph where about 50% of all simulated peers were on-line. The peers' arrival and departure were modeled by using the approach presented in Section 3.1. At the initial moment, each of the on-line peers had no more than 4 neighbors, but on average two of them were on-line. Therefore, average in-degree (calculated only for the graph organized by on-line peers) was less than 2.

3.5 Description of the Simulation

The network simulation was done during the simulation run. The simulation run is divided into equal intervals called steps. During each of the steps, network operations were monitored and statistics were collected. The statistical data from different simulation steps was used to evaluate and to analyze changes made by the developed algorithms and to investigate their influence on the system operations. The number of simulation steps was typically 100. As it will be shown, the majority of changes were done within the first 20 simulation steps. By the end of one step, statistical data was collected and all messages, which were still in the network, were discarded. This was done in order to avoid "phantom messages" from the previous simulation step because the significant part of statistics was message-related (e.g., the number of hops made). The next simulation step started with the topology achieved during the last step.

A simulation step consisted of simulation cycles. Each cycle was a control loop, which was used to achieve pseudo-parallelism of peers' operations. During a cycle, peers sequentially received control. While having a control, a peer could change its status (on-, off-line), generate queries, handle incoming messages, restruct its neighborhood, etc.

All activities performed by all peers within a cycle were assumed to have been made simultaneously. Therefore, all messages, which had been sent during a cycle, were accumulated in a message spooler. By the end of a cycle (when all of the peers had already received controls), messages were delivered from the spooler to receivers. Thus, every message could make only one hop during a cycle. To make a simulation step long enough for statistics collection, the number of such cycles within one simulation step must be related to the network size. For simplification, the number of cycles in each step was chosen equal to the number of peers in a network. For example, the size of a network is 4,000 peers, so each peer receives a control 4,000 times within one simulation step. On the other hand, a query, which had been generated at the beginning of a step, had at least a theoretical possibility of visiting all peers in a network to find required data.

4 Discussion on Simulation Results

The goals of the evaluation of the developed approach were to determine whether it could avoid flooding and whether the local activities could result in global self-organization under dynamic conditions.

Based on search traffic represented by the number of hops needed to find data, the proposed approach can be positioned between flooding-based and structured applications. It delivered significantly lower average number of search hops (about 20) than Gnutella-like flooding-based systems (Fig. 1) even if optimistic assumptions for Gnutella (TTL=3, 4 connections) were used. In comparison with highly structured systems, e.g., CAN, the content-oriented approach demonstrated bigger numbers of hops and, therefore, higher search traffic. The respective theoretical estimations for CAN were made with an assumption of n=2048, and d=5 (where d- is a number of dimensions corresponding

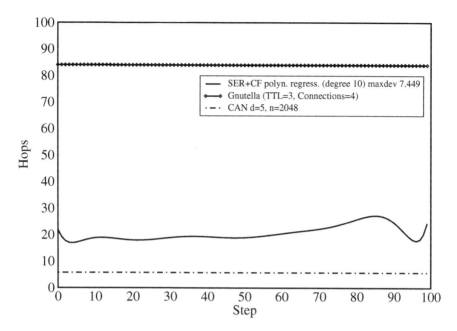

Fig. 1. Average Number of Hops per Successful Query

to the 10 neighbors). In this case, the average number of hops was estimated by using $\frac{dn^{\frac{1}{d}}}{4}$.

The positive effects were caused by content-oriented organization. The observations demonstrated that social neighbors were mainly used for forwarding. It means that queries were forwarded within groups sharing similar content. The egoistic neighbors were mainly used at the initial stage to reach those groups.

The obtained results demonstrated that local activities led to the global organization. In spite of dynamics, the network stabilized. The number of changes caused by organization activities reached a stable level within the first 5 simulation steps (Fig. 2). The observed self-organization was fast enough to adapt to the network dynamics. Each peer had on average 9.5 (max. number is 10) outgoing connections during the simulation.

The important issue of all P2P protocols is their scalability, i.e., changes of their behavior with network growth. The proposed approach was also tested under different network sizes in order to determine whether the data can be found within a reasonable number of hops. The respective results are represented in Table 1.

It is seen that in the chosen simulation conditions, the developed approach demonstrated almost linear scalability. In this way, the average number of hops needed to find a requested file is proportional to the size of the network. The observed effect corresponds to the worst case behavior; it is mainly caused by bad simulation conditions. It was assumed that:

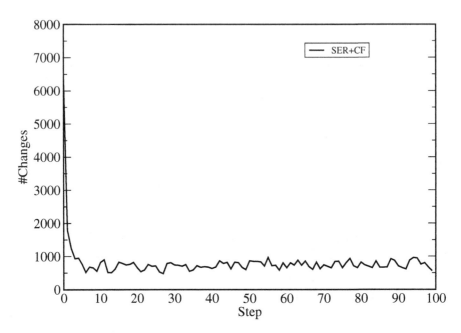

Fig. 2. Topological Changes Caused by Content-oriented Restructuring

Table 1. Average Number of Hops Per Successful Query vs. Size of the Network

	Size of a Network, peers			
Max Number of Neighbors	1,024	2,048	4,096	8,196
10	9.18677	20.4708	41.8841	91.4992
20	4.8982	7.46469	14.6508	34.3842

- Peers may ask for the data which is not available on-line. Since a query is forwarded until data is found or until query is discarded, it negatively influences the system performance.
- Data is not replicated. A search query visits more peers to find required data than would be required to in real systems where the popular data is significantly replicated.
- Each query is represented only by one search message. If a message is discarded (in congestion or due to an on-line - off-line transition), a query is lost.
- If a message is discarded in congestion, a sender is not informed since connection-oriented protocol is not used.
- A peer- search initiator does not use a time-out to resend a query. The peer will keep waiting and generates a new query only when it joins the network next time.

In addition, simulations used unidirectional connections between peers. In real systems, messages can be sent in both directions during communication (using

TCP protocol). Thus, the system performance can be improved once more by utilizing bidirectional connections.

The presented results demonstrated that flooding in file sharing networks can be avoided by using content-oriented self-organization and search. It was demonstrated that a network self-organizes under highly dynamic conditions by executing simple local algorithms. In contrast to DHTs, a tightly controlled network structure was not required for the correctness of operations that positively influenced the reliability of the system.

5   Conclusion

The operation of unstructured P2P applications can be significantly improved by employing content-oriented self-organization. The search mechanism can use content-related network topology to achieve focused search in order to avoid network flooding. At the same time, the good properties of unstructured systems can be preserved. The discussed principles can also be used to organize operations of other types of P2P applications like communication or service sharing systems that accept partial search.

References

1. Gnutella: The Gnutella protocol specification v0.4. http://www.limeware.com (2003)
2. Jovanovi, M., Annexstein, F., Berman, K.: Modeling peer-to-peer network topologies through small-world models and power laws. In: IX Telecommunications Forum TELFOR 2001, Belgrade, Yugoslavia (2001)
3. Ripeanu, M., Foster, I.: Mapping the Gnutella network: Macroscopic properties of large-scale peer-to-peer systems. In: Peer-to-Peer Systems, First International Workshop, IPTPS 2002, Revised Papers. Volume 2429 of Lecture Notes in Computer Science., Cambridge, MA, USA, Springer-Verlag, Berlin (2002) 85–93
4. Milojicic, D., Kalogeraki, V., Lukose, R., Nagaraja, K., Pruyne, J., Richard, B., Rollins, S., Xu, Z.: Peer-to-Peer Computing. Technical Report HPL-2002-57, HP Laboratory Paolo Alto (2002) Available: http://www.hpl.hp.com/techreports/2002/.
5. Internet2: Weekly reports. http://netflow.internet2.edu/weekly/ (2003)
6. Ratnasamy, S., Francis, P., Handley, M., Karp, R., Shenker, S.: A scalable content addressable network. In: Proceedings of ACM SIGCOMM 2001. (2001)
7. Stoica, I., Morris, R., Karger, D., Kaashoek, F., Balakrishnan, H.: Chord: A scalable Peer-To-Peer lookup service for internet applications. In: Proceedings of ACM SIGCOMM 2001. (2001) 149–160
8. Rowstron, A., Druschel, P.: Pastry: Scalable, decentralized object location, and routing for large-scale peer-to-peer systems. In: IFIP/ACM International Conference on Distributed Systems Platforms (Middleware). (2001) 329–350
9. Saroiu, S., Gummadi, P.K., Gribble, S.D.: A measurement study of peer-to-peer file sharing systems. In: Proceedings of Multimedia Computing and Networking 2002 (MMCN '02), San Jose, CA, USA (2002)

10. Chu, J., Labonte, K., Levine, B.: Availability and locality measurements of peer-to-peer file systems. In: SPIE ITCom: Scalability and Traffic Control in IP Networks. Volume 4868. (2002)
11. Vaucher, J., Babin, G., Kropf, P., Jouve, T.: Experimenting with gnutella communities. In: Distributed Communities on the Web (DCW 2002). Volume 2468 of Lecture Notes in Computer Science., Sydney, Australia, Springer Berlin (2002) 85–99
12. Pandurangan, G., Raghavan, P., Upfal, E.: Building low-diameter P2P networks. In: 42th IEEE Symp. on Foundations of Computer Science, Las Vegas, USA (2001) 56–64
13. Sen, S., Wang, J.: Analyzing peer-to-peer traffic across large networks. In: Proceedings of the second ACM SIGCOMM Workshop on Internet measurment workshop, ACM Press (2002) 137–150
14. Clip2: Gnutella measurement project. http://www.clip2.com (2001)
15. Witten, I., Moffat, A., Bell, T.: Managing Gigabytes: Compressing and Indexing Documents and Images. second edn. Morgan Kaufmann, San Francisco (1999)
16. Makosiej, P., Sakaryan, G., Unger, H.: Measurement study of shared content and user request structure in peer-to-peer Gnutella network. In: Design, Analysis, and Simulation of Distributed Systems (DASD 2004), Arlington, USA (2004) 115–124
17. Leibowitz, N., Ripeanu, M., Wierzbicki, A.: Deconstructing the Kazaa network. In: 3rd IEEE Workshop on Internet Applications (WIAPP'03), San Jose, CA (2003) 112–119
18. Gummadi, K.P., Dunn, R.J., Saroiu, S., Gribble, S.D., Levy, H.M., Zahorjan, J.: Measurement, modeling, and analysis of a peer-to-peer file-sharing workload. In: 19th ACM Symposium on Operating Systems Principles (SOSP-19), Bolton Landing, NY, USA (2003)
19. Sakaryan, G., Unger, H., Lechner, U.: About the value of virtual communities in P2P networks. In: 4th IEEE International Symposium and School on Advanced Distributed Systems (ISSADS 2004). Volume 3061/2004 of Lecture Notes in Computer Science., Guadalajara, Mexico, Springer (2004) 170–185

Improving Reliability of Distributed Storage

Ricardo Marcelín-Jiménez*

E.E. Dept., UAMI; Atlixco 186; 09340 México D.F.
calu@xanum.uam.mx

Abstract. A storage scheme is a distributed system that coordinates a set of network-attached components. Using this type of solution it is possible to achieve balance in time and space over the involved components. Although this approach was developed to support efficient global states recording, many storage applications, like web hosting or distributed databases, might profit from it to provide highly available and reliable services. We explore the impact of space and information redundancy in order to improve the integrity requirements of files stored according to this management principles.

1 Introduction

In its simplest form, distributed storage consists of spreading a collection of files across the components of a network. Of course, each application has special requirements. For a long term operation, the active components of a distributed storage system have a non-zero probability of crash failures. In an event of this type, information retrieving might be compromised unless some preventive actions are taken.

In a storage scheme, proper subsets of network-attached components are appointed to work as storage repositories. The size and composition of these subsets achieves a balanced solution where each component participates as many times as any other and none works as a full-time storage. Also, depending on the intersections between these subsets, a given scheme may resist more or less crash failures, i.e. the absence of a component may affect more or less subsets.

1.1 Related Work

Distributed storage is becoming a key procedure as long as telecomunications and computer systems depend on it not only to support the increasing number of services but also, to keep up with the inner operations of these very systems. Yianilos [Yianilos 2001] provides a sample of the many trends of this emerging technology. Marcelín and Rajsbaum [Marcelín & Rajsbaum 2003] introduced the idea of storage scheme as a distributed coordination procedure achieving balance in time and space, over the involved components. Marcelín [Marcelín 2005],

---

* (Visiting the E.E. Dept. of the CINVESTAV under contract Marina-CONACyT 2002C013199A).

A. Bui et al. (Eds.): IICS 2005, LNCS 3908, pp. 117–125, 2006.

evaluated the initial solutions in terms of reliability and time to failure. Storage schema are related to the so-called Redundant Arrays of Distributed Disks (RADD) [Mourad et al. 1996]. Nevertheless, storage schema are not a special purpose hardware, but rather provide logistics to manage storage devices already available.

Up to now, storage systems have addressed the information integrity issue using erasure codes [Bhagwan et al. 1999]. Rabin [Rabin 1989] provides a way to tolerate failures by dispersing each data item into several bit sequences of a smaller size. This method is more demanding on communication, because reconstructing information means multiple remote accesses. On the other hand, it has advantages in supporting backup copy storage.

1.2   Contributions

Given a storage scheme known to have a superior fault-tolerance, we wanted to improve its lifetime. For this purpose, we have tested the effect of incorporating information redundancy in combination with different forms of space redundancy: starting from a simple base case called kv1d, we have evaluated the impact of spare components with and without replacement, as well as two-folded and three-folded mirror systems, called kv2d and kv3d, respectively.

We assume that failure rates are i.i.d. following exponential distribution. This hypothesis allows us to use phase type distribution to model system behavior. We achieve analytic expressions for failure time distribution and mean time to failure.

The rest of this paper includes the following parts: Section 2 introduces the concept of storage scheme, describes the particular storage scheme which is the departing point of this work, as well as the different types of redundancy that will complement this original system. In section 3 we present the analytic tools that will help us to model the degradation process of the systems under study. Section 4 presents and comments on the results of the experiments we designed. Section 5 includes the concluding remarks as well as the recommendations for further work.

2   Variations on the Same Scheme

A *storage scheme* is a distributed coordination system that runs a set V of network components and evolves through *steps*. Every component is in charge of one disk of its own. At each step, a file F to be recorded is cut up and all of its corresponding fragments will be stored in a proper subset of the components, called a *block*. A sequence of blocks $B_1, B_2, \ldots, B_b$ of the same size is appointed to play the role just described, during succesive steps. Blocks are rescheduled in a fixed order at the end of a *cycle*.

The storage scheme of this work is based on a very simple collection of blocks which has turned out to be the most resilient to failures: We say that a "k out of v" scheme, or kv for short, is a storage scheme that runs on a set V of

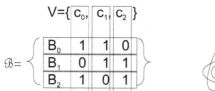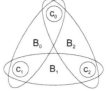

Fig. 1. A storage scheme $\mathcal{B}$ from a given V

v components and coordinates as blocks all of the subsets of size k, from V. Figure 1 shows an example of kv scheme, with parameters $v = 3$ and $k = 2$. In [Marcelín & Rajsbaum 2003], we introduced 4 different storage schema, including kv. In [Marcelín 2005] we evaluated their performance in terms of a reliability measure called, mean time to failure (mttf). Also, we showed that kv is the most reliable storage scheme to coordinate a given set of v components.

For any storage scheme, components are assumed to have a unique number $i \in (0, v - 1)$. During the execution, each component risks a crash failure. We assume that once it stops working, it is never restarted and it is considered permanently out of service [Deswarte 1991]. If a site in B_j crashes, all of the data stored in the block is useless, because the corresponding files cannot be reconstructed. A storage scheme is considered to be *destroyed*, when each of its blocks has at least one missing component.

Any system threatened of malfunctioning may incorporate some form of redundancy on their components or subsystems: Space redundancy implies the replication of physical components. Spare components and mirror systems are two examples of this approach. In time redundancy, a given operation is repeated in order to improve its probability of completion. Timed retransmissions used on link protocols, use this techique. Finally, information redundancy requires some coding techniques to detect and, if possible, correct a given error-bit. See error-correcting codes, like Hamming or Reed-Solomon, for instance.

In many storage scenarios, there is a file to be stored in a hard disk belonging to a network component. So, if this component has a stop failure, the information retrieval will be cancelled. The most frequent solution for this problem consists of storing a backup copy in a second component. The main drawback of this solution is that the alternate component reduces its effective available space in order to locate a file that might never be read from it. Besides, if the first and the second component fail, the file will be lost.

We propose an alternative approach based on the so-called "IDA: Information Dispersal Algorithm" developed by Rabin [Rabin 1989]. Let F be a file, F could be transformed into k files called dispersals. Each of size $|F|/m$, where $k > m > 1$. Then, the dispersals are stored in the k components that built up the corresponding block of a given storage scheme. From the algorithm properties it is granted that if any $k - m$ dispersals were lost, the original information can be reconstructed from the m surviving dispersals. In this case, the cost of the reconstruction could be accepted due to the "amortized" storage shared among the alternate components, and also due to the superior tolerance it exhibits.

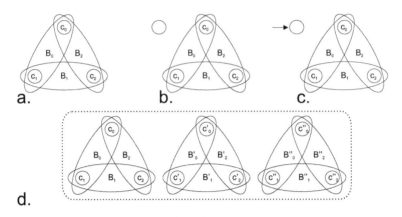

Fig. 2. Variations on a kv1d scheme

Information dispersal is a form of information redundancy. For the rest of this paper, we will assume that any storage operation uses IDA. Therefore, any file to be stored is transformed into k dispersals to be placed in a given block of the underlying kv scheme.

Besides IDA, we explore some forms of space redundancy to evaluate its impact on the reliability of kv schema. A one-dimensional storage scheme, kv1d, is just a simple kv scheme, with parameters k and v, obviously. A two-dimensional storage scheme, kv2d, is made up from two identical kv1d schema, working as a mirror of each other. Finally, a three-dimensional storage scheme, kv3d, is made up from three identical kv1d schema, working as a mirror of each other. Our goal is to evaluate the risk of destruction in each of the following cases: i) kv1d (fig. 2a), ii) kv1d having s spare components (kv1d+s), with and without replacement (fig. 2b and c, respectively), iii) kvnd, for $n = 2, 3$ (fig. 2d, for $n = 2$).

3   Tools and Methods

Consider a storage scheme whose conditions can be represented by $n+1$ states indexed by $0 \ldots n$. State 0 denotes a "like-new" state and state n a complete system failure. Other states are ordered and indexed in increasing degree of deterioration. The scheme's deterioration process can be described using a finite-state absorbing continuous-time Markov chain with a single absorbing state. The time to absorption distribution of such a Markov chain has received extensive attention in the literature of stochastic modeling and computational probability. Such a distribution, called phase-type distribution, has many attractive properties from modeling and computation perspectives [Kao 1997] [Neuts 1981].

Let $S = \{0, 1, \ldots, n\}$ be a finite set of states. Now consider a Markov jump process $\{X_t\}_{t \geq 0}$ with state-space $S = \{0, 1, \ldots, n\}$ and with exactly one absorbing state, say state n. Assume that all other states are transient. Then the intensity matrix of the Markov process looks as follows:

$$\Lambda = \begin{pmatrix} \mathbf{T} & \mathbf{t} \\ \mathbf{0} & 0 \end{pmatrix},$$

where it is understood that $\mathbf{0}$ is a n-dimensional row vector of zeros, $\mathbf{T}$ a $n \times n$ matrix and $\mathbf{t}$ is a n-dimensional column vector. Then we say that the restriction of the Markov jump process to the set of states $0, 1, \ldots, n-1$ is a terminating Markov process, since eventually absorption will take place. Moreover, the time of termination is called the life time of the terminating Markov process. *A phase-type distribution is the distribution of the life time of a terminating Markov process.*

We will assume that $P(X_0 = n) = 0$. Hence it is sufficient to specify the initial distribution of $\{X_t\}_{t \geq 0}$ for states $0, 1, \ldots, n-1$. Let $\mathbf{\Pi}$ denote the n-dimensional (row) vector such that $\pi_i = P(X_0 = i)$, $\sum_{i=0}^{n-1} \pi_i = 1$. We say that a distribution is phase-type with generators $\mathbf{\Pi}$ and $\mathbf{T}$ has a representation $PH(\mathbf{\Pi}, \mathbf{T})$. In the following we call $\mathbf{T}$ the intensity matrix of the phase-type distribution, and $\mathbf{t}$ the exit (rate) vector.

We introduce the following notation for the terminating Markov process $\tilde{X}_t = X_t|_{0,\ldots,n}$. The distribution of the terminating Markov jump process $\{\tilde{X}_t\}_{t \geq 0}$ at time t is $\mathbf{\Pi}e^{\mathbf{T}t}$. Let $X \sim PH(\mathbf{\Pi}, \mathbf{T})$, if t is a random variable describing the time to absorption of X, then

1. *The distribution function F of t is given by* $F(t) = 1 - \mathbf{\Pi}e^{\mathbf{T}t}\mathbf{e}$.
2. *The density function f of t is given by* $f(t) = \mathbf{\Pi}e^{\mathbf{T}t}\mathbf{t}$.
3. *The expected time to absorption $E(t)$ is given by* $E(t) = \mathbf{\Pi}[(-\mathbf{T})^{-1}(-\mathbf{T})^{-1}]\mathbf{t}$.

We note that $R(t) = 1 - F(t)$, also called *the survival probability*, is the probability that the terminating Markov process is alive at time t. While $F(t)$ is probability that the terminating Markov process is been absorbed at time t.

The phase-type distribution associated to the resulting Markov chain, features the failure model of a storage scheme under study. The expected time to absorption, from now on *mean time to failure* (mttf), measures the average time it takes to hit each of the blocks that make up the corresponding scheme.

It is known that if an individual component, a disk for instance, has a failure probability following an exponential distribution, with mttf λ_1, then having v replicas of the same component will reduce the mttf of the whole set to $\frac{\lambda_1}{v}$, unless some kind of redundancy is settled among these components in order to build up an enduring system. For the rest of our work we assume that each individual component has a mttf, $\lambda_1 = 1$.

To explain the Markov chain featuring the degradation of a kv1d storage scheme it is important to note that no matter how $v - k + 1$ components were dismissed, there would not be a single block unaffected. Therefore, starting from v available components the chain jumps to its next state with an agregated failure rate equal to $v\lambda_1$, for there are v different ways to eliminate any of the original components. From then on, the transition rate is consecutively reduced

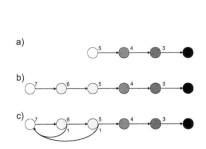

Fig. 3. kv1d Markov chains   **Fig. 4.** kv2d Markov chains

one unit each state, which means that number of remaining components is also decreasing. The final state represents the moment when not even a single block can be made up from the remaining $k-1$ survivors. Figure 3a) shows the Markov chain associated to a kv1d scheme with parameters $k = 3$ and $v = 5$.

A kv1d scheme having s spare components has an associated Markov chain similar to the one corresponding to a simple kv1d. The only difference is that the starting failure rate is equal to $(v+s)\lambda_1$. On the other hand, the destruction conditions are exactly the same as in the first case, i.e. the final state represents the moment when only $k-1$ components survive. If we want to model the replacement operation we must incorporate s jumps of speed λ_2 to the initial state. Starting from the second state on, this backwards transitions represents an operation that restarts the system to its initial conditions. Figures 3b) and c) show the Markov chains associated to the same kv1d scheme with parameters $s = 2$ spare components and replacement speed $\lambda_2 = 1$, respectively.

As for the kvnd $(n = 2, 3)$ scheme, it is clear that any given scheme of this type is alive as long as, at least, one of its kv1 subsystems stands in operation. Therefore, it can resist the massive failure of all but one of its subsystems. In other words, it could be possible to dismiss v components from any $n-1$ subsystems, as long as there is at least one block functioning in the surviving kv1d. Figure 4 shows the Markov chain associated to a kv2d scheme with basic parameters $k = 3$ and $v = 5$.

4   Results

Table 1, obtained from a Markov chain like that of fig. 3a), shows the mttf as a function of k and v for different cases of kv1d. If read by columns we will find that mttf< 1.0 when $k \geq v/2$. On the other hand, mttf> 1 when k is about equal to $\sqrt{(v)}$. Also, the lower the size of k, the higher the value of mttf. Nevertheless a very small block size is not a good option: first, because in the limit the best value would be $k = 1$, which is not a distributed solution at all. Second, because

Table 1. mttf of kv1d

kv1d	$v = 5$	$v = 7$	$v = 10$	$v = 15$
$k = 2$	1.2833	-	1.9290	2.3182
$k = 3$	0.7833	1.0929	1.4290	1.8182
$k = 4$	0.4500	0.7595	1.0956	1.4849
$k = 5$	-	0.5095	0.8456	1.2349
$k = 6$	-	0.3095	-	1.0349
$k = 7$	-	-	-	0.8682

Table 2. mttf of kv1d+s

$v = 5$	$k = 2$	$k = 3$	$k = 4$
kv1d	1.2833	0.7833	0.4500
kv1d+$s = 1$	1.4500	0.9500	0.6167
+$s = 2$	1.5929	1.0929	0.7595
+$s = 3$	1.7179	1.2179	0.8845

Table 3. mttf of kv1d+s and r

$v = 5, k = 3$	$s = 1$	$s = 2$	$s = 3$
kv1d+s	0.9500	1.0929	1.2179
kv1d+$s, r = 1$	0.9833	1.1833	1.3833
+$s, r = 2$	1.0167	1.2833	1.5833
+$s, r = 4$	1.0833	1.5119	2.1012

it may produce a bottleneck. Therefore, $k = \sqrt{(v)}$ seems to be a very good trade-off on the block size.

Table 2, obtained from a Markov chain like that of fig. 3b), shows the impact of the spare components on the mttf, for a fixed $v = 5$ and different combinations of k and s. It can be shown that any kv1d scheme with parameters k and v and s spare components has the same mttf value that a simple kv1d scheme with parameters k and $v + s$.

Table 3, obtained from a Markov chain like that of fig. 3c), shows the impact of the spare components (s) and the speed of replacement (r) on the mttf, for fixed values of $v = 5$, $k = 3$ and different combinations of s and r. It is assumed that the replacement time also follows an exponential law with a rate λ_2 equal to once, twice or four times the failure rate. It can be seen, as expected, that r plays a key role on the system's lifetime but (see the last value of the second column and the first value of the last column) a reasonable number of spare components may compensate a rather slow replacement.

Table 4, obtained from a Markov chain like that of fig. 4), shows for a fixed value $v = 5$ and different values of k, the effect of mirroring a simple kv1d to produce a kv2d and a kv3d under the same parameters. Also, we wanted to compare the mttf of each of these n-folded schema against the corresponding mttf

Table 4. kv1d's mttf vs kv2d's vs kv3d's

$v = 5$	kv1d	kv2d	kv(2v)1d	kv3d	kv(3v)d
$k = 2$	1.2833	1.6512	1.9290	1.8695	2.3182
$k = 3$	0.7833	1.0321	1.4290	1.1814	1.8182
$k = 4$	0.4500	0.6194	1.0956	0.7243	1.4849

of a simple kv1d having nv storage components, that we will call k(2v)1d and k(3v)1d, respectively. As expected, the mttf of kvnd is bigger than kv1d but, surprisingly, lower than that of k(nv)1d ($n = 1, 2$). A major problem we had when evaluating kvnd schema is that the state space grows with a rate $O(v^n)$.

5   Conclusions

We presented a specific family of distributed storage systems called storage schema. Network storage components are organized in subsets of a fixed size, called blocks. Blocks are properly scheduled to work as file repositories in order to achieve balance in time and space. Also, the size and composition of these blocks defines the tolerance resilience of the corresponding scheme.

We introduced different types of space and information redundancy that complement a basic storage scheme already studied, called kv1d, and evaluate the reliability parameters of the resulting combinations.

We have seen that, as long as possible, it is better to work with a simple kv1d storage scheme with a block size equal to around $\sqrt{(v)}$. It is also a good idea to leave more or less spare components depending on the speed of replacement. These rules of thumb seem to perform better when v grows. Nevertheless, what we mean by "as long as possible" is that communication problems may appear at some point. Scalability requires regionalization and mirroring may become a feasible solution.

For future work we are planning to study storage situations arising in real-life that might profit from the ideas presented here, i.e. P2P nets, web storage, distributed databases and the like. Additionally, we believe that the stochastic tools we have worked with, may help to model federated storage schema.

References

[Bhagwan et al. 1999]   Bhagwan, R., Moore, D., Savage, S. and Voelker G. 2002. "Replication Strategies for Highly Available Peer-to-Peer Storage" in International Workshop on Future Directions in Distributed Computing.

[Berenbrink et al. 1999]   Berenbrink, P. and Brinkmann, A. and Scheideler, C. 1999. "Design of the PRESTO Multimedia Storage Network." in International Workshop on Communication and Data Management in Large Networks. 2–12.

[Deswarte 1991]   Deswarte, Y. 1991. "Tolérance aux Fautes, Sécurité et Protection." in Construction des Systèmes d'exploitation Répartis, R. Balter, et. al. (eds.), INRIA, chapter 9.

[Kao 1997]   Kao, E.P.C. 1997. *An Introduction to Stochastic Processes*. Duxbury Press.

[Marcelín & Rajsbaum 2003] Marcelín-Jiménez, R. and Rajsbaum, S. 2003. "Cyclic Strategies for Balanced and Fault-tolerant Distributed Storage." LNCS 2847. 214–233.

[Marcelín 2005]   Marcelín-Jiménez, R. 2005. "Performance Measures for Distributed Storage." in Proceedings of the Design Analysis and Synthesis of Distributed Systems Conf.(DASD2005). Society for Computer Simulation. 53–62.

[Mourad et al. 1996]   Mourad, A.N., Fuchs, K.W. and Saab, D.G. 1996. "Site Partitioning for Redundant Arrays of Distributed Disks." Journal of Parallel and Distributed Computing. 33. 1–11.

[Neuts 1981]   Neuts, M.F. 1981. *Matrix-Geometric Solutions in Stochastic Models*. The Johns Hopkins University Press.

[Rabin 1989]   Rabin, M. O. 1989. "Efficient Dispersal of Information for Security, Load Balancing and Fault Tolerance." Journal of the ACM. 36(2). 335–348.

[Yianilos 2001]   Yianilos, P. 2001. "The Evolving Field of Distributed Storage." IEEE Internet Computing. Sep/Oct. 35–39.

Using Lamport's Logical Clocks to Consolidate Log Files from Different Sources

Roberto Gómez, Jorge Herrerias, and Erika Mata

ITESM-CEM, Depto. Ciencias Computacionales, Km 3.5 Lago Guadalupe,
51296, Atizapan Zaragoza, Edo México, Mexico
{rogomez, jherrerias, emata}@itesm.mx

Abstract. Event logging and log files are playing an important role in system and network security. Log files record computer system activities, are used to provide requirements of reliability, security and accountability applications. Information stored in log files can be obtained from different devices, not necessarily clock synchronized, and they do not arrive in the same order they are generated. Nevertheless, log information has to be coherent in time to be useful. To support the events we propose to use Lamport's logic clocks, originated at different sources, in a causal relationship. As a result the administrator will count all the events involved general idea in a computer incident. A model implementation is also presented.

1 Introduction

Log files keep information used in computer forensics to find system crash causes or to obtain evidence to define responsibilities. Accountability is an essential part, i.e. to be capable of being held responsible for something.

Every operating system, application or network device writes the activity records into one or multiple log files. The event logs implementation varies for different operating systems and applications; there is no industry standard for it. For example, on UNIX systems, the majority events are written to the text file called a Syslog, as well as the Windows systems maintain multiple binary files for multiple purposes: security log, system log.

In [1] Lamport presents the logical clock concept. A logical clock is a chronological capturing mechanism and causal relationships in a distributed system. As physical clocks cannot be perfectly synchronized, event timestamps derived from readings of physical clocks generally cannot be used to find out the ***order in which events happened.

Some approaches have been proposed in order to correlate log information originated at different devices. Most solutions need that time synchronized devices, and they propose to use NTP protocol. Nevertheless some of these devices reside in different time zones and NTP protocol is not a solution. In order to establish devices events reported secuency we propose to "stamp" every log using Lamport's logical clocks. This stamped logs will be stored in a database in order to help the administration to have a general panorama of the events occurred in a specific time period.

A. Bui et al. (Eds.): IICS 2005, LNCS 3908, pp. 126–133, 2006.

This paper is organized as follows. Section two describes the log management features. Section three summarizes all Lamport's logical clocks Theory. Section four presents some related work and our proposal. Section five discusses the experiments made to test our proposal. Section six draws some conclusions and shows future work.

2 Logs Management Overview

As mentioned in [2] application programs and subsystems use log services for recovery, to record security audit trails, and for performance monitoring. Preferably, a log service should accommodate very large, long-lived logs, and provide efficient retrieval and low pace overhead.

Generally logging facilities are used in computer systems and applications to provide requirements of reliability, security and accountability. Computer systems use logs to record or log, execution history to satisfy these requirements. Following a failure, the application can use this history to recover a previous state. The history can also be used to restore the current state of a system after the data structures for this state have been reviewed, allowing the application to evolve without excessive disruption. This technique is often used to move between different file systems incompability versions.

The logs can be used in the security domain. System logged history can be examined to monitor for, and detect, unauthorized or suspicious activity patterns which might represent security violations.

File logs can be found in several formats, divided in text and binary log files. Logs come in different flavors, so we need several approaches to deal with them. The most common type of log file is one composed entirely with text lines. Popular server's packages, like Apache (web), INN (Usenet news), and Sendmail (email) spew log text in voluminous quantities. Most logs on Unix machines look similar because they are created by a centralized logging facility known as syslog.

Sometimes it's not easy writing programs to deal with log files. Instead of nice, easily parseable text lines, some logging mechanisms produce nasty, gnarly binary files with proprietary formats that can't be parsed with a single Perl line. Luckily, Perl isn't afraid of these miscreants. Let's look a few approaches we can take when dealing with these files. Let look at two different examples of binary logs: Unix's wtmp file and NT/2000's event logs. One important issue in log management is log consolidation. It offers a way to organize, assure, correlate and control logs. All information is sent and stored in a central host, known as a logging host or loghost. It is a significant disk storage machine dedicated to receive these log messages sole purpose.

According to [3], a centralized scheme offers the following benefits: it is easier to analyze what may have happened (normal behavior versus curious event), less likely that a successful infiltrator could corrupt or alter relocated logs, and it simplifies the collected logs off-line archival to removable media, or even a line printer.

There are two scenarios when we want to consolidate logs to be considered. Both scenarios are based in a centralized scheme. The first scenario involves a unique host which manages all logs. Log information is used in an operations center which generates alerts depending in the information found in the log's repository. The principal disadvantage of this scenario is that it defines a unique point of failure. Complete log system depends on loghost availability.

The second scenario presents a stronger architecture. Logs are classified and treated according to a classification based on the log source. There is a loghost for any kind of generated log. This scenario gives more availability to the system, if the Windows syslog fails, we can count with the Unix loghost.

Both scenarios have to arrange logs in a repository. If logs sources are not synchronized on time, or they belong to different time zones, two related events can be badly interrelated. For example, considering that event A is a message sent by host 1 to host 2, and event B is the reception of this message. If the internal clock of host 1 advanced in one hour in respect to host 2 clock, it will seem that event B happened before event A. In order to avoid this kind of situations we propose to use logical clocks.

3 Lamport's Logical Clocks

One of the most important issues in a distributed system is the absence of a global clock. Distributed processes cannot rely on having an accurate view of global state, due to transmission delays. It has not sense to talk about a global state. The "time" and "state" traditional notions do not work in distributed systems. It is necessary to develop some concepts corresponding to "time" and "state" in ** uniprocessor system.

"Time" concept in distributed systems is different that the one used in centralized systems. This concept is used in distributed systems to order events generated in different hosts. Distributed system events are not total chaos. Under some conditions, it is possible to ascertain the events orders. Lamport's logical clocks try to catch this.

Lamport defines logical clocks to establish a distributed events global ordering. He assumes that the execution process is characterized by an events sequence; an event can be one instruction or procedure execution. It is also assumed that sending a message is one event, receiving a message is one event.

Lamport defines a "happened before" relation ($\rightarrow$) between two events. The relation is defined as follows:

- A $\rightarrow$ B if A and B are within the same process (same sequential thread of control) and A occurred before B.
- A $\rightarrow$ B if A is the event of sending a message M in one process and B is the event of receiving M by another process.
- if A $\rightarrow$ B and B $\rightarrow$ C then A $\rightarrow$ C.

Based in the previous statements, event A causally affects event B if A $\rightarrow$ B. Distinct events A and B are concurrent (A | | B) if we do not have A $\rightarrow$ B or B $\rightarrow$ A.

It is important to note that events are local to each process (in our case, device). They do not measure real time, only measure "events". Logical clocks are consistent with the happened-before relation and are useful for totally ordering transactions, by using logical clock values as timestamps.

In order to determinate a logical clock value in a process, Lamport defines some conditions.

Assuming that Ci is the local clock for process Pi, the following rules apply

- if a and b are two successive events in Pi, then $Ci(b) = Ci(a) + d1$, where $d1 > 0$
- if a is the sending of message m by Pi, then m is assigned timestamp $tm = Ci(a)$
- if b is the receipt of m by Pj, then $Cj(b) = max\{Cj(b), tm + d2\}$, where $d2 > 0$

d value could be 1, or it could be an approximation to the elapsed real time. For example, we could take d1 to be the elapsed local time, and d2 to be the estimated message transmission time. The latter solves the problem of waiting forever for a virtual time instant to pass.

We can extend the partial ordering of the happened-before relation to a total ordering on events, by using the logical clocks and resolving any ties by an arbitrary rule based on the processor/process ID.

If a is an event in Pi and b is in Pj, a $\Rightarrow$ b iff

- $Ci(a) < Cj(b)$ or
- $Ci(a) = Cj(b)$ and $Pi < Pj$

where < is an arbitrary total ordering of the processes.

We propose to use logical clocks to define a total ordering relationship between all the logs that a loghost receives. Every log will we stamped with its logical clock, and the system will define which event happened first.

4 The Proposed Scheme

There are several approaches to accomplish log consolidation. In [4] the authors propose a model to write a log based in network behavior different in applications. They argue that centralized logs do not contain enough information to determinate if logs were generated by a user, an application or by other kind of event. They propose to create a log which keeps all network's requests, such a way to be possible to establish a relationship between the user that manipulates the program, and the traffic produced by the program.

In the other hand, some authors establish the need to define a log standard to facilitate loss reading and analysis originated in different sources. In the intrusion detection area, it has been proposed a standard known as IDMEF [5]. It has been proposed the Intrusion Detection Message Exchange Format (IDMEF) to define data formats and exchange procedures to share interest information to intrusion detection and response systems, and to the management systems which may need to interact with them. In [6] the authors present a system to communicate an IDS and a firewall through the IDMEF standard.

The IDMEF model has been extended in [7], but with a different approach. The authors do not propose a standard for log events, instead they propose a format to make log recording easier and flexible. Any log can be converted to this format, in such a way that all logs can be analyzed with the same software.

Another approach is presented in [8]. The authors use small programs to read a log and recollect information and store it in a data bases. These programs need to known the log format they are going to read, so this can be considered a translation.

In [9] the authors present a log analysis and correlation overview, with special emphasis on techniques to manage tools within a network forensics context. They cover the most important parts of log analysis and correlation, starting from the acquisition process to the analysis. They introduce an IRItaly system which provides several tools to do a log analysis. The correlation process involves logs comparison between different machines.

Our proposal follows a centralized scheme. All devices generating logs send their data to a host, the loghost. Every time a log arrives it is stamped with a value according to the source and local time at the source. These values are stored in a database.

When a user wants to known all related data with a particular event it has to look for it in the database, and it will be ordered in a causal relationship with the rest of the events. This provides the user a complete view of all the events involved during an incident.

In order to establish a total events ordering, Lamport's logical clocks use an identifier process and an internal clock. The internal clock is the time in which log was generated, converted to an integer. We add hours, minutes and seconds to obtain a six digits number. For example if the event was generated at 15:47:38, the number will be 154738. Identifier process is formed combining host Internet address and process number to generate log. Internet address is translated to an integer, using the long inet_addr( ) unix syscall, and then the pid is added to it. For example if internet address is 10.45.69.89, (which representation number is 1497705738) and the pid is 3891, then the identifier process will be 14977057383891.

5   Implementation and Tests

In order to test our scheme we use three computers, running Red Hat Linux 9.0 over them. One has installed snort IDS, the other one has IPTables activated ant the third one received all logs generated by the two first.

5.1   Snort's Logs

Snort is a versatile, lightweight and very useful intrusion detection system. Snort is a lightweight network IDS, capable of performing real-time traffic analysis and packet logging on IP networks. It can perform protocol analysis, content searching/matching. It can be used to detect a variety of attacks and probes, such as buffer overflows, stealth port scans, CGI attacks, SMB probes, OS fingerprinting attempts, and more. Snort uses a flexible rules language to describe traffic it should collect or pass, and includes a detection engine using an architecture modular plug-in.

Plug-ins allows the detection and reporting subsystems to be extended. Available plug-ins includes database logging, small fragment detection, portscan detection, and HTTP URI normalization.

Logs are optional in Snort, and administrator has to active it. Snort logs packets in either tcpdump binary format or in Snort's decoded ASCII format to logging directories that are named based on the IP address of the foreign host.

Two examples of alerts/logs generated by snort are presented below.

[**] [1:1256:2] WEB-IIS CodeRed v2 root.exe access [**]
[Classification: Web Application Attack] [Priority: 1]
03/30-19:35:54.306411 68.153.97.216:4464 -> 192.168.1.1:80
TCP TTL:122 TOS:0x0 ID:2271 IpLen:20 DgmLen:112 DF
AP Seq: 0x949963A3 Ack: 0xA3F9CDE1 Win: 0x4510 TcpLen: 20

[**] [1:1002:2] WEB-IIS cmd.exe access [**]
[Classification: Web Application Attack] [Priority: 1]
03/30-19:35:54.555283 68.153.97.216:4477 -> 192.168.1.1:80
TCP TTL:122 TOS:0x0 ID:2302 IpLen:20 DgmLen:120 DF
AP Seq: 0x94A46F43 Ack: 0xA3CF89A0 Win: 0x4510 TcpLen: 20

5.2 IPTables Logs

IPTables, along with its companion netfilter, are collectively a software extension to the Linux operating system which implements a stateful firewall framework. It also enables other networking features such as network address translation (NAT). Although netfilter is a Linux extension, it is included in all 2.4 or 2.6 kernel major Linux distributions. Netfilter does not work with Linux kernels older than version 2.4.

Firewall treats packets leaving, entering, or passing through a host. Basically there is a chain for each of these. Administrator has to set up certain rules on each of these chains which decide what happens to data packets passing through them. Each rule has two parts: a part which says the rule how to match the packet, and a part which says what to do with the packet if it matches.

Administrator can configure IPTables to generate logs. Two examples of IPTables logs are presented below:

Dec 21 11:40:08 kernel: IN=eth0 OUT= MAC=[] SRC=xx.yy.zz.98
DST=aa.bb.cc.64 LEN=60 TOS=0x00 PREC=0x00 TTL=50 ID=1564 DF
PROTO=TCP SPT=33576 DPT=37624 WINDOW=5840 RES=0x00 SYN
URGP=0

Nov 11 07:06:36 valhalla sudo: cbrenton : TTY=pts/1 ; PWD=/home/cbrenton
; USER=root ; COMMAND=/sbin/iptables -A FORWARD -i eth0 -p tcp
--tcp-flags ALL SYN,FIN -j LOG --log-prefix SYNFINSCAN
Test XXX YYY ZZZ

One important feature of IPTables is log prefixing. The prefixing capability allows to define an iptables rule, and to specify a text string that should be recorded to the logs whenever that rule is matched.

It is possible to use this feature to include a timestamp, but this will limit our scheme to logs produced by IPTables.

5.3 The Data Recollection

All logs are sent to the loghost via the syslog facility. We use a mysql database to store all the data. The database has four fields: internal clock field, process identifier field, log itself and IP address. The user interrogates this database with a SQL query to get the information it requires.

Computers clock presented differences between them, but logs were continuously generated. When the user wants to list all the events with a total ordering it introduces an initial and a final time. The system displays all the events ordered according to the Lamport's logical clocks rules.

As a database loss record example we consider that the host running snort has the 10.10.10.2 internet address, and that the process running snort has the 4142 identifier. In the other hand the host with IPTables has the 10.10.10.5 address, and the process identifier is 3857. Stored information at the database is described below

Internal clock	Process identifier	log	IP address
101031	342123624142	log 1	10.10.10.2
101029	845440103857	log 2	10.10.10.5
101028	342123624142	log 3	10.10.10.2
101032	845440103857	log 4	10.10.10.5
101033	845440103857	log 5	10.10.10.5
101026	845440103857	log 6	10.10.10.5
101024	342123624142	log 7	10.10.10.2
101030	845440103857	log 8	10.10.10.5
101028	845440103857	log 9	10.10.10.5

Log is not showed, because it does not help to understand our scheme, and the entries are sorted according to their arrival time. We can see that some logs arrived at different order they were generated.

Once the events are sorted according to Lamports clocks, we obtain the following list:

Internal clock	Process identifier	log	IP address
101024	342123624142	log 7	10.10.10.2
101026	845440103857	log 6	10.10.10.5
101028	342123624142	log 3	10.10.10.2
101028	845440103857	log 9	10.10.10.5
101029	845440103857	log 2	10.10.10.5
101030	845440103857	log 8	10.10.10.5
101031	342123624142	log 1	10.10.10.2
101032	845440103857	log 4	10.10.10.5
101033	845440103857	log 5	10.10.10.5

The list show us the relationship between the different events.

6 Conclusions

We presented a scheme to consolidate logs produced by different devices with different local times. The scheme is based in Lamport's logical clocks. Our implementation shows that this scheme helps to have a general idea of all the events generated in a time period.

It is important to remark, that devices were not modified; all work is done at the loghost. Logs arrived and they are treated to stamp them.

Future work includes modify the system in order to include vector clocks, and to define a causal chain between the events represented by the received logs.

References

1. Leslie Lamport, Time, clocks, and the ordering of events in a distributed system. Communications of the ACM, Vol. 27, No. 7, July 1978, pp. 558–565.
2. Finlayson, D. Cheriton Log files: an extended file service exploiting write-once storage, Proceedings of the eleventh ACM Symposium on Operating systems principles, Austin, Texas, USA, 1987, pp. 139–148
3. D. Pitts, Log Consolidation with syslog, december 23, 2000, SANS Institute 2000–2002
4. Ahmad, A., Ruighaver, A.B., Design of a Network-Access Audit Log for Security Monitoring and Forensic Investigation, Proceedings of the 1st Australian Computer Network, Information & Forensics Conference , Perth, Nov 24, 2003
5. Internet Draft: draft-ietf-idwg-idmef-xml-12, The Intrusion Detection Message Exchange Format, IETF Intrusion Detection Exchange Format Working Group, July 8, 2004.
6. R. Gómez, J. Herrerías, An example of communication between security tools: Iptables – Snort, ACM Operating Systems Revies, submitted
7. M. Bishop, A Standard Audit Trail Format, Proceedings of the Eighteenth National Information Systems Security Conference, Oct. 1995, pp. 136–145
8. Allison, Jared, Automated Log Processing, login: The Magazine of Usenix & Sage, december 2002, volume 27 number 6, pp. 16–20
9. Dario V. Forte, Log Correlation Tools and Techniques. The art of Log Correlation. Proceedings of ISSA 2004 SouthAfrica, and HTCIA Conference 2004 Washington DC

A Simple Approach for Testing Web Service Based Applications

Abbas Tarhini[1,3], Hacène Fouchal[2], and Nashat Mansour[3]

[1] LICA/CReSTIC, Université de Reims Champagne-Ardenne Moulin de la Housse,
BP 1039, 51687 Reims Cedex 2, France
`Abbas.Tarhini@univ-reims.fr`
[2] GRIMAAG, Université des Antilles et de Guyane, F-97157 Pointe-à-Pitre,
Guadeloupe, France
`Hacene.Fouchal@univ-ag.fr`
[3] Computer Science Division, Lebanese American University,
PO Box 13-5053, Beirut, Lebanon
`nmansour@lau.edu.lb`

Abstract. The cost of developing and deploying web applications is reduced by dynamically integrating other heterogeneous self-contained web services. However, the malfunctioning of such systems would cause severe losses. This paper presents a technique for building reliable web applications composed of web services. All relevant web services are linked to the component under test at the testing time; thus, the availability of suitable web services is guaranteed at invocation time. In our technique, a web application and its composed components are specified by a two-level abstract model. The web application is represented as *Task Precedence Graph (TPG)* and the behavior of the composed components is represented as a *Timed Labeled Transition System (TLTS)*. Three sets of test sequences are generated from the WSDL files, the TLTS and the TPG representing the integrated components and the whole web application. Test cases are executed automatically using a test execution algorithm and a test framework is also presented. This framework wraps the test cases with SOAP interfaces and validates the testing results obtained from the web services.

Keywords: label transition systems, testing, verification, web service, web application.

1   Introduction

The development of web applications received significant attention in the past few years. They have been remarkably introduced into all areas of communication, information distribution, e-commerce and many other fields. The use of web services also provided a common communication infrastructure to communicate through the internet, and enabled developers to create applications that can span different operating systems, hardware platforms and geographical locations. Thus building reliable web applications and web services should be considered seriously.

Originally, web sites were constructed form a collection of web pages containing text documents and interconnected via hyper links. Only recently, the dramatic changes

A. Bui et al. (Eds.): IICS 2005, LNCS 3908, pp. 134–146, 2006.
© Springer-Verlag Berlin Heidelberg 2006

of web technology lead web applications to be built by integrating different components from variety of sources, residing on distributed hardware platforms, and running concurrently on heterogeneous networks. The construction of systems from different types of software components faces various complexities and challenges such as maintaining performance, reliability and availability of those systems. Thus the validation of such web applications remains the main challenge. A Web application might invoke multiple web services located on different servers with no design, source code or interface available. This forces designers to use black-box notions to select the relevant web services from the pool of services found on the internet.

The technique presented in this paper is testing on the fly during the building of web systems. That is, during the development process, we test the web application and its interaction with remote services to select only relevant web services that build a correct web system. First, we suggest a two-level abstract model to represent a web application. Then, we generate three sets of test sequences that are used to automatically test the web system. Next, an automated testing technique is presented: it selects all relevant web services that interact with our web application and integrates them into the system before invocation time. This will guarantee the reliability and availability of services in the web application. Moreover, we present a test framework adapted from [13] for supporting both test execution and test scenario management. In this work we do not deal with performance, we only need a correct behavior. Moreover, the generated test cases use only symbolic values for variables satisfying an adequate coverage criteria. In order solve the state explosion problem, for test execution we may use either, boundary values for variables, or, we use a heuristic to choose values. In both cases, the test coverage will not be complete.

The rest of this paper is organized as follows. In Section 2 we present a brief background on web service models and previous work done on testing web services. The modeling of web applications and needed definitions are presented in Section 3. Section 4 presents our technique for testing web applications. In this section we show how to generate and execute test cases. In Section 5 we present the testing framework that is used to configure, generate and execute test cases. We conclude the paper in Section 6.

2   Background

In this section, we present an overview of web service infrastructure and definitions, and a brief survey of previous work done on testing web services.

2.1   Web Services Overview

Web Services were defined differently by vendors, researchers, or standards organizations. IBM defined web services as self-describing, modular applications that can be published, located and invoked across the web [12]. They are Internet-based, modular applications that uses the Simple Object Access Protocol (SOAP) for communication and transfer data in XML through the internet [10]. In our study, we define Web Services

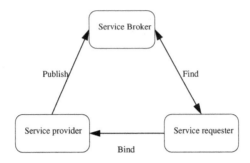

Fig. 1. Web service architecture

as self-contained component-based applications, residing on different servers, and communicating with other applications by exchanging XML messages wrapped in SOAP interfaces.

Web services infrastructure is based on service-oriented architecture(SOA) that involves three kinds of participants: service providers, service requesters and service broker (Figure 1). The provider publishes services to service broker. Service requesters find required services using the broker and bind to them [12].

This infrastructure uses the following standards to make web services function together: Web Services Description Language (WSDL), Universal Description, Discovery and Integration (UDDI), The Extensible Markup Language (XML), and Simple Object Access Protocol (SOAP).

After creating a web service, the service provider generates the corresponding WSDL file and publishes it on the internet. The WSDL file is a description of how to access the web service and what operations this service can perform. On the service broker, the UDDI registry holds the specification of services and the URL that points to the WSDL file of services. The service requester searches for a web service in the UDDI registry, then binds to it, and transmit massages and data using XML wrapped in SOAP interfaces.

2.2 Testing Web Services

Several aspects make testing web services a challenging task. The heterogeneity of web services that uses different operating systems and different server containers makes the dynamic integration of these services a non-easy task. Moreover, web services do not have user interfaces to be tested [11] and therefore they are hard to test manually. Consequently, test frameworks, techniques, and tools have been studied by several researchers.

Song et al. [13] proposed an XML-based framework to test web services. The framework consists of two parts: the test master and test engine. The test master allows testers to specify test scenarios and cases as well as performing various analysis and converts WSDL files into test scenarios. The test engine interacts with the web service under test and provides tracing information. [6] proposed ideas towards enabling testing web services by using Design by Contract to add behavioral information to the specification of a web service. The behavioral information includes contracts that describe behavior offered and behavior needed (pre and post conditions) by a web service. Then graph transformation rules are used to describe contracts at the level of models. Such contracts would help much during the execution of test cases; however, a list of issues are left open like creating XML-based language and UML-based notations for contracts.

[15] proposed a mobile agent-based technique to test web services. This approach needs the authentication of servers to allow mobile agents execute external code on them. It dynamically selects reliable web services at run time where no backup plan presented in case of unavailability of services satisfying the test criteria. [4] presented a white-box coverage testing of error recovery code in Java web services by provoking exceptions and evaluating how the web service handles them. This method covers many testing aspects, however, testing scenarios apply only to Java web services at a time web services are platform independent. Moreover, this technique requires the knowledge of web service code, at a time most web services are published as executable files and should be treated as black boxes, thus such techniques could be considered for in-house testing. [10] highlighted the difference between traditional applications and web services; web services use a common infrastructure, XML and SOAP, to communicate through the internet. The author presented a new peer-to-peer approach to testing web services by using test cases generated from the modification of existing XML messages based on rules defined on the message grammar. This approach is based on data perturbation. It uses data value perturbation (based on data type) and the interaction perturbation that tests communication messages (RPC communication and data communication). This approach relies on syntactic information about the XML messages; thus lacks behavioral information that are supported more in specification-based testing approaches which allow more detailed kinds of analysis.

Other testing tools and techniques focused on testing WSDL files and SOAP messages [8], and some recommended general best-practices that developers of web services can apply such as functional, regression and load testing [5]. [2] highlighted on what web services are and how to put to use. The author presented how to test web services manually through a web page and automatically through a programming language. Both approaches recommends to focus on what the web service expects as inputs and what it defines as its outputs. [14] proposed to extend WSDL files to support information useful for testing such as dependency information. By using these extensions, we can easily retrieve the necessary useful information for web service testing. This can greatly reduce the effort and cost to do these tasks and make the automation of these tasks possible. [7] surveyed testing techniques that can be applied to web services and detailed the advantages and drawbacks of some methods and tools. Then, the authors suggests fault injection technique as a promising line of research that can be applied to this problem.

Many papers have suggested testing Web services at invocation time, but performing a full-scale test of Web services integrated in Web applications before launch remains a considerable issue. Our testing technique selects and then associates all suitable web services to our web application before launch time; moreover, it suggests testing the functionality of the web service integrated in the web application by executing test cases generated from (1) the WSDL files and (2) the specification of both the component fulfilled by a web service and the specification of the whole web application. This method guarantees the reliability and availability of services in our web application by ignoring both all services that act errantly in a composed environment and hosts of web services that act maliciously at invocation times.

In the following section we introduce some basic notations, the modeling of a web application and the modeling of a single component in a web application which are used in subsequent discussions.

3   Modeling Web Applications

Web-based software systems are constructed by integrating different interacting-components from a variety of sources. The schedule of invoking the interacting-components is restricted by the requirements specification of the web application and by time constraints. These components interact with the main application as well with other components by exchanging messages (actions) that might also involve timing constraints. To model such systems, we suggest a two-level abstract model. The first level models the interaction of components with the main application. The second level of abstraction models the internal behavior of each component in the system. In the following subsections we describe each model and illustrate it with examples.

3.1   Web Application Representation

Since Web applications are composed of components that interact by exchanging messages restricted by timing constraints, our first level of abstraction models a web applications as a *Task Precedence Graph (TPG)*, where each node in the TPG is an abstract representation of a single component in the system and an edge joining two nodes represents the flow of actions (transitions) between components. Every edge is labeled with an action and its timing constraint.

Figure 2 illustrates a *TPG* representing a simple travel agency web application that is composed of four components: Main Component (MC), Hotel Reservation (HR), Car Rental (CR), and Weather Prediction (WP). The Main component (MC) is assumed to

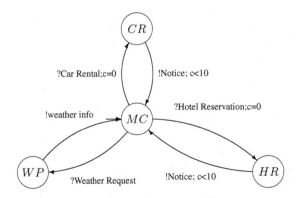

Fig. 2. An example of TPG representing a travel agency web application

be the background component that handles requests from the main web page in the web system. Each of the attached components is invoked whenever its corresponding input is selected and it returns the output back to the Main Component (MC). Thus, if the user wants to reserve a hotel, the transition labeled (?Hotel Reservation; c =0; -) is executed as soon as the input $?Hotel Reservation$ is invoked, and the clock c is set to zero, so that it counts the time taken by the web service to fulfill the user request. The output from the component HR should be sent back with in the time limit (c<10); if not, that means the invoked web service might be not available, thus, the MC component will request HR to contact another web service.

3.2   Single Component Representation

The second level of abstraction models every single component in the web application. In this level, we suggest to model each component as a *Timed Labeled Transition System* *(TLTS)*. Each state in the TLTS represents a state of the modeled component. An edge joining two states is labeled with an action and its corresponding timing constraint. It represents a transition from one state to another. We formally define an TLTS as follows:

Definition 1 (Timed Labeled Transition System (TLTS)). *An* **TLTS** *is defined by* $M = (S, A, C, T, s_0)$ *where S is a finite set of states, s_0 is the initial state, and A is a set of actions. A is partitioned into 2 sets: A_I is the set of input actions (written ?i), A_O is the set of output actions (written !o). C is a set of clocks.*

T is a transition set having the form $\{Tr_1.Tr_2...Tr_n\}$; Tr_i = **<s; a; d; EC; C_s>**, where: **s** $\in S$ and **d**$\in S$ are starting and destination states; **a** $\in A$ is the action of the transition; **EC** is an enabling condition evaluated to the result of the formula $a \sim b$ where $\sim \in \{$ <, >, $\leq$, $\geq$, = $\}$; C_s is a set of clocks to be reset at the execution of transition Tr_i.

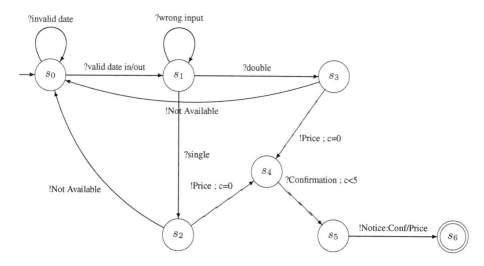

Fig. 3. An Example of TLTS representing simple hotel reservation

Figure 3 shows an example of TLTS representing a simple hotel reservation component (HR) with initial state s_0. A transition is represented by an arrow between two
states and labeled by the action, the timing constraint and clocks to reset (action; EC;
Cs). The TLTS in figure 3 is input-complete, if at state s_0 the user input an invalid date
the system stays in s_0; otherwise, it moves to state s_1 where the users may choose either
a *single* or a *double* room, thus, the system may move to either state s_2 or s_3. As soon
as the appropriate input is selected the corresponding price is given, and clock c is set to
zero in order to count the time for the conformation back from the user, then, the system
moves to state s_4. If the conformation is not sent with in the time (c<5) the session will
be timed-out.

4   Testing Methodology

Consider the web application illustrated in figure 2. In this work, this application is
thought to be a Component Based system (CBS) that contains a set of interacting components (MC, HR, CR, WP), where the requirements of each component is already
defined and represented as a TLTS. Assume that component HR will be fulfilled by a
web service; therefore, we have to find all suitable web services, having similar functionality, that satisfy the requirements of HR and do not act errantly in our composed
system (Figure 4), and then, link the selected services to our web application so that we
can use any of them at invocation time.

   This is usually done by searching the UDDI registry each time our system requires a
web service. The UDDI registry holds the URL's and the corresponding WSDL specification of services that are published by the service providers. After selecting the "optimal" web service, our system binds to the service's web site and invokes the Web
service. In this dynamic invocation model it may not be possible to know which web
service will be used until run time [9]. Moreover, searching and testing web services

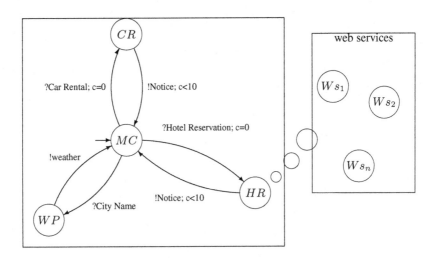

Fig. 4. An Example Web service oriented web CBS

whenever the system requires them would generate enormous network traffic and, still, may not find a suitable web service.

In our method, we suggest to select the web services during the development of our CBS. The method proceeds as follows: while building the CBS, if a component, HR, is implemented by a web service, the UDDI registry is searched and a set of WSDL files describing the candidate web services is found. Next, our task is to find all suitable web services and to eliminate all web services that does not satisfy the requirements of HR. Then, we test the selected web services to ignore all services that act errantly when integrated in our system. The new set of selected web services is saved into a log file linked to the component HR so that any of these suitable web services could be used later depending on its availability, without having to search the UDDI registry every time the service is needed. To reach our aim, we have to generate three sets of test sequencess. The first is used to select all adequate candidate web services that satisfies the requirements of our component. The second set is used to test the selected web services individually, and the third set is used to test the interaction of the suitable web services as a composed component in our web application. The generation of test sequences is detailed in section 4.2.

4.1   Testing Web Applications

Contrary to other testing techniques, our proposed testing method selects all suitable web services only once, during the testing of the web application, rather than selecting them each time the web application is invoked. This will help the developer to build a reliable and available web application. The links to all selected suitable web services are saved into a *log file* associated with the component to be fulfilled by the web service. The *log file* contains the *urls* of all suitable web services and the set of test cases used to test this component. Using this *log file*, the web application would have a wide range of finding available and suitable web services at invocation time. This method tests the web service individually (as a stand-alone component) and as a part of the web CBS. The method consists of four main steps described in the following algorithm:

Step 1: Search the UDDI registry for candidate web services. For each candidate web service found in the UDDI registry, we parse the WSDL file of web service under test (WSUT) to check whether the interface of this web service matches with the specification of our component. If the interface does not match, this process is stopped and we check another candidate web service in the UDDI registry; otherwise, we move into the second step.

Step 2: We connect to the web service's site and start testing the actual web service as a stand-alone component by sending SOAP messages generated from the **first set** of test cases, then we check the correctness of the information received as SOAP responses from the web service by matching them with the corresponding outputs in the test cases. If the web service does not pass this test, it is ignored and we start checking another web service; otherwise, we move to the third step.

Step 3: We continue testing the actual web service as a stand-alone component by sending SOAP messages generated from the **second set** of test cases, then we check the correctness of the information received as SOAP responses from the web service by matching them with the corresponding outputs in the test cases. If the web service does not pass this test, it is ignored and we start checking another web service; otherwise, we move to the fourth step.

Step 4: We test the interaction of this web service as a component in our system by sending SOAP messages generated from the **third set** of test cases, then we check the correctness of the information received as SOAP responses from the web service by passing those outputs to the respective components in the web CBS and monitor the behavior of the whole system, taking into consideration the time restriction on responses. If the web service does not pass this test, it is ignored.

If the web service under test (WSUT) passes the four steps of the above algorithm, then the information -(*including the url, the first and second sets of test cases*)- about WSUT is saved into a *log file* associated with the component to be fulfilled by a web service. Next, this process is repeated until all candidate web services are tested. In any of the above steps, information about errors occurred during testing is saved in an *error log file* associated with the component under test. If non of the web services matches our component under test, then the error log file should be considered to modify the requirements of that component.

4.2 Test Case Generation

To make a decision about selecting a web service that fulfills a component, we have to (1) find all adequate candidate web services, (2) test those web services independently (as a stand-alone components) and select the ones that fulfill the functional requirements of our component, and (3) test the reliability of the selected web services' interaction as a part of our web component based system. Thus, test sequences are divided into three sets. In this work, the generated test cases use only symbolic values satisfying an adequate coverage criteria.

The first set, which tests the adequacy of the web service independently, is generated from information found in the WSDL file of the web service. In this set, test cases are generated based on boundary value testing analysis [3]. Traditional boundary value testing typically involved either boundaries in numerical data types such as integers, floating point numbers, or real numbers or else the end points of enumeration types. In this work, for numerical data types, the negative and positive numbers would be bounded by the limitations defined in the XML schemas: the most possible negative number, zero, and the most possible positive number. With string data types, the boundary values are maximum length and minimum length as defined in the XML schemas, and for boolean it is true and false. The generated test cases contains information about (a) the input boundary values to be sent to the web service and (b) the output boundary values to be used for validating the output received from the web service. To illustrate, we consider the following WSDL file that describes a web service for weather forecasting taken from [1]. It takes as an input the $CityName$ and returns the corresponding $Humidity$.

```
<types>
<xsd:schema targetNamespace="http://www.capeclear.com/AirportWeather.xsd" xmlns:SOAP-ENC=
"http://schemas.xmlsoap.org/soap/encoding/" xmlns:wsdl="http://schemas.xmlsoap.org/wsdl/"
xmlns:xsd="http://www.w3.org/2001/XMLSchema">
...
</types>
<message name="cityName">
  <part name="arg0" type="xsd:string" />
</message>
<message name="getHumidityResponse">
  <part name="return" type="xsd:double" />
</message> ....
<portType name="Station">
<operation name="getHumidity">
  <input message="tns:cityName" />
  <output message="tns:getHumidityResponse" />
</operation> ...
```

Based on the boundary value analysis method, the **first set** of test cases for method *"getHumidity"* generated form the above WSDL file could rely on the following:

The Input argument is of type string:
maximum value: "00000000000000000000000000". minimum value: "null".
The Output is of type double:
maximum value: $2^{63} - 1$. minimum value: -2^{63}. zero: 0.

The **second set** of test sequences is used to test the behavior of the web service individually. Therefore, this set should be able to test the functionality of all possible actions in the service. Thus, we generate this set by traversing *all paths going from the initial state* of the TLTS representing the component to be fulfilled. To illustrate, consider Figure 3 that shows the TLTS for the HR component. Due to space limitation we only list three test sequences of the **second set** generated from the TLTS paths:

T1: <?invalid date;-;->
T2: <?valid date;-;->.<?single;-;->.<!Price;-;c=0>.<?Confirmation;c<5;-><!Notice;-;->
T3: <?valid date;-;->.<?double;-;->.<!Price;-;c=0>.<?Confirmation;c<5;-><!Notice;-;->

The **third set** of test cases tests the interaction of the web service as a part of our web CBS. Therefore, this set should perform a full-test coverage of the whole system. The whole system is covered by invoking all possible actions in the main web application as well as invoking the internal actions of the composed components. Thus, we generate this set by traversing *all paths going form the initial state* of the *TPG* representing the web CBS including the paths of the *TLTS* representing the inner actions of the composed components. To illustrate, consider figure 4 that shows the TLTS for the web CBS. A sample test sequences of the **third set** generated from the TLTS paths would be:

T4: <?HotelReservation;-; c=0>.<?invalid date;-;->
T5: <?HotelReservation;-; c=0>.<?valid date;-;->.<?double;-;->.<!Price;-;c=0>.
     <?Confirmation;c<5;-><!Notice;-; c<10>
T6: <?HotelReservation;-; c=0>.<?valid date;-;->.<?single;-;->.<!Price;-;c=0>.
     <?Confirmation;c<5;-><!Notice;-; c<10>
T7: <Weather Request;-c=0>.<?cityName;-;c=0>.<!WeatherInfo; c<10;->

A sample SOAP request and response message that would wrap the above test case (T_7) would look like:

```
...
SOAPAction: "http://www.myasptools.com/GetWeather"
    <?xml version="1.0" encoding="utf-8"?>
<soap:Envelope xmlns:xsi="http://www.w3.org/2001/XMLSchema-instance"
xmlns:xsd="http://www.w3.org/2001/XMLSchema" xmlns:soap="http://schemas.xmlsoap.org/soap/envelope/">
  <soap:Body>
    <GetWeather xmlns="http://www.myasptools.com/">
      <cityName>Paris</cityName>
    </GetWeather>
  </soap:Body>
</soap:Envelope>
...

    <?xml version="1.0" encoding="utf-8"?>
<soap:Envelope xmlns:xsi="http://www.w3.org/2001/XMLSchema-instance"
xmlns:xsd="http://www.w3.org/2001/XMLSchema" xmlns:soap="http://schemas.xmlsoap.org/soap/envelope/">
  <soap:Body>
    <GetWeatherResponse xmlns="http://www.myasptools.com/">
      <GetWeatherResult>
      <Humidity>70</Humidity>
      </GetWeatherResult>
    </GetWeatherResponse>
  </soap:Body>
</soap:Envelope>
```

In order to have an adequate state coverage, test sequences are generated by traversing, from the initial state, all paths of components' *TLTSs* (for the second set) and all paths of the *TPG* concatenated with the paths of the components' *TLTSs* (for the third set), still, we do not fear path explosion since both the web application and web service have a finite number of states to be covered by the test sequences and the test cases are assumed to be generated using only symbolic values for variables satisfying an adequate coverage criteria.

To assure a full-test coverage, test cases may use all possible values; however, this process is too expensive. In order solve the state explosion problem, for test execution we may use either, boundary values for variables, or we use a heuristic to choose values. However, in both cases, the test coverage will not be complete.

In the next section, we present the test framework that is used to implement our test method. It wraps the test cases with SOAP interfaces and validates the testing results back from the web services. It supports both execution and test scenario management.

5   Web Service Testing Framework

The framework that we use to test our web services is adapted from [13] with some modifications. It consists of two parts: test master and test engine (Figure 5).

The test master (1) extracts the interface information from the WSDL file and maps the signatures of the service into test scenarios, (2) extracts paths from the TLTS and maps them into test scenarios. The test cases are generated from the test scenarios in the XML format which is interpreted by test engine in the second stage. Test engine reads the test scripts produced by the test master and executes the test at the target web services, it also saves the execution trace into *log files* and sends the test results back to the test master. The actual test execution involves three phases:

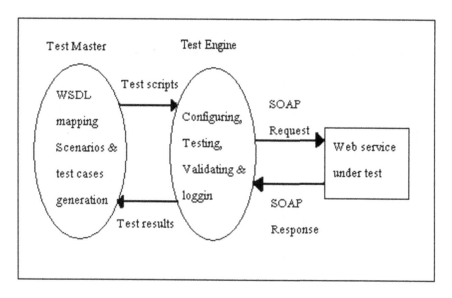

Fig. 5. Web Service Testing Framework

- Configuration: Configure the test scenarios from the WSDL and TLTS.
- Test: Generate the SOAP request messages, and invoke the particular service method with the respective input parameters.
- Validating: Check and assess the testing results in the SOAP response messages against the expected output specified in the test scripts, and save the suitable services in the log file.

6   Conclusion

This paper has presented a simple approach for building reliable web applications. A two-level abstract model is introduced to model the web application as a Task precedence graph (TPG) and the internal behavior of components as Timed Labeled Transition Systems (TLTS). One contribution of this paper is that it allocates all suitable web services that fulfill a component during the testing of the web application rather than during invocation time. This will give a wide range for rapid selection of available web services at invocation time. Another contribution is the full-coverage test cases that are generated form the WSDL files and the TLTS of the integrated components and the TPG of the whole web application. A third contribution is the Test-execution algorithm that generates two log files. The first log file contains all suitable web services that fulfill a component. The second is the error log files that contains information about non-suitable service that could be re-considered by the test architect. Finally, a testing framework is presented, it supports both execution and test scenario management.

Further research will focus on regression retesting method that may reveal any modification-related errors in the web application. We intend to implement our technique on a real industrial web application to prove its applicability. Moreover, a heuristic for test case selection will be studied.

References

1. ALTOVA. Web service description language for weather forecasting. In *www.altova.com*, November 2005.
2. T. Arnold. Testing web services (.net and otherwise). In *Software Test Automation Conference*, March 2003.
3. Boris Beizer. *Testing Techniques. Second Edition*. New York, VanNostrand Reinhold, 1990.
4. A. Milanova C. Fu, G. Ryder and D. Wonnacott. Testing of java web services for robustness. In *Proceedings of the International symposium on Software Testing and Analysis (ISSTA' 04) , July 11-14, 2004, Boston, Massachusetts, USA*, pages 23–33, July 2004.
5. J. Clune and L. Chen. Testing web services (methods for ensuring server and client reliability). In *Web Sphere Journal*, February 2005.
6. R. Heckel and M. Lohmann. Towards contract-based testing of web services. In *International Workshop on Test and Analysis of Component Based Systems, Bercelona*, March 2004.
7. N. Looker, M. Munro, and J. Xu. Testing web services. In *The 16th IFIP International Conference on Testing of Communicating Systems, Oxford*, 2004.
8. Vance McCarthy. A roadmap for web services management. In *www.oetrends.com*, November 2002.
9. N. Gold, C.Knight, A.Mohan, and M.Munro. Understanding service-oriented software. In *IEEE Software*, March 2004.
10. J. Offutt and W. Xu. Generating test cases for web services using data perturbation. In *Workshop on Testing, Analysis and Verification of Web Services. July 2004, Boston Mass.*, September 2004.
11. N. Davidson.The Red-Gate software technical papers. Web services testing. In *www.red-gate.com*, 2002.
12. IBM Web Services Architecture team. Web services overview. In *IBM*, 2004.
13. W. Tsai, R. Paul, W. Song, and Z. Cao. Coyote:an xml-based framework for web service testing. In *Proceedings of the 7th IEEE International Symposuim on High Assurance System Engineering*, October 2002.
14. W. Tsai, R. Paul, Y. Wang, C. Fan, and D. Wang. Extending wsdl to facilitate web service testing. In *Proceedings of the 7th International Symposium On High Assurance Systems Engineering*, 2002.
15. J. Zhang. An approach to facilitate reliability testing of web services components. In *Proceedings of the 15th International Symposium on Software Reliability Engineering (ISSRE' 04)*, November 2004.

Optimizing and Reducing the Delay Latency of Mobile IPv6 Location Management

Abbas Malekpour, Djamshid Tavangarian, and Robil Daher

Chare for Computer Architecture, Institute of Computer Science,
University of Rostock, Albert-Einstein-Str. 21,
18059 Rostock, Germany
abbas.malekpour@uni-rostock.de
http://wwwra.informatik.uni-rostock.de

Abstract. The long latency related with Mobile IPv6's home-address and care-of-address tests can considerably impact delay-sensitive applications. Applying the *ingress-filtering* in a proper way over the networks can prevent the source IP address spoofing which is used by the malicious nodes to launch some sort of attacks. We have suggested a new communication mode which is called Very Early Binding Update Mode (VEBU) for mobility in IPv6. The VEBU eliminates the long delay-latency associated with mobile IPv6 mobility messages either in start of a session or during a session after a handover. Our communication mode allows an optimistic mobile node (MN) to run in one less round-trip-time compared to the route optimization mode.

1 Introduction

Mobile IP is designed to solve the mobility problems which allows a flow of data streams between a MN and its Correspondent node (CN), and try to keep this communication as seamless as possible (i.e. with minimum possible delay latency) [1] [2].

MN is expected to be identified by its static "home address" anywhere in the internet regardless of its current location. MN also can be addressed by a temporary associated address at its current location when it is located in a foreign network (i.e. Care-of address). Packets destined to a MN can be directly routed to its new Care-of address. Communicating on the direct path between the MN and it's correspondent, raises some security concerns. Mobile IPv6 prepared some mechanisms (e.g. Return Routability) to solve this security concerns. Usually, these mechanisms are time costly which affects on the Quality of Service (QoS) of mobile networks. It is obvious that communicating on a longer path also cause more packet loss. There is a tradeoff between the security and optimization (i.e. having less delay-latency and packet-loss) of the mobile IP networks.

With the advent of different radio access mechanisms and increasing deployment of sophisticated applications in mobile end systems, IPv6-based networks will increasingly have to support Quality of Service (QoS) in mobile environments. It is necessary to decrease the delay latency of the MNs movements for the specific required level of quality of services (QoS). It is also essential to provide proper Quality

A. Bui et al. (Eds.): IICS 2005, LNCS 3908, pp. 147–158, 2006.
© Springer-Verlag Berlin Heidelberg 2006

of Service (QoS) forwarding treatment to the packets sent by or destined to MN as they propagate along different routes in the network due to node mobility.

Currently, the standard protocol for Mobile IPv6 does not support fast handover for time-critical and loss-sensitive applications. To address this problem, some extensions of Mobile IP for *Location Management* and *Handover* of mobile IPv6 are being developed. The location management is used to provide and maintain the current location of a MN, and keep track for its movement, while handover management (e.g. Fast Handover for Mobile IP or Hierarchical Mobile IP [5],[6]) is used to perform an uninterrupted session when it moves into different sub-nets during a session [7]. This paper is focused on Location Management of mobile IPv6.

Mobile IPv6 standard protocol has defined two mechanisms including "bidirectional tunneling" and "route optimization" for the location management of mobile IPv6 [2]. Both methods are not able to support the real-time applications (e.g. VOIP) for a desired level of QoS [14]. There are some enhanced approaches such as "Binding Update Backhauling"(BUB), "Early Binding Update" (EBU) and "pre-configure kbm" for dominating and reducing the related delay latency of mobile IPv6 location management.

This paper aims to analyze whether, and to what extent, the location management of Mobile IPv6 complies with the identified requirements of real time application scenarios. For any requirements that fail to be fulfilled, existing alternative approaches are to be found. Finally, we have suggested a solution which has reduced the delay latency of mobility management for the applied ingress filtering networks area.

Section 2 is a recap on background and related work on mobile IPv6. Section 3 will point on shortfalls of existing solutions and section 4 explains our enhanced communication mode.

2 Background and Related Works

This section firstly explains a general overview of mobile IPv6 and its standard communication modes. This overview helps to understand the rational behind the mobile IPv6 communication modes. In fact, this section tries to clear why a MN has to engage with these processes and consequently related delay latency. Finally the enhanced approaches which are tried to reduce this delay latency will be summarized.

2.1 Mobile IPv6 Standard Communication Modes

Mobile IPv6 uses two IP addresses per MN in order to separate localization semantics from identification semantics: A transient "care-of address" routes to the MN's current point of IP attachment. A static "home address" serves as an identifier at stack layers above IP. CN can send the packets to either address for MN. When sends to the care-of address, the packets reach the MN directly. Otherwise, the packets will be routed to the MN's "home network". MN registers its current Care-of address with a router on its home network, which is called Home Agent (HA). HA enables a MN to be addressed only with one static IP address (home address) regardless of its new current location address. HA intercepts the packets, encapsulates them, and tunnels them to the care-of address. Vice versa, the MN may send its packets from the care-of address directly to the CN, or it may tunnel them to the HA to have them sent from the home address. Relaying packets through the HA is called "*bidirectional tunneling mode*" and sending them directly is called "*route optimization mode*". These modes are the standard mobile IPv6 communication methods.

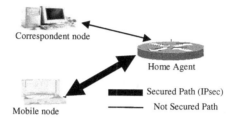

Fig. 1. Bidirectional Tunneling

Route optimization has the interesting properties that it saves a lot of routing overhead compared to bidirectional tunneling. However, route optimization bears a security challenge, since two communication peers do not necessarily have to be acquainted. [8] gives a detailed account on the Mobile IPv6 security design. Relevant to this document are the following two questions.

- When the CN receives a command to redirect node X's packets, how can it be sure that it is X itself, rather than a malicious third node, who has send this command?
- Assuming that the CN can somehow identify X as the originator of a certain redirection request, how can it rely on X actually being present at the IP address to which packets are to be redirected?

The first question raises an authentication issue, the second points to the lack of trust between the peers. There are a variety of possibilities how one could have realized authentication in Mobile IPv6. A desire to be independent from a global, trusted infrastructure motivates to a different strategy: return routability (see Fig. 2.).

In return routability procedure a MN sends to the CN two messages in parallel: a Home Test Init message (HoTI) and a Care-of Test Init message (CoTI). The HoTI message is tunneled to the MN's HA, and forwarded on to the CN. The HoTI message includes a random Home Init Cookie. The Home Init Cookie will be returned by the CN in the Home Test message (HoT). Both the HoTI message and the HoT message are protected by IPsec on the path between the MN and MN's HA [4]. The MN considers this a sufficient proof that the Home Test message was generated by the CN itself.

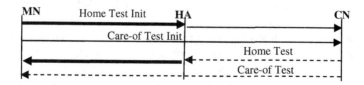

Fig. 2. Return Routability Message diagram

The CoTI message does not go through the MN's HA. It takes the direct path to the CN. The CoTI message includes a random Care-of Init Cookie. The Care-of Init Cookie will be returned by the CN in the CoT message which proofs the CoT message came from the right CN.

The HoT message contains a Home Keygen Token, a Home Nonce Index, and the Home Init Cookie copied from the HoTI message. The Home Nonce Index identifies a random value based on which the CN has computed the Home Keygen Token.

The MN will include the Home Nonce Index in the subsequent Binding Update message to allow the CN to reproduce the Home Keygen Token.

Likewise the HoT message, upon receiving the CoTI message, the CN sends back to the MN directly a Care-of Test message (CoT). The CoT message contains a Care-of Keygen Token, a Care-of Nonce Index, and the Care-of Init Cookie copied from the CoTI message.

The MN uses the Home Keygen Token and the Care-of Keygen Token to produce a secret key that called the Binding Management Key (kbm), shared with the CN.

After the return routability, the MN then generates a Binding Update message to be sent to the CN. The Binding Update message contains a *message-authentication code* (MAC) produced with the Binding Management Key. It also contains the Home Nonce Index and the Care-of Nonce Index [2].

2.2 Binding Update Backhauling

The binding update backhauling (BUB) is an alternative mode for communication in the mobile IPv6 networks [9]. The authors of the BUB have aimed to design a solution, which establish a security association at the start of the BUB mode for each session and use it during an ongoing session for any further binding update. They desired to have a protected binding update for high frequent movement scenarios. They also believe the BUB method is a solution for the scenarios, which both of the parties are MN (i.e. CN is also a MN) and may move from one sub-net to another sub-net at the same time (double jumping).

BUB mode, firstly initiates a BUB Test in parallel with Return Routability Test. BUB Test check whether the both parties are agreed on communicating in this mode or not. Having finished the BUB test, both parties will be establishing a bidirectional security association with the use of Diffie-Hellman between themselves [10]. Diffie-Hellman uses the binding management key (kbm) as a pre-shared secret for its signature. This security association will result a session key. The session key is used for authenticating any further BU. The authors believe, such a security association not only increases the security of BU but also eliminates the need for any further HoTI/HoT and CoTI/CoT messages during the ongoing sessions. In fact, the MN after the hand-over or updating the previous BU which is going to be expired, only sends a BU protected by session key. Having received the Binding Acknowledgment, the MN can start using its new address again.

As a result this mode has a big startup time for starting a session due to BUB Test, Return routability and Diffie-Hellman security association. But any further BU after the handover during a session does not need to run the return routability test again. Authors believe that there is no need for CoTI/CoT during a session but we think it has a risk of flooding a third party attack.

2.3 Early Binding Update

The Early Binding Update (EBU) mode is based on the rout optimization [11]. The EBU suppose that the home test must not necessarily execute after the handover during a session. The MN runs the home test whenever it feels a movement is imminent, or run the home test periodically. The MN sends a temporary binding update based on the most recent home test toward its correspondent in direct path after the handover, which is called Early Binding Update. This EBU carries a message-authentication code, which has been encrypted with a kbm. This kbm is produced by a one-way hash function only on the home keygen token.

An optimistic MN can start using the new care-of address after dispatching the EBU. The MN runs the care-of test (i.e. sending CoTI) and home registration in parallel with the EBU. The CN adds a Temporary Binding Cache Entry with a limit expiration time in its Binding Cache. The correspondent also replies to the CoTI with a CoT message.

A conservative MN does not use the new care-of address until receiving the early binding acknowledgment. Having received the CoT, the MN starts to send a standard BU towards its HA in direct path. The standard binding update use the kbm which has generated based on the concatenation of the home keygen token and care-of keygen token for producing the message-authentication code. Moreover, the CN will change the Temporary Binding Cache Entry to a standard Binding Cache Entry. If the CN does not receive a standard binding update in the specified time, it will remove the Temporary Binding Cache Entry. Moreover, if a CN does not support the EBU, it can easily ignore it. The Early Binding Update is fully backward compatible with the standard mobile IPv6.

This mode reduced the delay latency related to return routability but increased the risk of flooding third party attack.

2.4 Preconfigured Binding Management Key

This mode according to the following condition allows the communication parties to generate a "binding management key (kbm)" before they are going to communicate with each other. MN uses this kbm in any further binding update with its correspondent. In fact, the MN and its correspondent generate this key periodically in a long period of time. If the MN were to move every hour, 24 hours a day, every day of the year, this would require changing keys every 7 years [12]. This mode assumes the following conditions:

- MN and CN have reasonable reason for trusting each other (e.g. administered within the same domain)
- the CN can punish the MN if it has not proper behavior (e.g. contract or some other forces)
- correspondent has some diagnostic procedures which can prove the MN trustability

It is obvious that this mode is relatively fast but it is limited only for some special scenarios and not all.

3 Problem Description in Existed Solutions

Successful employment of mobile IPv6-based services, including VoIP, requires provision of end-to-end adequate QoS level across the heterogeneous networks to meet the desired expectation services.

Standard mobile IPv6 communication modes (i.e. route optimization and bidirectional tunneling) are both engaging with long-delay latency. Since Bidirectional tunneling exchanges all the packets via the HA, it causes a longer path for all data packets. Suppose a scenario that a student who studies in Germany has gone to a seminar in USA. Since he has his account from Germany; therefore, his home network is located in Germany. If this student wants to receive some file from the seminar's server, which is located in the seminar hall (perhaps with less than 10 meter distance) via his laptop, each data packet must fly from the seminar server in USA to the HA in Germany and then turn back to the laptop in the seminar hall again. Each packet instead of 10 meter, it must fly many thousand of kilometers which costs a long delay latency.

In other side route optimization besides its security problems [13], it needs at least 1.5 round-trip times (RTT) before starting any data exchange. In fact, it needs one RTT for return routability and half RTT for sending a BU. These RTTs in some scenarios may cost some seconds which is not acceptable for the expected level of QoS [14].

BUB tries to have the efficiency of route optimization in direct communication path while supporting for better security, especially for the case, that both communication parties are MNs. The BUB uses the Diffie-Hellman key exchange for generating a session key. Diffie-Hellman operations need heavy computations, which has a big overhead on the processors of mobile devices. This processing overhead can be more critical if the MN is involved with small session's scenarios. In other side, the lack of Care-of Test in this mode helps an attacker to easily flood a victim node somewhere in the internet. It is also noticeable that this mode has a big setup time (nearly 3.5 RTT). In Overall, if we ignore its security fault and suppose that the mobile devices have enough power of processing this mode can be a good choice for some scenarios.

The early binding update has solved the delay latency of MN after the handover due to the return routability test. The early binding update runs the home test whenever a handover is eminent or periodically. Therefore, it tries to maintain a fresh home test with its correspondent. The early binding update with use of the recent home test will send an early binding update. Then the Care-of Test will run and finally the standard binding update will be established. There is a time between the EBU and standard binding update, that an attacker can use the lack of Care-of Test for launching some sort of attack (i.e. flooding or denial-of-service attack). However, it has solved the delay latency after the handover but raised more security concerns and more mobility signaling. *Credit-Based Authorization for Binding Lifetime Extension* is a solution to dominate EBU security fault [16].

The "Pre-configure kbm" mode is one of the best solutions for mobility in mobile IPv6 but it is limited for the mentioned criteria that are not applicable in all scenarios. In this mode, a MN can starts or continue its communication after a handover in one RTT sooner than the standard route optimization. Next section is dedicated to our new approach which is a new communication mode for mobile IPv6.

4 Very Early Binding Update

Very early binding update is an enhanced mode for reducing the delay-latency of mobile IPv6 location management. This mode is not only needs less messages but also is more secure. VEBU has reduced this delay-latency by eliminating the return routability test and suggesting a new mechanism which allows a MN to start its communication with a correspondent without any delay even for a started session. VEBU presumes that ingress filtering is applied globally over the Internet. Ingress filtering prevents the attacker who wants to use source IP address spoofing in their attacks. This mechanism prevents the packets originated from a sub-net toward other subnet with the source IP address, which does not belong to the originated sub-net. Ingress filtering allows the provider to track and identify the source of any "denial-of-service" attacks being initiated by a customer [15].

The rational behind the VEBU mode is to send two dependent and integrated messages in both paths, one in direct path, and the other via the HA. These messages make some assurance for the correspondent that the MN is reachable in two addresses, home address and care-of address. The procedure is depicted in Fig. 3.

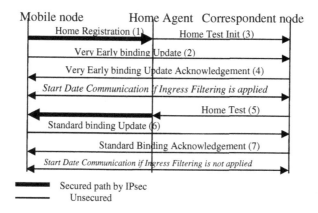

Fig. 3. Very Early Binding Update Message Diagram

The following seven steps show how the VEBU mechanism works. If *ingress filtering* is applied globally over the internet, only the first four steps are needed and the rest is not necessary otherwise we should go through the whole process. Any variable or function such as *Message Authentication Code* (MAC), kbm and Kcn which is not explicitly explained here, is fully backward compatible with the standard mobile IPv6 [2] ,[3].

1) MN uses IPsec with tunneling mode to send a binding update towards its HA. The MN generates and sends a "*mobile keygen token*" and related "*mobile nonce index*" in this message. The mobile keygen token may build as:

Mobile keygen token = first (64, HMAC_SHA1 (Kmn, (home address | nonce | 0)))

Each MN has its own secret key, Kmn, which is used to produce the mobile keygen token. This message can be assumed as follow:

- Source address = care-of address
- Destination address = home agent address

This binding update message contains:

- Mobile keygen token
- Mobile nonce index
- Home address

Note: according to [2] MN and HA are supposed to have a *pre-shared secret key* and know each other from a previous relationship. In fact, the MN cannot fool its HA and any cheating is track-able.

2) The MN also sends a VEBU in direct path towards its CN. This message contains a MAC, which has signed by the kbm generated only by the *MN keygen token* (in standard Mobile IPv6 it is generated by *home keygen token* and *care of keygen token*). This message must not carry the MN keygen and related nonce index. This message can be assumed as follow:

- Source address = care-of address
- Destination address = correspondent address

This Very Early Binding Update message contains:

- MAC (i.e. generated only by mobile keygen token)
- Home address

3) HA checks the validity of this binding update; if accepted, the HA will register this MN's care-of address and sends a HoTI message towards the MN's correspondent. This message is assumed as follow:

- Source address = home agent
- Destination address = correspondent address

This message also contains:

- Mobile keygen token
- Mobile nonce index
- Home address

4) Having received the both messages in both paths, the CN generates a MAC according to the received *mobile node keygen token* (i.e. Within the HoTI message) and checks integrity of the both messages by comparing the received MAC and generated MAC. The correspondent will add a *Tentative Binding Cache Entry* (TBCE) for this MN's care-of address. The life-time of TBCE should be defined very precisely otherwise, it may raise many security concerns such as third party flooding attack [16].

CN generates a *correspondent keygen token* and related nonce index. The correspondent keygen token may form as below:

Correspondent keygen token = first (64, HMAC_SHA1 (Kcn, (care-of address | nonce | 1)))

The CN will send nonce indices in direct path and the correspondent keygen token via the HA. Therefore, the CN forms a very early binding update acknowledgement (VEBUA) message as below towards the MN in direct path:

- Source address = correspondent address
- Destination address = care-of address

This message also contains:

- Home address
- Nonce indices

5) The CN also sends a *Home Test* message via the HA towards the MN. This message will carry the *correspondent keygen token*. In fact, the CN by sending the nonce indices in direct path and *correspondent keygen token* via the HA proves the MN's accessibility in both addresses by itself. This message may have the following form:

- Source address = correspondent address
- Destination address = home address

This message also contains:

- Correspondent keygen token

6) Having received the both messages by the MN, the MN will generate the related kbm (only with use of *correspondent keygen token*). The MN will send a *standard binding update* towards the MN in direct path. Only the right MN which is located in the claimed care-of address (i.e. the receiver of the nonce indices) and accessible via the home address (i.e. the receiver of the *correspondent keygen token*) can generate the wanted kbm. In addition, only this right mobile node receives the correspondent nonce index that can send it in the further standard binding update.

7) On the other side, the correspondent aga in checks the validity of this binding update. If it is consistent and accurate, firstly, it converts the *Tentative Binding Cache Entry* to a *standard binding Cache Entry* and secondly, the CN will reply to the binding update with a *Binding Acknowledgment* (7).

A very optimistic MN which is located in a known applied *ingress filtering* sub-net may starts using its new care-of address upon dispatching the (1) and (2) messages without any delay latency (step 1 and 2 can run in parallel). An optimistic MN may use its care-of address after dispatching the standard binding update (step 6). In fact, the optimistic MN can use its new care-of address about one round-trip time sooner than with standard binding updates. A conservative MN uses its care-of address upon receiving the Binding Acknowledgement (step 7).

We should consider that VEBU for the non-global ingress filtering networks area works like "route optimization" or EBU mode from delay latency point of view.

4.1 Different Location Management Scenarios

For the case of global ingress filtering network area, there is no more need for the standard binding update. In fact, the correspondent will respond to the VEBU only in direct path with a VEBUA, which has only the MN nonce index and nothing more.

If ingress filtering is not applied globally over the network, the following scenarios should be considered as follow:

A. Mobile Node Locates in Its Home Network
When a MN is located in its home subnet instead of sending two messages, it only sends a VEBU, which uses its home address as its source address and the rests are the same as the mentioned steps. The correspondent forms and sends a VEBUA towards the MN home address. This message carries the correspondent keygen token and its related nonce index.

B. Mobile Node Moves to a Foreign Network
For the ongoing session (i.e. started in home network) the MN goes through the 7 mentioned steps only instead of MN's keygen token, it uses the received correspondent's keygen token (i.e. received at home) and the rest is the same as before. On the other side, for the started sessions (i.e. started in a foreign network), the process completely runs the same as the mentioned seven steps.

5   Very Early Binding Update Advantages

This section tries to show the benefits of our communication mode, VEBU, compared to the other communication modes:

1) The new care-of address can be used immediately after sending the (1) and (2) approximately without any delay even for the start of a session (see Fig. 2.). If ingress filtering is not deployed in general, VEBU and EBU have same delay latency but VEBU supports for better security.

2) Mobility messages are reduced in mobile node wireless network:

Route optimization messages = 2 (home registration) + 4 (return routability) + 2 (binding update) = 8 messages
Very Early Binding Update messages = 1 (home registration) + 2 (very early binding update/acknowledgement) + 2(standard binding update) = 5 messages

It is noticeable that in case of ingress filtering, only the first four steps are needed. Therefore, VEBU reduced the mobility messages to less than half (3 messages).

3) VEBU has integrated its mobility messages by means of sending two dependent messages in two paths that one of them is protected by IPsec. This forces the attacker to sniff both messages in both paths to launch any sort of attack. Since one of the paths between the MN and its HA is protected by IPsec; therefore, sniffing these messages are not possible. In fact, the attacker cannot fool a MN by sniffing the mobility messages in wireless link and reply them instead of the CN. This attack is one of the possible attacks against MN in route optimization mode which can disrupt the MN communication.

4) If ingress filtering can not be applied on the whole internet; the VEBU at least can be one of the best choices for the mobility under the administrative domains which ingress filtering is applied for all its sub-domains hierarchical.

6   Analysis According to the Round-Trip Time (RTT)

Since the behaviour of the VEBU strongly depends on the ingress filtering, VEBU will be discussed in two parts:

1) Ingress filtering area: An optimistic MN can use its new care-of address immediately after the dispatching of the VEBU message and home registration message. In this case, there is no delay latency after the each handover. However, a conservative MN can use its new care-of address upon the receiving of VEBUA. Therefore, even for a conservative MN, VEBU reduced at least one RTT.

2) Non-ingress filtering area: a very optimistic MN can use its new care-of address immediately after the dispatching of the VEBU message and home registration message. An optimistic MN can use its new care-of address upon dispatching the standard binding update which needs the below average RTT ("_" symbol shows the path between two parties):

$$Max \ (RTT \ of \ MN\_HA\_CN, \ RTT \ of \ MN\_CN) \approx RTT \ of \ MN\_HA\_CN$$

A conservative MN can use its new care-of address upon the receipt of the standard binding acknowledgement. In this case, the delay latency is the same as route optimization:

$$Max \ (RTT \ of \ MN\_HA\_CN, \ RTT \ of \ MN\_CN) + RTT \ of \ MN\_CN$$

As a conclusion, this mode has the least delay latency compared with the route optimization and all its enhanced communication modes for the applied global ingress filtering scenarios.

7 Conclusion

The RFC 3775 has suggested the bidirectional-tunneling and route optimization modes. These modes are not applicable for all application scenarios especially for real-time scenarios. This paper has suggested a communication mode that minimized the delay latency of mobility in IPv6 layer. VEBU mode basically depends on ingress filtering. Many of the current networks have already applied the ingress filtering. Anyway, if ingress filtering is not globally applied, this mode needs to precisely define the life-time of TBCE on the CN. Since the TBCE plays the same role in VEBU and EBU, therefore, any solution for the TBCE can be applied here in VEBU.

Sniffing the mobility messages on the wireless subnets in VEBU mode, has no use for the attackers, because the mobility messages on wireless subnet are integrated with the mobility messages on the secured path to the HA.

References

1. Perkins, C., Ed., "IP Mobility Support for IPv4", RFC 3344, August 2002.
2. Johnson, D., Perkins, C. and J. Arkko, "Mobility Support in IPv6", RFC 3775, June 2004.
3. Deering, S. and R. Hinden, "Internet Protocol, Version 6 (IPv6) Specification", RFC 2460, December 1998.
4. Arkko, J., Devarapalli, V. and F. Dupont, "Using IPsec to Protect Mobile IPv6 Signaling Between Mobile Nodes and Home Agents", RFC 3776, June 2004.
5. Soliman, H., Castelluccia, C., El Malki, K. and L. ellier, "Hierarchical Mobile IPv6 mobility management (HMIPv6)", draft-ietf-mipshop-hmipv6-04.txt (work in progress), December 2005.

6. Koodli, R., Editor, "Fast Handovers for Mobile IPv6", draft-ietf-mipshop-fast-mipv6-03.txt, October 2004.
7. International Telecommunication Union, Telecommunication Standardization sector, SSG – LS 2 – E, San Diego, 9–11 August 2004
8. Nikander, P., Arkko, J., Aura, T., Montenegro, G. and E. Nordmark, "Mobile IP version 6 Route Optimization Security Design Background", Internet-Draft draft-ietf-mip6-ro-sec (work in progress).
9. Helsinki University of Technology "Binding Update Backhauling" draft-haddad-mip6-cga-bub-00, April 2004
10. Krawczyk, H., "SIGMA: the 'SIGn-and-MAC' Approach to Authenticated Diffie-Hellman and its use in the IKE protocol", Advanced in Cryptography – CRYPTO 2003
11. Christian Vogt, Tobias Kuefner, Roland Bless, Mark Doll, University of Karlsruhe, Early Binding Update, Draft-vogt-mipv6-early-binding-updates-00, February 2004
12. Charles E. Perkins, IETF Mobile IP Working Group, "Preconfigured Binding Management Keys for Mobile IPv6", draft-ietf-mip6-precfgKbm-00.txt, 5 April 2004
13. Nikander, P., Arkko, J., Aura, T., Montenegro, G. and E. Nordmark, "Mobile IP version 6 Route Optimization Security Design Background", Internet-Draft draft-ietf-mip6-ro-sec (work in progress)
14. ITU-T Y.1541 Network Performance Objectives for IP Based Services
15. Paul Ferguson and Daniel Senie. Network ingress filtering: Defeating denial of service attacks which employ IP source address spoofing. RFC 2827, IETF Network Working Group, May 2000.
16. Vogt, C. and J. Arkko, "Credit-Based Authorization for Mobile IPv6 Early Binding Updates", Internet-Draft draft-vogt-mobopts-credit-based-authorization (work in progress).

Compositional Constraints Generation for Concurrent Real-Time Loops with Interdependent Iterations*

I. Assayad and S. Yovine

VERIMAG, Centre Equation, 2 av. de Vignate, 38610 Gieres, France
{Ismail.Assayad, Sergio.Yovine}@imag.fr

Abstract. In this paper we describe an assume/guarantee based execution constraints synthesis algorithm for concurrent threads executing on parallel platforms. Threads are loops which can have several control points, such as the activation of loop iterations and the interaction with other threads. Real-time applications such as multimedia applications are usually specified using this kind of concurrent interacting threads. The proposed compositional algorithm outputs a set of sufficient constraints on the control points in order to meet timing objectives. The paper first presents the timed system model we use to specify such applications. Then, the constraints synthesis algorithm is presented and illustrated on a real-time video application.

Keywords: Execution constraints synthesis, Compositionality, Concurrent loops.

1 Introduction

Embedded systems design is being strongly driven by software, which is becoming a dominant part of embedded systems. This trend is leading to a significant grow in the workload of embedded processors as software gradually shifts towards an increasing computational complexity, requiring the execution of tasks such as image, audio, and video compression and recognition. Indeed, it has been observed that the increase of computational requirements is difficult to meet by processor development alone.

Multiprocessor architectures are an appealing hardware solution to provide high computational power at low-cost, compared to single-processor architectures which are becoming too costly in terms of power consumption, time-to-market and design complexity [1].

Moreover, there is a trend towards heterogeneous multiprocessor architectures integrating multiple processor cores, and other specialiazed hardware components on a single chip.

Besides, embedded software programming tends to use parallel programming, both because applications are composed of intrinsically concurrent tasks and to

---

* Partially funded by MEDEA+ project NEVA.

A. Bui et al. (Eds.): IICS 2005, LNCS 3908, pp. 159–170, 2006.

better exploit at software-level the physical parallelism provided by multiprocessor hardware [2].

The increasingly complex hardware and software interactions bring in additinal challenges when it comes to meet non-functional constraints concerning timing, memory, energy, ... Thus, building correct parallel real-time embedded systems is an extremly complex activity. The grand challenge consists in synthesizing correct-by-construction parallel code that complies with the non-functional requirements of the application and constraints of the hardware architecture.

One of the key issues here is scheduling. There is a broad litterature on scheduling real-time systems, in particular the well established theory developed after RMA [3]. Synthesizing a scheduler consists in assigning priorities to tasks. There are today available commercial tools which are used in several application domains such as automotive and avionics. An inconvenience of such theory which weakens its usability for heterogeneous systems, is that each new class of models requires developing a new analysis technique.

Another approach consists in viewing scheduling analysis as a flow-analysis problem for event streams [4, 5, 6]. This approach handles heterogeneous components which interact, but it is mostly focused on system-level scheduling, and it is not amenable to synthesis.

Existing work deals essentially with either (1) the problem of the sechedule length optimisation of a data flow DAG describing the body of a cyclic process, (2) the problem of scheduling non interacting real-time loops or either (3) parallel interacting tasks without explicit deadlines constraints [7]. These process models are restrictive because they do not address the standard process model used in real-time systems, namely, the concurrent cyclic processes model. A few work has been done in this direction for the parallel execution of loops. In [8], the authors used a set of prerequisite constraints similar to the ones computed by our constraints generator algorithm, and produced memory efficient or run-time constraints derivation algorithms.

An alternative approach to handle heterogeneity consists in using timed automata, and applying algorithmic controller-synthesis techniques to construct a taylor-made scheduler [9]. This allows taking into account complex dependencies and interactions, as well as the control and observation points of the applications. It also allows compositional reasoning to both ease integration of components and schedulers. The major drawback of this approach is complexity. Though there are some techniques to alliviate this issue, they are either focused on modelling issues [10], or restricted to monoprocessor architectures [11].

In this paper, we compute a sufficient execution constraints for each thread separately but taking into account its environment composed of the other threads which interfer with its execution. For this purpose we give in this paper an assume/guarantee rule to synthesize the set of the constraints of a system of concurrent threads subject to real-time constraints in a compositional way. This compositional reasoning owes its attractiveness to its application to parallel composition, since it replaces operational reasoning, with a complexity increasing exponentially in the number of parallel components, by reasoning compositionally on the basis of given specifications. The complexity of this way of reasoning increases linearly only w.r.t. the number of those specifications.

The constraints generated by our algorithm can be used, for instance, to implement a scheduler of a parallel system composed of concurrent processes subject to explicit timing constraints, or to determine if two or more real-time applications can be composed together in a safe manner w.r.t. their timing and bandwidth usage constraints.

The paper is structured as follows. We present our model in section 2 and controller-synthesis algorithm in section 3. In section 4 we apply our approach on a real-time industrial application.

2   Model

Hereafter we introduce some definitions and notations that will be necessary for understanding the following sections.

2.1   Syntax and Definitions

Iterations Control. We note b_q the start time of a state q and e_q its finish time. Also, for a set of **valuations** X we note $C(X)$ the set of constraints containing elements from X. We also note τ_c and τ_u and the set of **controllable** and **uncontrollable** transitions respectively and we note $\tau = \tau_c \cup \tau_u$ the set of all transitions. Each thread is a loop. Each loop has two distinguished states, called *first* and *last*. The next iteration can either begin its execution immediately after the termination of the current one or a laps of time later. In the first case, the thread goes from the state *last* to the state *first* without idling. In the second case, the scheduler delays the execution of the iteration. We say that the transition *last* → *first* is controllable, i.e., *last* → *first* ∈ τ_c. Depending on the iteration activation control mechanism, the threads can be periodic, i.e., iterations are periodically fired, or sporadic, i.e., the execution of the next iteration begins a laps of time after the finish time of the preceeding iteration.

Dependencies. For a computation q in the thread loop body, we note (q, i) the ith instance of q, that is the instance of q executed in the ith iteration. For two computations q and r we note $(r, j) \rightarrow (q, i)$ the precedence dependency between the computation instance of r in the iteration j and the computation instance of q in the iteration i. By default, **if no instance index is given** then the dependency concerns computations instances of the same iteration number. That is:

$$r \rightarrow q \quad \Longleftrightarrow \quad \forall k \geq 1 \ (r, k) \rightarrow (q, k)$$

An execution of the thread must respect this dependency relation between computations: the execution of a computation instance (q, i) can begin only after the end of all its predecessors. We note $Prd((q, i))$ the set of computations instances belonging to the other threads, i.e., threads other than the q one, and preceeding

(q, i). We also note b_i^q, e_i^q and δ^q respectively, the start time, the end time and the execution duration respectively of (q, i). We thus have:

$$e_i^q = b_i^q + \max_{(r,j) \in Prd((q,i))} w_{ji}^{rq} + \delta^q + \epsilon_i$$

where w_{ji}^{rq} is the waiting time due to the precedence relation $(r, j) \rightarrow (q, i)$, and $\epsilon_i \geq 0$ is either null, when the transition t leading to q on the thread is uncontrollable (i.e. $t \in \tau_u$), or a positive number according to the restriction of t by the scheduler, when the transition is controllable (i.e. $t \in \tau_c$). Finally, we note σ_i^q the relative end time of the computation (q, i) (compared to the iteration firing time).

Thread. The behavior of a thread is modelled by an automaton A, where A is a tuple (Q_A, E_A, d_A, τ_A) s.t.:

- $Q_A = \{q_0, q_1, \ldots, q_n\}$ is the set of the control states of the automaton A representing the thread computations,
- $E_A : Q_A \rightarrow N$ is the function which associates execution times to states: $E_A(q_j) = \delta^{q_j}$, where δ^{q_j} is the execution time of q_j,
- d_A is the execution time deadline of the thread iteration,
- $\tau_A = \tau_c \cup \tau_u$ is the set of controllable and uncontrollable transitions.

System. A system is a tuple $(A_1, \ldots, A_r, Dep)$ of $A_i, i \in [1, r]$ automata, each one modelling the behavior of a thread, and Dep, a set of dependencies between states instances.

2.2   Semantics

Let the parallel composition of r threads $A_1 \parallel A_2 \parallel \ldots \parallel A_r$.

System States. For each automaton A, we note $S_A : N \rightarrow \mathbb{R}^{2 \cdot |Q_A|}$ the state of A where $S_A(i)$ is the vector $\langle b_i^{q_1}, b_i^{q_2}, \ldots, b_i^{q_k}, e_i^{q_1}, e_i^{q_2}, \ldots, e_i^{q_k} \rangle$ of state $(q_1, \ldots, q_k)$ *valuations*) valuations of the ith-iteration. In the same way, we denote the system $A_1 \parallel \ldots \parallel A_r$ state by a function $S_{A_1 \ldots A_r} : N \rightarrow \mathbb{R}^{2 \cdot \Sigma_{i=1}^r |Q_A|}$, where the image $S_{A_1 \ldots A_r}(i)$ of the ith-iteration is the vector $\langle S_{A_1}(i), \ldots S_{A_r}(i) \rangle$. A component $S_{A_j}(i)$ denotes the state of an automaton A_j, explained above, at the ith-iteration. For instance, the initial state, $S_{A_1, \ldots, A_r}^0$ is:

$$S_{\parallel_j A_j}^0(q^k) = \langle \bot, \bot \rangle_{i,j} \forall k > 0$$
$$S_{\parallel_j A_j}^0(q^0) = \langle b_{A_j}^{q_i}, e_{A_j}^{q_i} \rangle_{i,j}$$

where $b_{A_j}^{q_0} = t_0^j, 1 \leq j \leq r$, and all the other valuations are equal to $\bot$. For simplicity, we noted $b_{A_j}^{q_i}$ and $e_{A_j}^{q_i}$ the start time and the end time of the state q_i of A_j for first iteration (number 0).

System Transitions. The semantics of the transition $l \xrightarrow{(A,q,k)} l'$ is:

1. $q \rightarrow q'$ is a transition of the automaton A.
2. $\forall (p, k') \in Prd((q, k))$ $e_{k'}^{p} \neq \bot$, that is q can terminate only if each of its predecessors p has already terminated.
3. $b_k^{q'} = e_k^q = b_k^q + w_k^q + \delta^q$ with $\delta^q \in N$ is the execution time of q and w_k^q is the waiting time due to the dependencies $(p, k') \rightarrow (q, k)$, $(p, k') \in Prd((q, k))$ that is:

$$w_k^q = \max_{(p,k') \in Prd((q,k))} w_{k'k}^{pq}$$

$$w_{k'k}^{pq} = \begin{cases} 0 & \text{if } e_{k'}^p - b_k^q < 0 \\ e_{k'}^p - b_k^q \end{cases}$$

$$= \max\{0, e_{k'}^p - b_k^q\}$$

$w_{k'k}^{pq}$ is the waiting time due to $(p, k') \rightarrow (q, k)$

4. If the transition $l \xrightarrow{(A,q,i)} l'$ corresponds to the activation of a new iteration, that is the transition $last(A) \rightarrow first(A)$ we have:

$$e_k^{last} = b_k^{last} + w_k^{last} + \delta^{last}$$
$$b_{k+1}^{first} = b_k^{first} + p \quad \text{[if A is periodic]}$$
$$b_{k+1}^{first} = e_k^{last} + \epsilon, \quad \epsilon \geq 0 \quad \text{[if A is sporadic]}$$

w_k is defined as previously according to the dependencies and $\delta^{last} \in N$ is the execution time of the state *last*.

System Executions. An execution of the system is an infinite sequence ρ s.t. $\rho = S_0 S_1 S_2 \ldots$ where for each k, $S_k \rightarrow S_{k+1}$ is a transition of the system. We note Execs the set of all execution sequences for all possible initial states.

Good System Executions. We say that S_k is good if for all n and for all automaton A $\left(e_n^{last(A)} - b_n^{first(A)} \leq d_A \vee e_n^{last(A)} = \bot \right)$ is true. We say that a sequence $\rho = S_0 S_1 S_2 \ldots$ is good if S_k is good for all k. Finally, We note Execs' the sub-set of Execs composed of good system execution sequences.

3   Constraints Synthesis

3.1   Outline of the Approach

Constraints Synthesis Problem. We consider r threads $A_1, \ldots, A_r$. We are interested in the two following constraints synthesis problems categories for the system $A_1 \parallel \ldots \parallel A_r$:

1. for each automaton A_j and iteration index i, Find t_{ij} s.t.
   $\mathcal{E} \subseteq$ Execs', where:
   $\mathcal{E} = \{\rho \in \text{Execs}/\forall (j, S, i) b_i^{first(A_j)}(S) = t_{ij}\}$

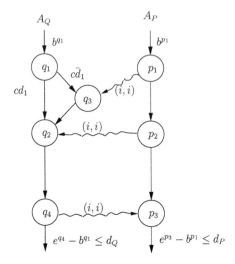

Fig. 1. Concurrent automata A_P and A_Q

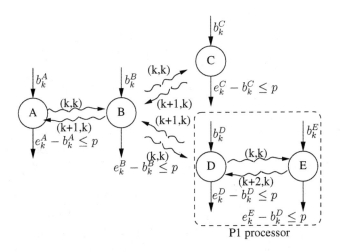

Fig. 2. Timed system model of the video sub-system

2. for the periodic automata case, find S^{init} s.t.
   $\mathcal{E} \subseteq \text{Execs}'$, where:
   $\mathcal{E} = \{\rho \in \text{Execs}/S^0 = S^{init}\}$

In the next sections we will describe the synthesis algorithm and give two examples: the problem of example of figure 1 falls into category (1) mentionned above, and the problem of application of figure 2 falls into category (2).

Outline of the Algorithm. For an automaton A and a constraint ϕ We define A/ϕ as the behaviour of A constrained by ϕ, that is, the set of executions of A that satisfy ϕ. We also note $Env(A)$, the environment of A, i.e., the set of automata which are in interaction with A by means of precedence dependencies, storage sharing constraints or computation resources sharing constraints. The synthesis algorithm is based on the following assume/guarantee kind-of rule.

For all i:

$$(1) \quad \emptyset \neq A_i/\Psi_i(w) \subseteq \text{good}(A_i),$$
$$(2) \quad (A_i/\Psi_i(w))||(Env(A_i)/\Phi_i(b,w)) \neq \emptyset$$
$$(3) \quad \Delta_i = \forall w.(\Psi_i \Rightarrow \Phi_i)$$

$$(4) \quad ||_i A_i/\Delta_i \subseteq \text{good}(||_i A_i)$$

Where $\text{good}(A_i)$ is the set of good executions of A_i, and $\text{good}(||_i A_i)$ is the set of good system executions (see section 2.2).

(1) means that $\Psi_i(w)$ characterizes a non-empty subset of good executions of A_i;
(2) means that $\Phi_i(b,w)$ characterizes a set of begin times of threads interacting with A_i that are consistent with the subset of good execs of A_i;
(3) we should note here that w's are determined by b's, because execution times are fixed.

It remains to find an assignment of b's that makes (4) non-empty.
So, the synthesis algorithm consists in finding Ψ_i and Φ_i.

3.2   Synthesis

We consider an automaton A_i inside a system composed of several concurrent loops. Before presenting the synthesis algorithm, we describe in the following the three main steps in the synthesis of the constraints Δ_i. We use the two automata A_P and A_Q depicted in the figure 1 to illustrate the technique.

Computing Ψ_i. This step computes a set of constraints noted W_i on the waiting times variables, i.e. $\langle w \rangle$, for each automaton separately, of the form $X_i \Leftarrow W_i \wedge I_i$ where X_i is the result of the backward constraints propagation on the automaton A_i starting from the *last* state, W_i is the constraint on the waiting times variables $\langle w \rangle$ of A_i and I_i is an invariant of A_i. Notice that W_i contains only $\langle w \rangle$ variables. The I_i formula may contain the waiting times valuations, i.e., $\langle w \rangle$, the start and the end time valuations $\langle b, e \rangle$. The computation of X_P, W_P and I_P for the automaton A_P are explained in table 1. A_P has no conditional branch. Thus, W_P is the sufficient and necessary condition on waiting times, i.e., $X_p \Leftrightarrow W_P \wedge I_P$, Notice that in the example of table 1, b's and e's variables are contained in σ's (in deed, σ is the relative end time, see section 2.1). For lack of space, the details of the constraints propagation process are not given for A_Q.

Computing Φ_i. It's a relation which links uncontrollable variables, i.e,. the waiting times $\langle w \rangle$ of A_i, and control points, i.e., the activation times $b^{first(A_i)}$ and $\langle b^{first(A_k)} \rangle_{k \in Env(A_i)}$ of A_i and its environment. This relation characterizes the

Table 1. Details of the constraints propagation process on P

$$
\begin{array}{c}
\hline
\text{Constraints propagation on P:} \\
\end{array}
$$

Constraints propagation on P:

$$X_P \equiv \wedge \begin{pmatrix} (\sigma^{p_3} \leq d_P \wedge \sigma^{p_3} = \sigma^{p_2} + \delta^{p_3} + w^{p_3}) \\ (\sigma^{p_2} \leq d_P - \delta^{p_3} - w^{p_3} \wedge \sigma^{p_2} = \sigma^{p_1} + \delta^{p_2}) \\ (\sigma^{p_1} \leq d_P - \delta^{p_3} - w^{p_3} - \delta^{p_2} \wedge \sigma^{p_1} = \delta^{p_3}) \end{pmatrix}$$

X_P can be expressed as a conjunction of an invariant of P, I_P, and a constraint on w's, W_P, as follows:

$$\begin{aligned} X_P &\equiv (\sigma^{p_1} \leq d_P - \delta^{p_3} - w^{p_3} - \delta^{p_2}) \wedge I_P \\ &\equiv (w^{p_3} \leq d_P - \delta^{p_3} - \delta^{p_2} - \delta^{p_1}) \wedge I_P \end{aligned}$$

$$I_P \equiv \begin{pmatrix} (\sigma^{p_3} = \sigma^{p_2} + \delta^{p_3} + w^{p_3}) \\ \wedge (\sigma^{p_2} = \sigma^{p_1} + \delta^{p_2}) \\ (\sigma^{p_1} = \delta^{p_3}) \end{pmatrix}$$

$$W_P \equiv (w^{p_3} \leq d_P - \delta^{p_3} - \delta^{p_2} - \delta^{p_1})$$

Finally, we obtain Ψ_P. Notice that since P does not contain a branch, W_P is a necessary and sufficient property on w's, that is, no need to compute the weakest precondition:

$$X_P \Leftrightarrow W_P \wedge I_P = \Psi_P$$

possible interactions of A_i with $Env(A_i)$. Several interactions may, in deed, exist since these automata can have conditional branchs. For instance, A_Q has two execution paths corresponding to the conditions $cond_1 = cd_1$ and $cond_2 = \overline{cd_1}$. This causes two possible interactions of A_P with A_Q, that is, $\Phi_Q^{cond_1}(w^{q_2}, b^{q_1}, b^{p_1})$ when $cond_1$ is true and $\Phi_Q^{cond_2}(w^{q_3}, w^{q_2}, b^{q_1}, b^{p_1})$ when $cond_2$ is true, and two interactions of A_P with A_Q, that is, $\Phi_P^{cond_1}(w^{p_3}, b^{q_1}, b^{p_1})$ when $cond_1$ is true and $\Phi_P^{cond_2}(w^{p_3}, b^{q_1}, b^{p_1})$ when $cond_2$ is true. For a given interaction , $\Phi_i^{cond_j}$ is computed as follows: for each state $(q, i) = (q_{k_0}, i)$ of the automaton A verifying (1) (q, i) belongs to the domain of definition of the function Prd (see section 2.1), and (2) (q, i) is executed when $cond_j$ holds; we compute $\phi(w_{(q,i)})$, by using: $w_{(q,i)} = \max_{(q',j) \in Prd((q,i))} w_{(q',j) \to (q,i)}$ where for each $w_{(q',j) \to (q,i)}$ the following relation holds:

$$\begin{pmatrix} \left(\wedge \begin{pmatrix} \sigma^{(q',j)} + b_i^{first(A)} > \sigma^{(q,i)} + b_j^{first(A')} \\ (w_{(q',j) \to (q,i)} = 0) \end{pmatrix} \right) \\ \vee \\ \left(\wedge \begin{pmatrix} (\sigma^{(q',j)} + b_i^{first(A)} \leq \sigma^{(q,i)} + b_j^{first(A')}) \\ \begin{pmatrix} w_{(q',j) \to (q,i)} = \sigma^{(q,i)} - \sigma^{(q',j)} \\ + b_j^{first(A')} \\ - b_i^{first(A)} \end{pmatrix} \end{pmatrix} \right) \end{pmatrix}$$

Table 2. Interactions of P with Q

Sub-interactions of P with Q when the branch condition cd_1 holds:

$$\Phi_P^{cd_1} \equiv \left(\vee \begin{array}{l} (\pi^{q_1 p_1} + \sigma^{q_4} < \sigma^{p_2} \wedge w^{p_3} = 0) \\ (\pi^{q_1 p_1} + \sigma^{q_4} \geq \sigma^{p_2} \wedge w^{p_3} = -\pi^{q_1 p_1} + \delta^{q_1} + \delta^{q_2} + \delta^{q_4} + w^{q_2} - \delta^{p_1} - \delta^{p_2}) \end{array} \right)$$

$$\equiv \left(\vee \begin{array}{l} (\pi^{q_1 p_1} + \sigma^{q_4} < \sigma^{p_2} \wedge w^{p_3} = 0) \\ (\pi^{q_1 p_1} + \sigma^{q_4} \geq \sigma^{p_2} \wedge \pi^{q_1 p_1} + \sigma^{q_1} > \sigma^{p_2} \wedge w^{p_3} = -\pi^{q_1 p_1} + \delta^{q_1} + \delta^{q_2} + \delta^{q_4} - \delta^{p_1} - \delta^{p_2}) \\ (\pi^{q_1 p_1} + \sigma^{q_4} \geq \sigma^{p_2} \wedge \pi^{q_1 p_1} + \sigma^{q_1} \leq \sigma^{p_2} \wedge w^{p_3} = \delta^{q_2} + \delta^{q_4}) \end{array} \right)$$

Sub-interactions of P with Q when cd_1 is false:

$$\Phi_P^{\overline{cd_1}} \equiv \left(\vee \begin{array}{l} (\pi^{q_1 p_1} + \sigma^{q_4} < \sigma^{p_2} \wedge w^{p_3} = 0) \\ (\pi^{q_1 p_1} + \sigma^{q_4} \geq \sigma^{p_2} \wedge w^{p_3} = -\pi^{q_1 p_1} + \sum_i \delta^{q_i} + w^{q_3} + w^{q_2} - \delta^{p_1} - \delta^{p_2}) \end{array} \right)$$

$$\equiv \left(\vee \begin{array}{l} (\pi^{q_1 p_1} + \sigma^{q_4} < \sigma^{p_2} \wedge w^{p_3} = 0) \\ (\pi^{q_1 p_1} + \sigma^{q_4} \geq \sigma^{p_2} \wedge \pi^{q_1 p_1} + \sigma^{q_1} > \sigma^{p_1} \wedge \pi^{q_1 p_1} + \sigma^{q_3} > \sigma^{p_2} \wedge w^{p_3} = -\pi^{q_1 p_1} + \sum_i \delta^{q_i} - \delta^{p_1} - \delta^{p_2}) \\ (\pi^{q_1 p_1} + \sigma^{q_4} \geq \sigma^{p_2} \wedge \pi^{q_1 p_1} + \sigma^{q_1} \leq \sigma^{p_1} \wedge \pi^{q_1 p_1} + \sigma^{q_3} > \sigma^{p_2} \wedge w^{p_3} = \delta^{q_2} + \delta^{q_3} + \delta^{q_4} - \delta^{p_2}) \\ (\pi^{q_1 p_1} + \sigma^{q_4} \geq \sigma^{p_2} \wedge \pi^{q_1 p_1} + \sigma^{q_1} > \sigma^{p_1} \wedge \pi^{q_1 p_1} + \sigma^{q_3} \leq \sigma^{p_2} \wedge w^{p_3} = \delta^{q_2} + \delta^{q_4}) \\ (\pi^{q_1 p_1} + \sigma^{q_4} \geq \sigma^{p_2} \wedge \pi^{q_1 p_1} + \sigma^{q_1} \leq \sigma^{p_1} \wedge \pi^{q_1 p_1} + \sigma^{q_3} \leq \sigma^{p_2} \wedge w^{p_3} = \pi^{q_1 p_1} - \delta^{q_1} + \delta^{q_2} + \delta^{q_4} + \delta^{p_1}) \end{array} \right)$$

Table 3. Interactions of Q with P

Sub-interactions of Q with P when the branch condition cd_1 holds:

$$\Phi_Q^{cd_1} \equiv \left(\vee \begin{array}{l} (\pi^{q_1 p_1} + \sigma^{q_1} > \sigma^{p_2} \wedge w^{q_2} = 0) \\ (\pi^{q_1 p_1} + \sigma^{q_1} \leq \sigma^{p_2} \wedge w^{q_2} = \pi^{q_1 p_1} + \delta^{p_1} + \delta^{p_2} - \delta^{q_1}) \end{array} \right)$$

Sub-interactions of Q with P when cd_1 is false:

$$\Phi_Q^{\overline{cd_1}} \equiv \left(\wedge \begin{array}{l} \left(\vee \begin{array}{l} (\pi^{q_1 p_1} + \sigma^{q_3} > \sigma^{p_2} \wedge w^{q_2} = 0) \\ (\pi^{q_1 p_1} + \sigma^{q_3} \leq \sigma^{p_2} \wedge w^{q_2} = \pi^{q_1 p_1} + \delta^{p_1} + \delta^{p_2} - \delta^{q_1} - \delta^{q_3} - w^{q_3}) \end{array} \right) \\ \left(\vee \begin{array}{l} (\pi^{q_1 p_1} + \sigma^{q_1} > \sigma^{p_1} \wedge w^{q_3} = 0) \\ (\pi^{q_1 p_1} + \sigma^{q_1} \leq \sigma^{p_1} \wedge w^{q_3} = \pi^{q_1 p_1} + \delta^{p_1} - \delta^{q_1}) \end{array} \right) \end{array} \right)$$

In the relation above, A' is the automaton to which (q', j) belongs and $\sigma^{(q,i)}$ is the relative end time of (q, i) compared to the firing time of iteration number i, under the condition $cond_j$. The expression of w_{q_i} may moreover contain some unknown waiting times variables w_{q_k}, $k < i$, in which case they are recursively computed in function of the appropriate control points of $Env(A)$ under $cond_j$. Finally, $\Phi_i = \bigvee_j \Phi_i^{cond_j}$. The details of this calculation process are illustrated on the example of figure 1: the relations $\Phi_P^{cd_1}$, $\Phi_P^{\overline{cd_1}}$, $\Phi_Q^{cd_1}$ and $\Phi_Q^{\overline{cd_1}}$ are given in table 2 and table 3 respectively, where the symbol $\pi_{q_1 p_1}$ notes $b^{q_1} - b^{p_1}$, $\Phi_P = \Phi_P^{cd_1} \vee \Phi_P^{\overline{cd_1}}$ and $\Phi_Q = \Phi_Q^{cd_1} \vee \Phi_Q^{\overline{cd_1}}$.

The Execution Constraints. The set of execution constraints of the automaton A_i, named $\Delta_i(b^{first(A_i)}, \langle b^{first(A_j)} \rangle_{j \in Env(A_i)})$, is obtained by mean of quantifiers elimination:

$$\Delta_i = \forall w \quad \left(\Phi_i(\langle w \rangle, \langle b^{first(A_k)} \rangle) \Rightarrow \Psi_i(\langle w \rangle) \right)$$

On the example of A_P and A_Q where we considered unit execution times for the threads computations: $\delta^{q_i} = 1$ for all i, and the same execution deadlines: $d_P = d_Q = 10$, the algorithm generates the two constraints $\Delta_Q \equiv (b^{q_1} + 2 \geq b^{p_1})$ and $\Delta_P \equiv (b^{p_1} + 5 \geq b^{q_1})$ for P and Q respectively.

4   Application

In this section we illustrate our algorithm on a video sub-system application whose timed model is given in figure 2. Each of the tasks A, B, C, D and E is a periodic process. The tasks have the same period and are subject to the following non-functional constraints: memory buffers capacities, deadlines, computation resources sharing.

Synthesis. Hereafter we apply our synthesis algorithm to compute the scheduling constraints for this model. We compute then compose each thread execution constraints to obtain the system constraints. We give below the result of each step of the algorithm for each of the loops A, B, C, D and E.

(1) `Computing` Ψ_i. This step gives the following constraints on waiting times variables:

$$\Psi_e = (w^e \leq p - \delta^e)$$
$$\Psi_d = (w^d \leq p - \delta^d)$$
$$\Psi_c = (w^c \leq p - \delta^c)$$
$$\Psi_b = (w^b \leq p - \delta^b)$$
$$\Psi_a = (\delta^a \leq p)$$

(2) `Computing` Φ_i. For each loop, we compute the interaction with its environment. Firstly, storage resources sharing constraints due to input/output buffers capacities are expressed in $\mathcal{B}$:

$$\mathcal{B}_d = (\delta^e + b^e - b^d \leq 2p) \quad (\text{buffer1 \& buffer2})$$
$$\mathcal{B}_a = (\delta^b + b^b - b^a \leq p) \quad (\text{b\_buffer1})$$
$$\mathcal{B}_b = \left(\wedge \begin{matrix} \delta^d + b^d - b^b \leq p & (\text{b\_buffer2}) \\ \delta^c + b^c - b^b \leq p & (\text{b\_buffer2}) \end{matrix} \right)$$

Second, computation resources sharing constraints are expressed in $\mathcal{M}$. By taking into account the periodicity property of the loops, we obtain the $\mathcal{M}_e$ and $\mathcal{M}_d$ formula.

$$\mathcal{M} = \left(\vee \begin{matrix} \delta_e + p_e \leq p_d + p \\ p_e \geq p_d + \delta_d + p \end{matrix} \right)$$

Finally, the precedence constraints are given in $\mathcal{D}$:

$$\mathcal{D}_d = b^d - b^e + \delta^d \leq 0 \wedge w^e = 0$$
$$\mathcal{D}_c = b^b - b^c + \delta^b \leq 0 \wedge w^c = 0$$
$$\mathcal{D}_d = b^b - b^d + \delta^b \leq 0 \wedge w^d = 0$$
$$\mathcal{D}_b = b^a - b^b + \delta^a \leq 0 \wedge w^b = 0$$
$$\Phi_x = \mathcal{B}_x \wedge \mathcal{M} \wedge \mathcal{D}_x \text{ for each } x \in \{a, b, c, d, e\}$$

(3) **The system constraints** is thus Δ, the conjunction of each of the threads constraints:

$$\Delta = \Delta_b \wedge \Delta_c \wedge \Delta_d \wedge \Delta_e$$

For the following execution times data values

$$\delta^a = \frac{1}{30}, \delta^b = \frac{1}{30}, \delta^c = \frac{1}{30}, \delta^d = \frac{1}{60}, \delta^e = \frac{1}{60}$$

and a real-time processing constraint of $p = \frac{1}{15}$, we synthesized:

$$\Delta_b \equiv (b_b = b_a + \tfrac{1}{30})$$
$$\Delta_c \equiv (b_c = b_b + \tfrac{1}{30})$$
$$\Delta_d \equiv (b_d = b_b + \tfrac{1}{30})$$
$$\Delta_e \equiv \left(\vee \begin{array}{l} ((b_e \geq b_d + \tfrac{1}{60}) \wedge (b_e \leq b_d + \tfrac{1}{20})) \\ ((b_e \geq b_d + \tfrac{5}{60}) \wedge (b_e \leq b_d + \tfrac{7}{60})) \end{array} \right)$$

5 Conclusion

We have described a constraints synthesis algorithm for the parallel composition of timed automata modelling concurrent threads. The threads are subject to real-time constraints. This algorithm uses the compositionality approach. It is based on the assume/guarantee paradigm to synthesize a constraints set for each of the threads separately taking into account the interference of its environment. We illustrated the algorithm on an industrial real-time application composed of five interdependent concurrent real-time threads.

The constraints generated by our algorithm can be used, for instance, to implement the scheduler of a parallel system composed of concurrent processes, or to determine if two or more real-time applications can be composed safely together w.r.t. their timing and bandwidth usage constraints.

Current theoretical work concerns extending the approach to handle non-deterministic execution times.

References

1. Lance Hammond, Basem A. Nayfeh, and Kunle Olukotun. A single-chip multiprocessor. *Computer*, 30(9), 1997.
2. Manfred Schlett. Trends in embedded-microprocessor design. *IEEE Computer*, 31(8):44–49, 1998.
3. Giorgio Buttazzo C. *Hard Real-Time Computing Systems Predictable Scheduling Algorithms and Applications*, volume 23 of *Real-Time Systems Series*. Springer, 2nd edition, 2005.
4. K. Gresser. An event model for deadline verification of hard real-time systems. In *Proceedings 5th Euromicro Workshop on Real-Time Systems*, pages 118–123, Oulu, Finland, 1993.
5. Lothar Thiele, Samarjit Chakraborty, and Martin Naedele. Real-time calculus for scheduling hard real-time systems. In *In Proceedings International Symposium on Circuits and Systems (ISCAS)*, Geneva, Switzerland, 2000.

6. Kai Richter, Razvan Racu, and Rolf Ernst. Scheduling analysis integration for heterogeneous multiprocessor soc. Technical report, Institute of Computer and Communication Network Engineering, Technical University of Braunschweig, 2003.

7. A. Siebenborn, O. Bringmann, and W. Rosenstiel. Worst-case performance analysis of parallel, communicating software processes. In *CODES'02*, pages 37–42, May 2002.

8. A. van der Werf, J.L. van Meerbergen, E.H.L. Aarts, W.F.J. Verhaegh, , and P.E.R. Lippens. Efficient timing constraint derivation for optimally retiming high speed processing units. In *the 7th International Symposium on High-Level Synthesis*, pages 48–53, May 1994.

9. O. Maler, A. Pnueli, and J. Sifakis. On the synthesis of discrete controllers for timed systems. In *STAC'95*, volume 900 of *LNCS*. Springer Verlag, 1995.

10. K. Altisen, G. Goessler, and J. Sifakis. Scheduler modeling based on the controller synthesis paradigm. *Journal of Real-Time Systems, Special Issue on Control Approaches to Real-time*, 20:55–84, 2002.

11. Ch. Kloukinas and S. Yovine. Synthesis of Safe, QoS Extendible, Application Specific Schedulers for Heterogeneous Real-Time Systems. In *Proceedings of 5th Euromicro Conference on Real-Time Systems (ECRTS'03), Porto, Portugal, July 2003*, pages 253–267, Porto, Portuga, July 2003.

Application Signaling Protocols as Basis for QoS in IP-Based Wireless Networks

Robil Daher, Djamshid Tavangarian, and Abbas Malekpour

Chair for Computer Architecture, Institute of Computer Science,
University of Rostock, Albert-Einstein-Str. 21,
18059 Rostock, Germany
firstname.surname@uni-rostock.de

Abstract. The wireless resources such as bandwidth in case of wireless networks (WNs) are very restricted compared with wired networks. Thus, providing integrated service for WNs could lead to high traffic and instable performance because of the high link error. However, some application signaling protocols transport information about their resource requirements; this information is similar to that transported by QoS-signaling protocol. The usage of these application signaling protocols to perform a kind of QoS can reduce the control traffic generated on the wireless side effectively. In this respect, new structure of QoS is presented, where a wireless access server (WAS) communicates with the applications server, and the base stations in order to provide a kind of QoS. This method is applied on SIP-based WLAN telephony. The experiments on our implemented software presented relatively small delay times, in average: 13 ms for flow reservation and 16 ms for updating the wireless state in WAS. This provides an effective structure of QoS for VoIP applications.

Keywords: Application Signaling Protocol, IP-based Wireless Networks, Quality of Service, SIP, Telephony, WLAN.

1 Introduction

The technical advance of wireless networks (WNs) and their applications recently creates a revolution in the mobility, where the mobile internet access is worldwide growing drastically [6]. However, while the wide area WNs such as GPRS and 3G have concentrated on voice traffic more than data traffic, the IP-based WNs such as WLAN are basically built for data traffic [1], which causes many drawbacks for applying real time traffic in such WNs. Therefore, the Quality of Service (QoS) forms an essential factor for developing this kind of WN's technology.

However, due to the fact that WN resources on the wireless side, such as bandwidth, are very restricted compared with the wired side, a mechanism for Resource Reservation and Admission Control (RRAC) is definitely required in order to control and manage the congestions effectively. Thus, providing service differentiation in such WNs is insufficient for QoS [4], [12], whereas providing service integration can avoid the severe performance degradation under high traffic load via an admission control.

A. Bui et al. (Eds.): IICS 2005, LNCS 3908, pp. 171–180, 2006.

The MAC-based solutions for RRAC provide an effective structure with minimal signalling traffic on the wireless side [4]; however, such solutions are designed for uni-cell mode RRAC [7], where resources are reserved only for flows inside the cell. Furthermore, such solutions require the modification of the MAC-layer frame and methods. The enhancement of these solutions to multi-cells mode RRAC, where resources are reserved along the path between flow initiator and receiver, increases the system's complexity drastically. Moreover, a cross-layer interaction between MAC and IP–layers is required to achieve the flow reservation in multi-cells mode [7]. Therefore, the IP-based solutions offer lower cost for applying RRAC in such WNs; however, they generate more signalling traffic on the wireless side.

In other words, all known solutions that provide integrated service for WNs generate extra overhead according to their signalling traffic. This reduces the WN's capacity available for users, and affects the whole performance of WN.

On the other hand, by many client/server-based applications, especially the real time application, the application signalling protocol carries information about the required resources. For instance, in case of SIP-based VoIP application, information about the resource requirements is integrated in the SDP-header of the SIP-message [8]. This information, which includes codec type, codec bit rate and frame size, could be used to calculate the required bandwidth [14]. However, similar information must be sent again by the used IntServ signalling protocol, which reduces the performance of the network. We think that the usage of such application signalling protocols in WNs to provide resource requirement for IntServ-QoS instead of IntServ signaling protocol will decrease the control overhead on wireless side without reducing the provided QoS, and thus increase the performance of wireless access.

In this paper, we present the problem in details in section 2, and then introduce our QoS-method in section 3. In section 4, we propose an application of our QoS-mechanism on WLAN telephony using SIP protocol. Our experiments and results are presented in section 5. Finally, we conclude this paper in section 6.

2   Traffic Issues of IntServ-QoS Signaling Protocol

In case of IntServ, the applications need to specify their required services from the network; thus, a signaling protocol is used for indicating the application requirement to network elements. This signaling protocol carries QoS-related information from the end systems requesting QoS guarantees to network elements. The following steps are typical for a QoS-signaling protocol [5]:

1. Application requests for resources;
2. Network element looks at required resources and unreserved resources;
3. Network element admits or rejects the request.

IntServe uses soft connection approach, where the connection state is maintained only for a limited amount of time [5]. As long as the connection is active, the state needs to be refreshed at regular intervals. This state refreshment produces extra traffic in the network.

The Resource Reservation Protocol (RSVP) is designed to provide IntServ for packet-switched networks such as WLAN and WiMAX. However, because of the restriction of bandwidth and high link error in WNs, directly applying the RSVP may lead to high overhead and instable performance. This reduces the resources available for users, and as a result degrades the whole performance.

Consequently, besides the signaling overhead generated by the application itself in order to build and maintain a session, additional signaling overhead is generated by IntServ signaling protocol in order to maintain certain QoS for this session. In other words, the use of IntServ in WNs generates extra overhead in wireless medium according to QoS-signaling traffic. This reduces the available WN's capacity for users, and degrades the whole performance and QoS of WN.

3 Application Signaling Protocols for Signaling QoS in WNs

In case many client/server-based applications, especially real-time applications, the application signaling protocol through setting-up and managing a session carries information about the required resources from client to server, or through the server. For instance, in SIP-based VoIP applications, building a session between user A and B starts when A sends SIP-Invite-Message to B through the proxy. The SIP-Invite-Message in its SDP-header contains information about the required resources of the flow from A to B, such as codec type, codec bit rate, and frame size [8][14]. If B accepts the session, it answers with SIP-Ok-Message, which similarly includes information about the required resources of the flow from B to A. On the other hand, when A, or B ends the session, it sends SIP-Bye-Message to the other user through the proxy, in case of firewall-proxy. When any one of A or B changes its session parameters, it informs the other through the proxy with the corresponded SIP-message [8]. The transferred information of resource requirement through the proxy relatively match the information needed for per-flow reservation and admission control by IntServ. However, InServ is appropriate for layer-3-based QoS, when the physical layer offers stable performance expressed as bandwidth, delay, and packet loss, such in some high bandwidth wired network like Ethernet.

On the other hand, the nature of the wireless medium causes high link error and instable bandwidth by the wireless network. As a result of the mobility, the bit rate of wireless link varies over the time according to the received signal strength [7]. Therefore, the mobile stations (MSs) must reactivate their per-flow reservation dynamically after each critical change of the achieved bandwidth in comparison to the reserved bandwidth, or after any handoff process. This also requires cooperation with the MAC-layer of the used wireless network.

Thus, when the required resources of the requested flow and the wireless state of the desired connection between the corresponded MSs are known, the achieved bandwidth between these MSs can be calculated. Consequently, the real load of each base station (BS) as well as MS can be calculated and measured over the time. This helps to detect and avoid overload cases of BSs, and as a result to organize the reservation processes on each BS.

The use of Application Signaling Protocols for Signaling QoS (ASPSQ) in IP-based WNs provides underlying structure to transport the application's resource requirements and flow reservation state to the wireless networks. On the other hand, the wireless state of the participated MSs in a session must be separately obtained, as we explain in the following subsections.

3.1 ASPSQ-System Architecture

To avoid using additional infrastructure on the wireless side that employs the wireless resources, we concentrate on the wired side of the BS; a BS is the central point of a cell, like the Access Point (AP) in case of IEEE 802.11 [1]. The BS builds a bridge between the wired side and the wireless side; therefore, it can be used to observe the bit rate variation of each wireless link on the physical layer.

In this paper, we present an approach that depends on moving the traffic generated by QoS-mechanism from the wireless side to the wired side; this approach is built on two main points:

1. Using each application signaling protocol to transport information about the requested resources to an external server, called wireless access server (WAS). WAS is a logical entity.
2. Checking the bandwidth on the wireless side periodically via the use of a logical entity called wireless links observer (WLO) that runs on each BS. WLO observes the associated MSs and their wireless links quality, and informs the WAS about the current wireless links state periodically or after a critical change. WLO sends this information as a links state message (LSM) to WAS.

Under the assumption that the bandwidth of the wired side is much higher than that of the wireless side, the additional traffic generated on the wired side according to our method could be tolerated.

This concept does not require any software or hardware modification on the client's side; clients of all supported application signaling protocols can be used in this system.

3.2 Operations of ASPSQ-Mechanism

Each WLO informs the WAS about the wireless links state by sending a wireless state message (WSM) to WAS periodically or after a critical change. WSM contains an IP-table of all associated MSs to the corresponded BS, and additionally includes information about the achieved bandwidth of each MS. The IP-table is used to resolve the relationship "MS-to-BS" through building a session, so that WAS can decide the admission control of the checked session on the stated BS.

Through ASPSQ-mechanism, a session of a determined application between two MSs (X and Y) can be built according to the following steps, as illustrated in Fig.1 and Fig.2:

1. X sends a request to the application server according to the corresponded signaling protocol;
2. Application server communicates with WAS over a proprietary protocol, and transfers the flow 4-tuples: Server-ID (IP and Port-Nr.), Source-IP, destination-IP, and the required bandwidth. The application server sends this information as wireless access request (WAR). WAS responds according to the following algorithm:

```
Check X location; // resolution of relationship
   MS-to-cell
If the free capacity of X's cell is greater than or
equaled to the required bandwidth
{Check Y location;
      If the free capacity of Y's cell is greater
      than or equaled the required bandwidth
      {
           response to application server with
           Ok/reserved
      } else {
           response to application server with
           rejected (destination cell is busy)
      }
} else {
   response to application server with
   rejected (source cell is busy)
}
```

3. Application server continues the session building if the WAS's response is "Ok"; otherwise the application server breaks the session and informs X over the corresponded signaling protocol.

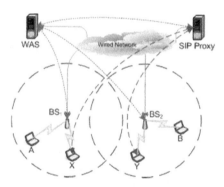

Fig. 1. Logical connections between network elements in an ASPSQ-system in a wireless network

In case X or Y belongs to a wired network, only MS that belongs to the wireless network will be checked. When an MS changes its achieved bandwidth due to the variation of transmission bit rate, the WLO informs WAS about the new state. The WAS then commands the appropriate application server to change the session parameters of the corresponded session participants, or even to end this session.

In ASPSQ- mechanism there is no need for refreshing the flow reservations, because the application server according to the used application signaling protocol is responsible for providing state information of the corresponded flows. Thus, no extra traffic for purpose of refreshing flow reservations may be generated.

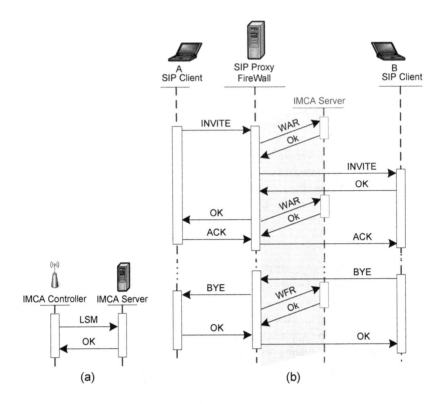

Fig. 2. Usage of SIP protocol as signaling protocol for QoS in WLAN telephony

4   QoS for SIP-Based WLAN Telephony

We apply our mechanism of QoS on the WLAN telephony, where the SIP protocol is used as signaling protocol for this service.

SIP protocol currently becomes the most important protocol for IP-Telephony and a basic signaling protocol for the 4G wireless network [13]. The central element of an SIP-System is proxy server, which control and manages the sessions between the user agents (UAs). This proxy server cooperates with two other servers: the registrar server for registration of UAs, and the location server for resolution of URI-addresses into IP-addresses [8]. The Figure 2.b shows the building process of an SIP session in relation to our QoS-mechanism.

WLAN consists of two main elements: AP as BS, and station (STA) as MS. In this system, an WLO must run on each AP in order to check the list of associated STAs and their links quality and bandwidth. WLO check the wireless links state periodically, each "τ" time interval. WLO sends this information to WAS through LSMs generated periodically or after a critical change. Due to the transmission bit rate variation of WLAN, the medium busy time (MBT) should be used to express the load of each AP as well as STAs [7].

The communication between WLO and WAS, and between WAS and application servers can be achieved over the Intelligent Management of Cell's Access (IMCA) protocol, which we developed in previous studies [3], [7] for load balancing and QoS purposes in WLAN. However, the current version of IMCA must be enhanced with few additional requests to integrate the functions of this QoS-mechanism. The IMCA protocol is bit-based protocol and can be carried over UDP or TCP/IP. IMCA protocol supports the centralized architecture as well as the decentralized architecture [7]. In this study, we use the controller/server architecture, where an IMCA controller (I-controller) runs on each AP and performs the functions of WLO. The IMCA server (I-server) supports the WAS functionality. In the rest of this paper, we use the terms I-server and I-controller to indicate WAS and WLO, respectively, unless explicitly mentioned to the contrary.

When the proxy receives an Invite-Message from A, it sends a Wireless Access Request (WAR) to the I-server, which temporarily reserves a flow on the related APs. If the proxy receives an Ok-response from B, it sends a new WAR to the I-server to reserve requested bandwidth from B to A. However, when the bandwidth reservation is performed for both flows, from A to B and from B to A, the proxy server can continue building the session. If in any process of flow reservation, the proxy receives reject-response from I-server, it breaks the session. Finally, when B ends the session by sending Byte-message, the proxy sends a Wireless Free Request (WFR) to I-server that removes the flows reservation of this session, and then response with Ok.

The main challenge of using this mechanism in WLAN is that the small cell size in WLAN creates frequent handoffs. Besides the handoff latency, the time needed by WLO to check the new STA-list of the new AP, and then to inform WAS that must response to the new changes when they critical to the load of the new AP. Finally, if needed, WAS must inform the corresponded application servers to control their applications bandwidth. These operations may cost relatively large time, which may affect the whole QoS in the new APs negatively. Small values of handoff latency of and the time interval "τ" are required for performing controlled load IntServ-QoS in WLAN [5].

5 Measurements and Results

Our first experiments have concentrated on the WAS and WLO latency time in order to investigate their effects on the real time applications.

5.1 Experiments Description

A special WLAN network based on standard IEEE 802.11b is used in DCF (Distributed Coordination Function) mode. This network consisted of three notebooks, one AP and two STAs. The AP was built upon the software "Hostap" (http://hostap. epitest.fi) and the WLAN card NetGear MA401. Linux Fedora Core 1 has been used as platform for this AP. The STAs were supplied with MS-Windows XP and the WLAN cards RoamAbout from Enterasys. For traffic generation and monitoring on

IP-level, the software MGEN (http://mgen.pf.itd.nrl.navy.mil) has been used. On other hand, to check the list of the associated STAs and their MAC-addresses as well as their links quality and achieved bandwidth, we had to modify the Hostap driver software in order to outputs the needed statistics in a file at runtime. The I-controller is built in java and is configured to check the stated output file of the driver periodically, where many time intervals were tested. The I-server is also built in java; the platform of I-server had MS windows XP running on a separated computer connected with AP through a FastEthernet switch. We used PostgreSQL database on another computer running Linux.

5.2 Results and Discussion

We measured two kinds of time delays; firstly the time delay (T1) between checking the WLAN-driver's statistic output by I-controller and the saving of the processed information in the database of I-server; and secondly the time delay (T2) between sending an WAR to the I-server and receiving an Ok from it. The Fig. 3 shows the results of T1 and T2.

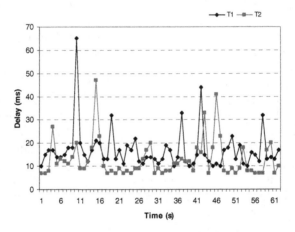

Fig. 3. Results of the measured T1 and T2 for time interval $\tau=1s$

The delay values of T1 are relatively low; the maximal value is less than 70 ms, where the average value is approximately 16 ms. The greatest delays were produced by database accesses (3 - 15 ms); however, the usage of static tables instead of database may decrease these delay times in an effective way. Through the T1 measuring, changes of STA bandwidth and new handing-off STAs are simulated. On the other hand, T1 does not includes the time delay (d) between the actual critical change of wireless state and its output in the statistics file output of driver. The time delay (T1+τ+d) forms the maximal possible delay between the actual change of wireless state and saving this information in the database. Unfortunately, our tools could not measure the delay "d", but we think "d" is relatively small time; therefore, the time "d" was eliminated in our evaluation. We selected $\tau=1s$ by our experiments to simplify the observation process. However, the lower is the time "τ", the higher is the processing overhead of the processor, but the more precise is the obtained results of wireless state, which can then provide better prediction of QoS.

Similarly, the delay values of T2 are relatively low; the maximal value is less than 50 ms, where the average value is approximately 13 ms. The sum (T1+T2) could be considered as the time delay between checking the associated STAs list and the acceptance or rejection of an WAR. Accordingly, an average delay of 29 ms could be required for any effective flow reservation. This value is relatively low in comparison to real time application requirements; it remains less than the maximal delay (150 ms) determined for VoIP-applications [9], [10], [11]. In overall, the delay times (T1 and T2) can be reduced via better optimizing for the implemented software, especially the database.

Consequently, we suggest that the development of any application signaling protocol for WN should take the QoS-signaling requirements into consideration, so that the control traffic for signaling QoS can be drastically reduced on the wireless side.

6 Conclusion

This paper presented a mechanism called Application Signalling Protocol for Signalling QoS (ASPSQ) in IP-based wireless networks (WNs). We presented an approach to use applications signalling protocol in order to transport needed information for resource reservation and admission control, so that the generated traffic by QoS-signalling protocol on the wireless side can be reduced. We proposed our method structure and operations. We also introduced an application of this method in the field of WLAN telephony, where the SIP protocol is used as signalling protocol. Our experiments concentrated on the latency times of the implemented part of the ASPSQ-mechanism in WLAN. The results showed that delay times needed to check the wireless state variation are relatively small; the average value was 16 ms. Similarly, the times needed to reserve a flow; the average value was 13 ms. These relatively small times could form an effective structure of QoS for VoIP applications.

References

1. IEEE Standard 802.11 (08/1999), Part 11: Wireless LAN Medium Access Control (MAC) and Physical Layer (PHY) specifications.
2. IEEE Standard 802.16 (2004), Part 16: Air Interface for Fixed Broadband Wireless Access Systems.
3. R. Daher, H. Kopp, and D. Tavangarian: "Active Load Balancing in Wireless LAN hotspots", GI 2004, September 2004
4. Ming Li, B. Prabhakaran, Sathish Sathyamurthy: "On Flow Reservation and Admission Control for Distributed Scheduling Strategies in IEEE802.11 Wireless LAN", MSWiM'03, San Diego, California, USA, September 2003
5. Sanjay Jha and Mahbub Hassan: "Engineering Internet QoS", Artech House, INC. ISBN: 1-58053-341-8, 2002

6. Rajiv Chakravort and et al.: "Performance Issues with Vertical Handovers-Experience from GPRS Cellular and WLAN Hotspots Integration", PERCOM'04, 2004
7. Robil Daher and Djamshid Tavangarian: "Load Observation and Control Model for Load Balancing with QoS in WLAN", IST Summit, Dresden, Germany, June 2005
8. J. Rosenberg, H. Schulzrinne, et al.: "IETF RFC 3261 - SIP: Session Initiation Protocol", June 2002
9. ITU-T Recommendation G.114, One-way transmission time, May 2003
10. ITU-T Y.1540 Internet protocol data communication service - IP packet transfer and availability performance parameters, 2002
11. ITU-T Y.1541 Network performance objectives for IP-based services, 2002
12. Cisco, White Paper: "DiffServ – The Scalable End-to-End QoS Model", www.cisco.com, 2001
13. Nilanjan Banerjee, Wei Wu, Kalyan Basu, and Sajal K. Das: "Analysis of SIP-based mobility management in 4G wireless networks", Computer Communications 27 (2004), October 2003
14. M. Handley and V. Jacobson: "IETF RFC 2327 - SDP: Session Description Protocol" April 1998

3D Emotional Agent Architecture

Félix F. Ramos, Luis Razo, Alma V. Martinez, Fabiel Zúñiga,
and Hugo I. Piza

Multi-Agent Systems Development Group,
Centro de Investigación y de Estudios Avanzados del Instituto Politécnico Nacional,
Prolongación López Mateos Sur No. 590, Guadalajara, Jalisco, México
{framos, lrazo, vmartine, fzuniga, hpiza}@gdl.cinvestav.mx
http://www.gdl.cinvestav.mx

Abstract. This chapter presents architecture to design emotional agents evolving in an artificial 3D environment. The agent behavior and environment emulator are independent of implementation. To achieve this, a Language of Interface for Animations in 3D called LIA-3D, is presented. The agent and environment simulator uses LIA to establish communication with each other.

1 Introduction

The problem we try to solve is how to generate suitable behaviors to virtual creatures participating in virtual environments. This work is part of GeDA-3D a platform to design and run dynamic virtual environments [1, 2]. GeDA-3D provides facilities to manage the communication among agents and mobility services used to share other services. The architecture to design emotional agents presented in this work allows the user to develop behaviors for agents which participate in the environments generated using the declarative virtual editor proposed in [1]. The agent architecture proposed has following characteristics: The agent is able to receive a goals-specification that contains a detailed definition about the way the agents' goals must be reached. The agent behavior is based on skills, thus an agent must be able to add skills into his global behavior. Skills are mobile services registered in GeDA-3D which could be added to agent behaviors. The personality and emotion of agents make difference in behaviors of agents having the same set of skills. We use a model of generic personality and an emotion simulation methodology [3] in which a defined personality and emotion module is used. This module uses a personality defined for each agent and the current emotional state to the simulation. These characteristics are used in the case of study presented in this paper. To display results we use a language LIA-3D we propose. It consists mainly of two parts: the language implemented in XML and the motor of 3D. This language was designed in XML to facilitate the communication with other applications as the motor of 3D created in java.

The chapter is organized as follows. Section 2 shows the overall architecture. Section 3 describes the emotional agent architecture. Section 4 introduces LIA (Animation Interface Language). Section 5 shows the case of study and finally, section 6 summarizes the conclusions.

A. Bui et al. (Eds.): IICS 2005, LNCS 3908, pp. 181–194, 2006.

GeDA-3D is designed to integrate distributed applications, this feature allow us to execute each agent which belongs to the editor in a distributed way. Therefore, the virtual-environment editor, rendering and the agents work in a distributed environment. This allows us to see a well-updated simulation, because the hard work often performed by the agents is distributed.

This architecture can be used in simulations, guide learning and specifically in behavior-based scene generation. This last one is based on the principle which provides that with the same goal and the same scene the goal achievement can generate different animations, because you only indicate to the agent where to go or which goal to accomplish, but not how to accomplish it, subsequently the way of doing it can change.

2 Overall Architecture

The whole solution extends GeDA-3D [2]. GeDA-3D is a platform used to integrate and manage distributed applications. It provides facilities to manage the communication among agents and mobility services. The main idea is to allow this architecture to support a declarative virtual environment editor in order to take advantage of its services. Figure 1 shows the overall architecture of the platform; according to their competencies, the components of the platform have been grouped in four main modules: Virtual-Environments Editor, Rendering, GeDA-3D and Agents Community.

The virtual-environments editor serves as an interface between the platform and the user. That is, it provides means for a modeler to specify the physical laws governing

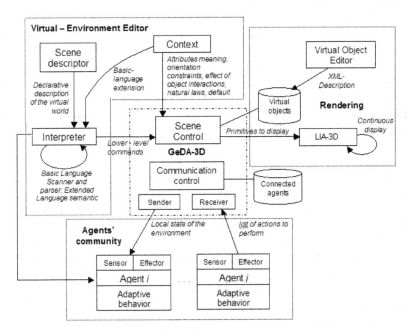

Fig. 1. Overall Architecture

an environment, and to describe a virtual scene taking place in such environment. It also translates the high-level descriptions into lower-level commands which will be required by the different components across the platform.

Rendering addresses all the issues related to 3D-graphics, it allows the design of virtual objects and the display of the scene. This is done by LIA-3D, the scope of this work.

Agents' community is composed by the agents in charge of ruling the virtual objects behavior. These agents are the scope of this work.

3   Emotional Agent Architecture

As we mentioned above, the objective is to create 3D-animated scenes as a result of a high-level description. The declarative virtual environment editor would generate a sketch or scene describing the environment and the goals the agents will perform.

The reason of creating this kind of scenes is to watch a behaviors-based scene simulation. The user specifies what the agents will do (using a declarative language), instead of how they have to do it. Therefore, the same scene specifications might produce different simulations.

Figure 2 shows the GeDA-3D agent architecture that allows users to develop behaviors which take part of the scene.

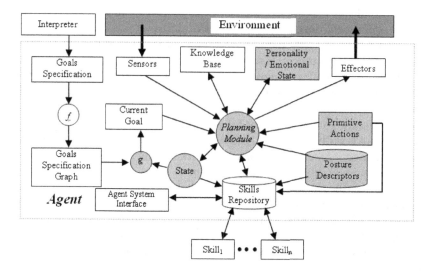

Fig. 2. Emotional Agent Architecture

We use process algebras to specify the way in which we want an agent (or a set of agents) to accomplish its (their) goals. We have based the syntax in LOTOS [4]. LOTOS has a defined syntax and semantic, and because LOTOS semantic is defined operationally, it is possible to implement this semantic in an interpreter, which for a behavior expression can enumerate the set of possible next actions. This property allows us to implement a function that gives the next goal to try to reach in a specific time in order to accomplish the whole specification (functions f and g in figure 2). In this context we use goals instead of actions. A method to generate a goals-specification and the way an agent can handle it is shown in [5].

A GeDA-3D agent has a knowledge base to represent environment facts. Each fact is represented by an oration of propositional logic or first order logic. This knowledge base provides the two main operations performed over a knowledge base: Add orations into the knowledge base and ask for knowledge. This knowledge base uses an automatic inference method to ask for knowledge and an automatic method to remove contradictory orations when the agent adds a new one. When an agent asks for the fact α, this is true if knowledge base is $\vdash \alpha$.

The syntax and semantic used on this knowledge base is the same used in propositional logic and first order logic. The method to relate an oration to a specific fact in the world (the meaning of an oration) depends on the agent and the specific problem.

As a GeDA-3D agent evolves into scenes, this knowledge base is commonly used to provide the agent with an initial knowledge of the world. This allows developing behaviors focused on the scenes and avoiding time spent recognizing the world before trying to accomplish the goals-specification.

3.1 Skill Based Behaviors

In order to build agents behaviors we adopted a philosophy of skills-based behaviors, that is, the agents behaviors are based on a set of skills.

A skill is a task an agent knows how to do, and in order to perform it, the agent probably would need to execute a sequence of primitive actions, for example catching a static object or an object in movement. A skill has an algorithm that controls its specific behavior and it could be implemented by using any of the existent paradigms, for example Evolutionary Algorithms [6, 7], Neural Networks [8], Finite Automata, etc. We have focuses on evolutionary computation.

The agent adds skills to its global behavior and these skills are shared in GeDA-3D as mobile services. At execution time, these skills are moved to the environment where the agent is executing them or they can be executed remotely.

GeDA-3D has the capability of managing mobile agents and provides a platform where mobile programming is supported and performed with certain ease. In this context, a mobile application is not forced to remain in the system where it was started; instead it has the ability to move from a system to another containing an object (agent, resource) to interact with. In [9] the model of the mobility platform in GeDA-3D is shown.

In order to achieve a shared mobile skill, skills are based on the architecture shown in figure 3. Agent system interface and mobility module are in charge of skill mobility and this modules are interfaces of mobility services provided by GeDA-3D.

Skill control sets the parameters to fit the skill to a specific agent and it controls the skill state (in execution, stopped, terminated). Although an agent adds a skill, this one might be stopped for a while. The agent and environment states, and the agent descriptors are gotten directly from the agent. Therefore, when a new skill will be

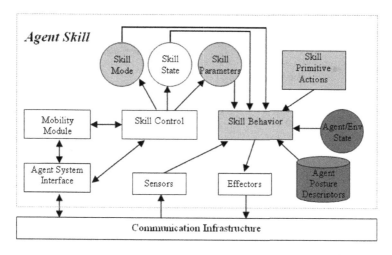

Fig. 3. Agent Skill

added, the user only has to define the skill primitive actions, the specific skill behavior and the skill mode. The skill mode is directly related to the agent emotional state, and it defines the way that the emotional state affects the agent behavior.

When a skill is executed to an agent, this skill generates a set of primitive actions to the agent to perform. Thus, if *Ap* represents the primitive actions to the agent *A*, and *Sp* represents the set of the possible primitive actions the skill *S* can produce, then it will be possible to add *S* in *A* if $Sp \subseteq Ap$.

3.2   Personality and Emotional Module

In each human being the personality determines some important aspects of the behavior as the way to react to diverse situations of life, as well as the emotional status of a human is an additional significant characteristic that can affect directly the behavior. Using these two attributes within the Emotional Agent Architecture as an accurate Personality and Emotional Module we obtain emotional interaction and realistic simulation as the result. In our work we have used the following two attributes: the personality as a constant and invariable value that defines the special character of the agent and the emotional status as a variable value, which is updated each time, influenced by the natural environment interaction, moreover changed by internal decay of the emotional status of the agent.

This section describes the methodology used to implement agents with personality and emotions. The methodology employs a model for both, the generic personality and the emotion simulation. Using this scheme we apply it into a personality and emotion module defined by our implementation. Thus an application occupies for each agent a current emotional state. To update the current emotional state we need to use inner attributes like personality and emotion as parameters. These parameters are used in the internal update and decay functions. These functions also receive an external environment influence variable from a specified environment appraisal. In

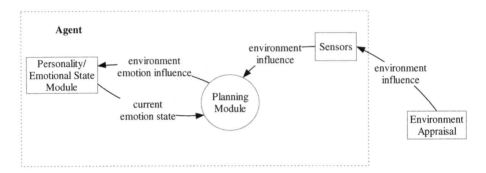

Fig. 4. Top-view of the emotional agent emotion state module and environment influence interaction

resume this description is the update sequence of the current emotional state according to the environment influence on the agent and the previous emotional context (see the fig.4). The update belongs to an infinite inner cycle that keeps the agents' "personality/emotional state" updated. In this way, emotional agents are sensible to their environment and can react to the external emotional stimulus according to the definition of the states of their personalities and emotions.

This module manages values of personality and emotions each one defined as vectors with a length equal to the total of emotions. Each emotion is a dimension in a vector. The elements of these vectors follow a specific personality model as the OCEAN model [10] that uses a five dimension vector. The size of the vector depends on the model's definition or our necessities. Also we applied our implementation on a methodology for the creation of generic personality and emotion model defined by Egges et al. [3].

In this work, we define the personality as a vector value of n dimensions length, as the next expression

$$p = [\alpha_1, \ldots, \alpha_n]^{\mathrm{T}} \; \forall i \in [1, n]: \alpha \in [0,1]$$

Also we have the emotional status vector value at the time t. It's a vector value of m dimensions length, where m is defined as the number of emotions used in the model, it could be different of n, the initial value is $e_0 = 0$

$$e_t = [\beta_1, \ldots, \beta_m]^{\mathrm{T}} \; \forall i \in [1, m]: \beta \in [0,1]$$

The emotional environment influence is defined as

$$a_t = [\delta_1, \ldots, \delta_m]^{\mathrm{T}} \; \forall i \in [1, m]: \delta \in [0,1]$$

So we have to define a personality-emotion influence Matrix as P_0 with a length denoted by $m \times n$.

After the product of the matrix P_0 and the personality vector p is realized

$$u_t = P_0 \cdot p = [\varepsilon_1 \ldots \varepsilon_m]^{\mathrm{T}}$$

The result is the u_t vector. Then taking each ε_i value of this vector the diagonal matrix P is built. The matrix values define how strong can be an emotion given by the p personality.

In other words, the P matrix defines a probability to obtain a high or a low value of an emotion. It depends on the personality definition; this matrix helps us at the update emotion functions as we see below.

$$P = \begin{bmatrix} \varepsilon_1 & 0 & \cdots & 0 \\ 0 & \varepsilon_2 & & \vdots \\ \vdots & & \ddots & 0 \\ 0 & \cdots & 0 & \varepsilon_m \end{bmatrix}$$

Finally we defined a default constant we named C_e initially with a value 0.01. This constant is used to define a vector in the decay function implementation that we define in the next section.

3.2.1 Updating the Emotional State

In this implementation we make use of an emotional model that employs two specific functions described after. These functions update the emotional state in general. The first one generates the updating value for the emotional state. The second one makes an internal emotion change or internal emotion decay. In this implementation we simplify the functions used by Egges et al. [3] and use them specifically for our implementation because the linear implementation simplifies the emotions manage in our architecture. The difference is that we use less parameters than Egges uses [3], besides we use these two functions to compute the emotional state in a t time given as described in the next equation.

The definition of our update emotional state function $\psi_e(p, a)$ consist in a linear implementation that uses the values of personality and the values of the emotional environment influence. We define the return value of this function as the next expression

$$\psi_e(p, a) = P \cdot a$$

Where we use the P matrix in a product between the a vector of environment influence. Finally with the C_e constant value, we define the decay function. It returns as value the next vector expression; we can see that in this case we do not use the p value,

$$\Omega_e(p) = \begin{bmatrix} -C_e & \cdots & -C_e \end{bmatrix}^T$$

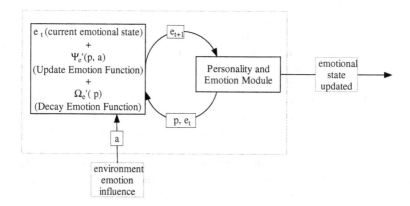

Fig. 5. A graphical overview of one updates cycle of the emotional state

Where C_e = 0.01 as default value. The defined functions are used in the architecture as illustrated in fig. 5 that shows the internal architectural performance. The next emotion status vector value is computed adding these functions as defined by next expression to the current emotional state.

$$e_{t+1} = e_t + \psi_e(p, a) + \Omega_e(p)$$

3.2.2 Environment Model and Influence

In order to have an efficient and accurate work using this emotional model, we include an environment model that could communicate to the agents an emotional influence. In such a way the environment model must affect the inner decisions, actions of the agent with the purpose of helping it to choose a behavior from a set available. The model we use takes into account the action. That is the model must answer to an action with a value or emotional cost. This model is useful to the agent to choose best suited behaviors.

In the case of study described in section 5, we define an emotional value for each action of the agent in the environment; it is done in order to produce the influence in the agents' emotional state, even more desirable it is to define the individual influence of environment event for each agent. Such influence is quantified by the agents' sensors. Then sensors send this information to the Planning Module. This last one sends just the emotional environment influence to the Personality and Emotional State Module influencing the state which updating the values. Then according to the personality these changes influence its decisions.

For example, if an emotional agent predator is hungry and perceives a prey close. Such a situation will change the predator's inner emotional state and his behavior will turn huntress, thus his future actions must be affected by this emotional change. Following this rule the predator will try to hunt the prey to stop his sense of hunger. The satisfaction of a need conforms to a regulation mechanism of his inner status and keeps the agent in equilibrate state.

4 Language of Interface for Animations in 3D (LIA·3D)

LIA-3D is a language independent of the application to manage virtual environments. It is constituted mainly of two parts, one of which is the language implemented in XML and the other it is the motor of 3D. This language was designed in XML to obtain a greater facility in the communication with other applications, the motor of 3D created in java guarantees us that LIA·3D is multiplatform.

To use LIA·3D it is not necessary to have great knowledge neither of 3D nor of programming. The user only needs to know XML in order to make actions, (once developed the avatars by the user) these actions will be performed by each one of the avatars in the virtual environment.

By means of this language the single user will have to create an application in some programming language that communicates to the server by means of socket to send thus the chain in XML, which indicates the action to execute.

4.1 Architecture

The user will have to make the chain in XML according to the language specification if an error arises at the execution time, an XML event indicating the type of error will be returned as result, these events are defined within the language.

Actions: This module selects the type of avatar with which the wished action will be made, thus, although in the environment exist a human being avatar and a bird avatar, this module is able to distinguish the type of avatar that could accomplish the selected actions.

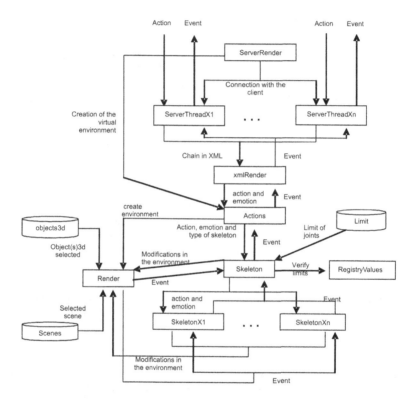

Fig. 6. Architecture of LIA-3D

Skeleton: In this module all the actions that can be realized by the avatar are specified, like the basic actions of a skeleton, like moving a movable body element (as a leg), to advance, etc. The elaborated actions are developed in the type of skeleton; the user can choose any type of skeleton he/she wishes.

SkeletonX1 . . . Xn: are modules which specialize in the movements depending on the type of skeleton with which it is desired to make an action, since it is not the same design an animation of the walking way of a biped and a quadruped.

RegistryValues: It contains one or many structures used to store a bounded number of each joint of a skeleton. The RegistryValues purpose is to evaluate the maximum and minimum limits of each joint to avoid an erroneous movement. For example, if we indicate to an avatar of a human being to turn his head at an angle of more than 180° he will not allow this because such a movement is not natural for a real person.

Render: This module has the following two objectives: the first one is to load the environment that consists of all objects 3D conforming with/to it. The user is who describes by means a file the position of each avatar, and object within the environment. The second objective of this module is to display all the events occurred within the graphical virtual environment, that is, its evolution in real time.

ServerThreadX1 . . . Xn: These modules receive the actions avatar must realize in the XML specification described in 4.2, which will be parsed in the obtained order, therefore the action and its parameters that are due to show in the virtual environment. The amount of these modules will depend on the number of users connected to the environment.

ServerRender: This main objective is to offer connections to the clients and it initializes the virtual environment calling the Render. The connections to the clients are necessary to present the evolution of the system.

XmlRender: This module parses the XML chain structured according to the LIA·3D specification from the ServerThreads, and indicates to the Actions module which action must be realized together with necessary parameters to show the changes in the environment.

Objects3D: This module is a sort of database containing all the objects 3D that the user can use to design his virtual environment 3D. The objects of Objects3D can be classified as avatars that are those having a skeleton, and others that are unanimated objects.

Scenes: Similarly to the Objects3D this module contains a set of scenarios defined. Those scenarios can be used by virtual world creators. These module contains not just the virtual representation but also all the context relevant to the scenarios [1, 2].

Limit: It stores limit maximum and minimums of movements of all joints of a skeleton. It helps the user to order a more natural movements and thus to have representations as realistic as possible.

4.2 Language

The objective of LIA·3D language is to manage a virtual environment by a sequence of instructions in order to display the evolution of that virtual environment. LIA-3D is based on XML because it has become a standard of communication and mainly because it allows increase easily the expressiveness of LIA-3D and the user can manage it without special knowledge of 3D. That is, a client (GeDA-3D) indicates in a declarative way which avatars must be placed in a certain position in the virtual environment and which actions must be executed, but not the way they must be executed.

After the virtual environment has been created we only have to manipulate the avatars, for which the actions defined within LIA·3D will be used, these actions will indicate to avatars which parts of their skeletons must be modified to obtain a particular result.

The client (GeDA-3D) must know the LIA-3D language specification in order to build the XML chains containing the actions the virtual creatures must execute. These chains are received by the ServerThreads (clients). Next these chains are sent to the XmlRender to be parsed and to obtain the actions together with its parameters. Once this is achieved, this last one sends actions and parameters to the Actions module which selects the type of avatar that must realize the actions described. Together with the actions to be realized by the virtual creatures the emotion with which the actions are realized must be indicated. The emotions are specified by the client (GeDA-3D) in VHML [11] which reunites main characteristics of several languages that describe different aspects related to the avatar's emotions (face animation, dialogues, etc.), the part that uses LIA·3D is the face animation.

With the integration of the actions defined in LIA·3D and the face animation of VHML, more convincing animations are obtained, in this way we can indicate to an avatar which action will be executed and which emotional state will be present in the display at the time of executing it. For example, if within the environment there is an avatar that represents a person, we can give him a command to walk certain distance sadly, the walking action is defined in LIA·3D and the emotional status "sad" is declared in VHML. This will result in displaying a special way of walk that express sadness.

VHML counts with a part of animation of the body, but this section does not indicate actions as LIA·3D does, in this way LIA·3D facilitates a lot the work of the user, it helps him to avoid creating an animation moving each joint of a skeleton, this work is already done by LIA·3D. We consider that these facilities must be included in future improvements of VHML.

Resuming user only needs to know LIA·3D he doesn't need to bother about how animation is made internally. The structure of the language is simple; the next code is an example of an action:

```
<action>
        <walk>
                <avatar> 1 </avatar>
                <steps> 3 </steps>
                <turn> -30 </turn>
        </walk>
</action>
```

As previously indicates the action of the avatar includes the necessary parameters to realize the action. The answer to an action LIA-3D is an event that indicates if there is an error or not. In the case of an error the type of error in the action is indicated. For example, if the client indicates the walk action to the avatar, and there is for instance a collision with another object 3D contained in the virtual environment, LIA·3D will respond with a collision event. Next code shows an example:

```
<event>
            <collision>
                        <object1> 1 </object1>
                        <object2> 4 </object2>
            </collision>
</event>
```

With this event the user will be able to know if the solicited action finalizes satisfactorily.

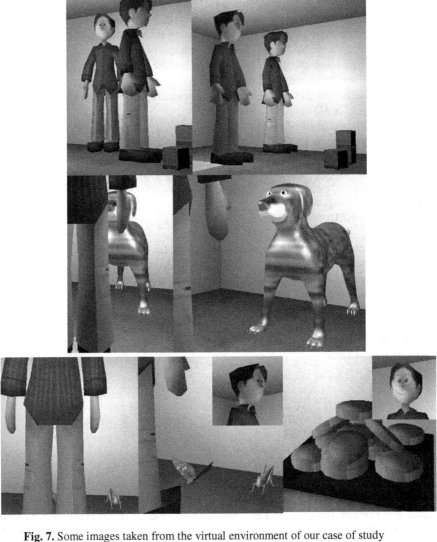

Fig. 7. Some images taken from the virtual environment of our case of study

5 Case Study

It consists in a virtual environment where two agents interact. The user can declare items into the boxes. These items could be gold, an insect or a dog. When one of the agents opens one box, he can find gold, if it does, he gets surprised and earns the gold and increments his gold points, or if he finds an insect, the agent reacts stunned and leaves the box quickly, if the dog appears, the dog runs trying to bite the agents, and the agents react running with fear; in the case that one agent earns too much gold and another doesn't, the first agent can change his inner emotional status, affected by this event, and he gets angry and may try to strike his rich agent partner, or if one agent only finds a lot of insects and dogs, he can lose his confidence and get sad and angry.

This case study represents the single scenario: two 'human' agents are in a small room, in which a lot of boxes are kept. Each box has different contents. These contents can be something good as gold coins or something bad as insects or a dog. The simulation consists in the emulation of these two agents. They have to open all the boxes, one at a time, they must try to find all the gold coins running the risk of discovering the undesired contents as insects or a mad dog, (see fig. 7).

This simulation works using the genetic algorithm that works with trajectories and some options to make selections to chose the right way to reach the next point, to walk or to take a box, to avoid a dog if it is the case or to reach another agent to give him a punch.

6 Conclusions

This paper is proposed an emotional agent-architecture and LIA-3D a language independent of application. The emotional agent architecture and LIA-3D are part of GeDA-3D [2]. The objective of our architecture is generating realistic animation for virtual creatures evolving in the virtual environments including emotions in their execution. Maybe the most important characteristic of this architecture is that it allows specifying goals but not the way to get those goals. On the other hand, the LIA-3D language presented is based on XML to improve efficiency aand openness, this last means that language can be enriched by new necessitated structures for specific events. To prove the emotional architecture and the language LIA-3D we develop a very simple example using our both modules of GeDA-3D. The results of the example are very successful, but the main drawback is the time to get results of the render module. This problem will guide our next studies. However a solution of this problem is to get a film of the solutions that can be displayed after all processing.

Face to face with another works of this kind of simulations as Animus [13] or the Oz project [12], in this work we can show the functionality in a 3D scenario with the help of LIA-3D, also we can change the behavior of the agents using the emotional agent implementation, these attributes are not included in the Animus or in the Oz projects [12], Animus only works with reactions established before the simulation runs, our work change these reactions in relation to the environment influence and the actual emotional status providing more believable and real behavior. The Oz project works only in a terminal display which gives the actions and changes of the scenario in text mode; our implementation shows all the actions in a 3D scenario.

References

1. H. Iván Piza, Fabiel Zúñiga, Félix F. Ramos. *A Platform to Design and Run Dynamic Virtual Environments*. IEEE Cyberworlds 2004, November in Japan. ISBN 0-7695-2140-1.
2. Félix Ramos, Fabiel Zúñiga, H. Piza. *A 3D-Space Platform for Distributed Applications Management*. International Symposium and School on Advanced Distributed Systems 2002. Guadalajara, Jal., México. November 2002. ISBN 970-27-0358-1
3. Arjan Egges, Sumedha Kshirsagar, Nadia Magnenat-Thalmann. *Generic personality and emotion simulation for conversational agents. Computer Animation and Virtual Worlds*. Volume 15, Issue 1, Pages 1–13. Published Online: 8 Mar 2004.
4. L. Logrippo, M. Faci, M. Haj-Hussein. *An Introdiction to LOTOS: Learning by Examples*. University of Ottawa. Protocols research group. Department of computer science.
5. Fabiel Zúñiga, H. Piza, Félix Ramos. *Specifying Agent's Goals Using Process Algebras*. LNCS Advanced Distributed Systems. International Symposium and School on Advanced Distributed Systems. Guadalajara, Jalisco, México. Enero 2005.
6. J. H. Holland. *Adaptation in Natural and Artificial Systems*. University of Michigan Press, Ann Arbor, 1975.
7. D. B. Fogel. Evolutionary Computation. Toward a New Philosophy of Machine Intelligence. IEEE Press, Piscataway, NJ, 1995.
8. Xin Yao. A review of Evolutionary Artificial. Neural Networks. Commonwealth Scientific and Industrial Research Organisation Division of Building, Construction and Engineering. Australia.
9. Felix F. Ramos, Fabiel Zuñiga, Antonio Alcala, Ivan Piza. *Specification of Distributed Systems Using Multi-Level Petri nets*. 2003 IEEE International Conference on Systems, Man & Cybernetics. October 5–8, 2003 – Hyatt Regency, Washington, D.C., USA.
10. P.T. Costa and R.R. McCrae. Normal personality assessment in clinical practice: The NEO personality inventory. Psychological Assessment, (4):5–13, 1992.
11. Andrew Marriott: VHML – Virtual Human Markup Language. School of Computing, Curtin University of Technology, Melbourne, Australia in conjunction with HF2002 and OZCHI2002, 29th November, 2002.
12. W. Scott Neal Reilly Believable Social and Emotional Agents, School of Computer Science Carnegie Mellon University, May 1996.
13. Daniel Torres, Pierre Boulanger *The ANIMUS Project: A Framework for the Creation of Synthetic Characters*, Department of Computing Science, University of Alberta. 2003.

A Distributed Preflow-Push
for the Maximum Flow Problem

Thuy Lien Pham, Marc Bui, Ivan Lavallee, and Si Hoang Do

Laboratoire de Recherche en Informatique Avancée, Université Paris 8, France
tl.pham@univ-reims.fr,
{Marc.Bui, Lavallee}@univ-paris8.fr, sihoang@free.fr

Abstract. We present a new algorithm that solves the problem of distributively determining the maximum flow in an asynchronous network. This distributed algorithm is based on the preflow-push technique. Sequential processes, executing the same code over local data, exchange messages with neighbors to establish the max flow. This algorithm is derived to the case of multiple sources and/or sinks without modifications. For a network of n nodes and m arcs, the algorithm achieves $O(n^2m)$ message complexity and $O(n^2)$ time complexity.

1 Introduction

We consider a connected directed graph with a positive function of capacity on arcs. There are two special nodes in graph, called source and sink. Such a graph is referred as a "network". The maximum flow problem is stated as follows: in this network we wish to send as much flow as possible from the source to the sink, without exceeding the capacity of any arc.

The maximum flow problem is widely studied in both applications and theory. Its applications can be found in diverse fields such as engineering, scheduling, traffic management...Recently, it has been applied in some new domains, such as coding network and wireless ad hoc networks [16]. The fundamental algorithmic techniques for solving the problem are presented in [5], [8], [9], [3], [4] and [2]. There have been a number of survey papers and books on theoretical and experimental analysis of algorithms, see e.g. [7], [10], [11], [12]. A detail comparison about the complexity of existed algorithms can be found in [1].

In general there are two principal categories for solving the problem:

1. Augmenting path method introduced by Ford-Fulkerson [5]. The algorithms of this category maintain balance constraints at every node of the network except the source and sink nodes, and incrementally augment flow along paths from the source node to the sink node.
2. Preflow-push method introduced by Golberg-Tarjan [2] who takes the original idea of preflow from Karzanov [9]. The idea of preflow-push algorithms is to flood the network so that some nodes haves excesses (or buildup of flow). The algorithm discharges excesses at nodes by sending flow forward toward the sink node, or backward toward the source node: nodes send flow on individual arcs based on the knowledge it has about itself and its neighbors. This algorithm of

A. Bui et al. (Eds.): IICS 2005, LNCS 3908, pp. 195 – 206, 2006.
© Springer-Verlag Berlin Heidelberg 2006

Goldberg-Tarjan makes decisions locally and hence, is suitable for a distributed version in the asynchronous network.

There are two synchronous distributed algorithms presented in [13] that based on the first method to find the maximum flow in network with $O(n^3)$ message complexity and $O(n^2)$ time complexity, where n is the number of nodes in network. In employing synchronizer technique to that algorithm, an asynchronous algorithm has proposed with message complexity and time complexity respectively is $O(kn^3)$ and $O(n^2 log n/log k)$ where k is an integer, $2 < k < |N|$. Takkula [14] has proposed an asynchronous algorithm using second approach but it is not efficient on both number of exchanged messages and execution times.

In this paper, we present an asynchronous distributed algorithm which determines the maximum flow of network based on the Goldberg-Tarjan's technique. We consider the graph as a network with bidirectional communication links. We assume each node initially knows capacities of outgoing arcs from and incoming arcs into it, moreover source node knows the number of nodes in graph. In this network, each node executes the same local algorithm, which consists of sending messages over adjacent links or waiting for incoming messages to process them. Our algorithm takes $O(n^2 m)$ message complexity and $O(n^2)$ time complexity. It can be applied to case of multiple sources and/or sinks without any modifications.

The rest of paper is organized as follows. In Section 2, we briefly introduce the maximum flow problem and Goldberg-Tarjan technique. In Section 3, we present a high-level and detailed description of our distributed algorithm. The proofs and complexity analysis of algorithm is presented in Section 4. Concluding remarks are given in Section 5.

2 Background

2.1 State of the Art

Maximum Flow Problem. We consider a network $G=(N,E)$ consists of a set N of nodes with a set E of arcs (directed edges), the source node s and the sink node t. Let's $n=|V|$, $m=|E|$. For each arc $e \in G$, there is an associated capacity $c(e)$, with $c(e)>0$.

A flow is a function $f: E \to R^{\geq 0}$ satisfying the capacity constraints and the flow conservation constraints:

1. $0 \leq f(e) \leq c(e), \forall e \in E$
2. $\displaystyle\sum_{(u,v)\in E} f(u,v) = \sum_{(v,w)\in E} f(v,w), \forall v \in V \setminus \{s, t\}$

The value of a flow f is defined:

$$ f = \sum_{(s,v)\in E} f(s,v) = \sum_{(v,t)\in E} f(v,t) $$

The maximum flow problem is to find a flow of maximum value.

Residual Network. The residual network of G induced by a flow f is $G_f=(N, E_f)$ where E_f, set of residual arcs, is constructed as follows. For $\forall e \in E$:

- If $f(e) = 0$: e is also an arc in E_f with capacity $r(e) = c(e)$.
- If $0 < f(e) < cap(e)$: e is also an arc in E_f with capacity $r(e) = c(e)-f(e)$. Add another arc e^{rev} in reverse direction of e with capacity $r(e^{rev}) = f(e)$ into E_f.
- If $f(e) = cap(e)$: e is not in E_f but an arc erev in reverse direction of e with the capacity $r(e^{rev}) = cap(e)$ is added into E_f.

Any residual arc $(u,v) \in E_f$ has capacity $r(u,v) > 0$; i.e., any arc in G_f can admit more flow. An example of a residual network is shown in the figure 1.

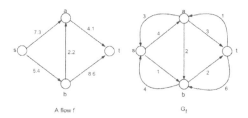

Fig. 1. Example of residual network

The residual network is actually network of remaining capacities on arcs.

Working on residual network, while the augmenting path algorithms maintain feasibility and attempt toward optimality, the preflow-push algorithms attempt toward feasibility. We will describe only the preflow-push technique in the following section.

2.2 Golberg-Tarjan's Preflow-Push Technique

For a node v, we call:

$$excess(v) = \sum_{(u,v)\in E} f(u,v) - \sum_{(v,w)\in E} f(v,w)$$

the *excess* of v. It is the difference between the total flow into v and the total flow out of v. The flow conservation constraint states that all nodes except s and t have zero excess.

By a relaxion on this constraint that no node in $V\backslash\{s,t\}$ has negative excess at intermediate steps, Karzanov has introduced notion of *preflow*. A preflow f is a function $f: E \rightarrow R^{\geq 0}$ with:

- $0 \leq f(e) \leq c(e), \forall\ e \in E$
- $excess(v) \geq 0, \forall\ v \in V \backslash \{s,t\}$

A node is *active* if its excess is positive. When such a node exists, the current flow is infeasible. The idea is then to *push* its excess flow to neighbors *closer* to the sink. To do this, Goldberg-Tarjan suggested a height function (or distance function) *height* on nodes of network such that valid heights satisfy: $height(t) = 0$ and $height(v) \geq height(u)+1, \forall(u,v) \in E_f$. In fact, $height(v)$ is a lower bound on the shortest path (on number of arcs) from node v to the sink t. A push is performed only from a higher node to a lower node. An residual arc $e = (v,u)$ is *admissible* for v if $height(v) = height(u)+1$.

Let v is an active node, $e = (v,u)$ is an outgoing residual arc from v. A push of $\delta=min\{excess(v), r(e)\}$ across e then sends δ unit flow from v to u. It increases *excess(u)* by δ and decreases *excess(v)* by δ. If e is an arc of G, a push across e increases the flow across e by δ and a push across e^{rev} decreases the flow across e by δ.

The Goldberg-Tarjan's algorithm searches for admissible arcs from an active node to push flow (source node is initially active). If no more admissible arcs exist, the heights are increased (lift the nodes) in order to create admissible arcs. Eventually the algorithm stops with no active nodes. At that stage the flow is feasible for the first time and also maximal.

```
Algorithm Preflow-push
begin
      height(s) := |V|, height(t) := 0
      compute the exact distance labels height(v), ∀v ∈V\{s,t}
      forall outgoing arcs e from s do saturate e
/*main loop*/
      while the network contains an active node do
            select an active node v
            push-lift(v)
end
Procedure push-lift(v)
begin
      if the network contains an admissible arc (v,u) then
            push min{excess(v),r(v,u)}units of flow from v to u
      else
            set height(v) = 1+ min{height(u) | r(v,u) > 0}
end
```

3 Our Distributed Algorithm

The Model of Computation. We assume that each node in the network G corresponds to a sequential process that executes asynchronously a program. Each arc (v,u) in G corresponds to a bi-directional communication link between process v and process u. All processes execute identical programs over local data. Processes may start executing the algorithm either at any arbitrary moment or upon receiving a message which triggers their execution of algorithm. Communications are in message-passing mode.

First, we describe how the algorithm operates in a global manner. Then, we will describe the local algorithm that each node must execute in to obtain the final result.

3.1 A High-Level Description

The execution of algorithm proceeds in two phases. The first phase sets heights of all nodes. The second phase establishes the maximum flow: each node either scans the downhill arcs and pushes as much flow as possible or lifts to continue transmitting flows.

(1) Initialization of node heights

We assume that the source node knows the number of nodes in graph, n. This phase will set sinks' heights to 0 and sources' heights to n. The heights of other nodes are set in breadth first search way. For starting, sinks scan its adjacency arcs and sends along init messages carried the height tag set to zero. When an init message arrives at a node, node's height is checked. If it is zero (for the first time the node receives this message) or strictly greater than message's height tag plus one, it is updated to new value. Once node's height is updated, the node will propagate init messages to neighbors over its incoming arcs of G and send messages informing its new height to neighbors over its outgoing arcs of G.

When the last init message reaches the source, the source will set its *excess* enough to saturate its outgoing arcs, and algorithm goes through the following second phase.

(2) The excess is pushed from the source downhill towards the sink

In this phase, we maintain the rule that only a higher node can push to a lower node.

The receipt of the last init message at source invokes a procedure which discharges its excess by pushing flow to neighbors. For the source, this procedure realizes saturating its outgoing arcs. When flow arrives to a node, it makes node's excess positive. Then this node will execute the same procedure above to transmit its excess to downhill neighbors. This procedure scans admissible arcs and tries to push as much flow as possible across. In our algorithm, a positive capacity link $e = (v,u)$ (also is an outgoing arc from v in residual network G_f at that moment) is admissible for v if $height_v \geq height_u+1$, that differs from the sequential algorithm because of our change below. When the node has no downhill neighbors, flow becomes trapped locally at node. At this moment, we must lift the node, and the flow is transmitted again.

There is a difference between our choices with sequential Golberg-Tarjan's algorithm of which responses to the following question: how much should we lift the node? Because a node, after lifting and pushing excess across the link, will continue to scan and choice another node to push if its excess remains positive. So we will increase node's height to a threshold which is just enough for that node can push all its remaining excess. This accelerates the execution of algorithm. To seek this threshold fast, for each node we can maintain a list of neighbor's heights in increasing order.

As we are in an asynchronous distributed network, there are moments when one node wants to transmit flow to a node which is lifting with its new height is greater than sender's height and still has not updated in sender's local data yet. This happens only when a node receives a push from a lower sender. Then the node must reply a non-successful message (which denotes that push is not permitted) in order to tell the sender to retire sent flow. Eventually, no more flow can reach the sink. As we continue to lift, the remaining excess flow eventually flows back towards the source. The algorithm will terminate when all the flows either are pushed into the sink or returned to the source.

3.2 Detail Description

Nodes. Node v maintains variables indicated in algorithm block 1 below, including the value of excess flow $excess_v$; its current height $height_v$; a list of neighbors $neighborlist_v$ with their current heights $height_v[u]$, $\forall u \in neighborlist_v$ and residual capacities of link (v, u), $r_v[u]$, $\forall u \in neighborlist_v$. For node v, $r_v[u]$ expresses existence of an outgoing arc from v to neighbor u in the residual network G_f reduced by flow f at that moment: when $r_v[u]$ is zero, there is no outgoing arc (v,u) in G_f. Node v has also a variable $type_v$ that denotes what kind it is. We define three possible kinds of nodes in the network: SOURCE, SINK, and NORMAL. In addition we have a variable *nbInitHeightMsgs* which is used for SOUCE nodes to count number of received init messages. Finally, a node has a state variable $state_v$.

Node states. A node is either *inactive* when node's excess is zero or *active* otherwise. Initially, all nodes are in the inactive state. The sink is always inactive. In the beginning of second phase, the source is active.

Messages. Messages (INIT-HEIGHT, h) are used in the first phase, where h is sender's height. On receiving this message, the receiver runs algorithm block 5 in which you can see the propagation of these messages. If receiver is SOURCE, the last INIT-HEIGHT message makes it active and procedure *push*() is invoked. This type of messages will not be used any longer.

Messages (PUSH-REQUEST, *value*) is used in the routine *push*(). Upon receipt of this message, the node checks sender's height in local data. If this value is not greater than its height, it will reply an answer message (PUSH-REQUEST-ANS, *value*, NOK) back to sender. Otherwise, the node accepts this push; updates its excess, its state (other SINK nodes) and capacity of correspondent link. If it is not a SINK node, it will call routine *push*() to discharge its excess flow. If this routine has terminated but the node still has excess then the procedure *lift*() will be invoked. The processing of PUSH-REQUEST messages is detailed in algorithm block 8.

About the sender of PUSH-REQUEST message, upon receipt of an answer (PUSH-REQUEST-ANS, *value*, NOK) (see algorithm block 9) it recovers sent flow by adding its excess to *value*, resets its state and updates capacity of correspondent link, calls routine *push*() and also *lift*() if it remains excess but has no admissible link.

Another type of message is (NEW-HEIGHT, h). We use these messages for updating a new height of a node. Upon receipt of this message, receiver updates sender's height in local data. Note that we can maintain the list of neighbor nodes in increasing order of node heights. This helps to determine fast the local variable height in algorithm block 10.

init-height(). This procedure propagates (INIT-HEIGHT, $height_v$) messages to neighbors over incoming arcs into v of G, and update new height of v in local data of neighbor nodes over outgoing arcs from v of G.

push(). This routine is presented in algorithm block 7. When a node (except SINK nodes) receives any message that makes its excess positive, it becomes active and executes the routine *push*(). This routine implements sending as much flow as possible to neighbor nodes over admissible links, i.e. neighbors are lower than node and correspondent links' residual capacities are positive. The node scans admissible links, and sends across PUSH-REQUEST messages with a value of flow set to minimum of its excess and link's residual capacity. The node also updates immediately his local variables such as value of excess, residual capacity of correspondent link. Once there are no more admissible links or node's excess is zero, the routine at node is stopped.

lift(). This procedure is called when the routine *push*() has stopped but the node's excess remains positive. First, the node calculates a new height such that this new height is just enough for the node can send all of its remaining excess. Then, the node sends NEW-HEIGHT messages to all its neighbors for updating its new height (see algorithm block 10).

When all nodes (except SOURCE nodes) are in state *inactive*, this means there are no more messages have been changed, the algorithm terminates.

---

1. Node variables

```
type_v  : (SOURCE, SINK, NORMAL)
state_v : (inactive, active)
excess_v : real;
height_v : integer;
neighborlist_v : list of neighbors;
height_v[u], ∀ u ∈ neighborlist_v : interger;
r_v[u], ∀ u ∈ neighborlist_v : real;
nbInitHeightMsgs : integer;
```

---

2. The Algorithm (as executed at each node)

```
/*As the first action of each process at node, the algorithm
must be initialized */
initializaton();
/* main loop */
while (true) do
     wait for incoming messages msg;
     process msg;
end while
```

---

3. initialization()

```
excess_v = 0;
state_v = inactive;
height_v = 0;
for all u ∈ neighborlist_v do
     if (u, v) is an incoming arc into vψin G then
          r_v[u] = 0;
     else
          r_v[u] = capacity of (v, u);
     end if
height_v[u] = 0;
end for
nbInitHeightMsgs = 0;
if type_v = SINK then
     init - height();
end if
```

---

4. init-height()

```
for all u ∈ neighborlist_v do
     if r_v[u] = 0 then
          Send (INIT-HEIGHT, height_v) to u;
     else
          Send (NEW-HEIGHT, height_v) to u;
     end if
end for
```

---

5. *Upon receipt of (INIT-HEIGHT, h) from w*

```
height_v[w] = h;
if type_v ≠ SOURCE then
    if (height_v = 0)||(height_v >(h + 1)) then
        height_v = h + 1;
        init - height();
    end if
else
    nbInitHeightMsgs_v = nbInitHeightMsgs_v + 1;
    if nbInitHeightMsgs_v = number of outgoing arcs of v then
        height_v = |V|
        excess_v = Σ_{u ∈ neighborlistv} r_v[u];
        state_v = active;
        push();
    end if
end if
```

---

6. *Upon receipt of (NEW-HEIGHT, h) msg from w*

```
height_v[w] = h;
```

---

7. *push()*

```
if type_v = SINK then
    while (excess_v > 0) && (∃u ∈ neighborlist_v such that (r_v[u]
    > 0) && (height_v[u] < height_v)) do
        δ = min{excessv, rv[u]} ;
        excess_v = excess_v - δ;
        r_v[u] = r_v[u] - δ;
        Send (PUSH-REQUEST, δ) to u;
    end while
end if
```

---

8. *Upon receipt of (PUSH-REQUEST, δ) msgfrom w*

```
if height_v[w] > height_v then
    r_v[w] = r_v[w] + δ;
    if (state_v = inactive)&&(type_v ≠ SINK) then
        state_v = active;
    end if
    excess_v = excess_v + δ;
    if type_v ≠ SINK then
        push();
        if excess_v > 0 then
            lift();
        end if
    end if
else
    Send (PUSH-REQUEST-ANS, δ, NOK) to w;
end if
```

---

9. Upon receipt of (PUSH-REQUEST-ANS, δ, NOK) msg from w

```
excess_v = excess_v + δ;
state_v = active;
r_v[w] = r_v[w] + δ;
push();
if excess_v > 0 then
     lift();
end if
```

---

10. lift()

```
if (type_v ≠ SOURCE)&&(type_v ≠ SINK) then
```
$$ht = min\{h\,|\,\textstyle\sum_{u \in neighborlist^v: height^v[u] \le_h} r_v[u] \ge excess_v\}$$
```
     height_v = ht + 1;
     for all u ∈ neighborlist_v do
            Send (NEW-HEIGHT, height_v) to u;
     end for
     push();
end if
```

3.3 Termination and Correctness Proof of the Algorithm

The algorithm will terminate because the number of messages exchanged is bounded. We will analyze and determine this upper bound in the following section. This type of termination is said "message termination".

When the algorithm terminates, there are no active nodes except the sources. Since source height is always equal to n, the residual network at this time contains no path from the source to the sink, so the flow is maximal.

4 Complexity of the Algorithm

4.1 Communication Cost

We first determine the total number of messages using in the first phase of algorithm. We have propagated init messages in breadth first search way and it is easy to see that the number of messages used for this is $2mn$.

To estimate the upper bound on the number of messages exchanged during second phase of algorithm, we use results in following lemmas.

Lemma 1. *The height of any node is bounded by* $2n - 1$, *where* $n = |V|$.

Proof: During the execution of algorithm, when a node v lifts, it is moved upward to a threshold h enough for v to push all its remaining excess. Then there are two cases:

Case 1. For admissible nodes u that $height_u < h - 1$: pushes from v to u will saturate links (v, u) in network, i.e. flow sent across (v, u) is $\delta = r_v[u]$. Such a push is called *saturating* (and *non-saturating* otherwise). Then after these pushes, there is no more such positive capacity link (v, u).

Case 2. For admissible nodes u that $height_u = h - 1$: pushes from v to u can saturate (v, u) or not, i.e. we can have two positive capacity links (v, u) and (u, v) after these pushes, but we have a constraint which is $height_v = height_u + 1$.

So after lifting v and discharging remaining excess of v, there exists no positive capacity link (v, u) from v such that $h = height_v > height_u + 1$, i.e. it doesn't exists any outgoing arcs (v, u) from v in residual network such that $height_v > height_u + 1$. As source nodes do not change heights n, height of any node v is bounded by the longest length (on number of arcs) of any path from v to s in the residual network, i.e. $height_v < 2n$.

Lemma 1 implies that total number of lifts of a node does not exceed $2n$. When this node lifts, there is a NEW-HEIGHT message transmitted across links from it. So total of NEW-HEIGHT messages across this link during second phase of algorithm does not exceed $4n$. This implicates total of NEW-HEIGHT messages across all links during second phase does not exceed $4mn$.

Lemma 2. *There are at most $3n^2/2 - 5n/2$ lifts and at most nm saturating pushes during the execution of algorithm.*

Proof: Using result of Lemma 1, and as there are no arcs (v, u) such that $height_v > height_u + 1$ in residual network, so the sum of node heights in network is bounded by $(n+1)+(n+2)+...+(2n-1) = 3n(n-1)/2$. In the beginning of second phase, this sum is at least n, so it increases by at most $3n(n-1)/2 - n = 3n^2/2 - 5n/2$. Each time when a node lifts, its height increases by at least one unit. So the total number of lifts during the execution of algorithm does not exceed $3n^2/2 - 5n/2$.

Now we consider an arc $(v, u) \in G$. For a saturating push across link (v, u), it must have $height_v \geq height_u + 1$, and for a saturating push across link (u, v) it must have $height_u \geq height_v + 1$. As $height_v$ and $height_u$ are inferior to $2n$, so number of saturating pushes across a link (vu) does not exceed n. This implies that the total of saturating pushes is at most nm.

Lemma 3. *The algorithm performs at most $2n^2(1+m)$ non-saturating pushes.*

Proof: The principle to prove lemma given here is due to [6,13]. Let A denote the set of active nodes. Consider a potential function $\Phi = \Sigma_{v \in A} height_v$. Initially $\Phi = 0$. During the execution of algorithm there are two possible cases:

Case 1. A node v wants to push his excess but there is no admissible link. In this case its height increase by $\varepsilon \geq 1$ units. So Φ is increased at most ε units. Since $height_v < 2n$, the total increase in Φ due to lifts is bounded by $2n^2$.

Case 2. There is an admissible link for node to push flow across. A saturating push on link (v, u) may create a new excess at node u, node u becomes active, and therefore increasing Φ by $height_u$ which is bounded by $2n$. According to the result of lemma 2, the number of saturating pushes does not excess nm, so Φ can increase $2n^2m$ over all saturating pushes. A non-saturating push across link (v, u) will deactivate v and may or may not activate u. Thus Φ decreases by $height_v$ but may increases by $height_u = (height_v - 1)$. In either case, Φ decreases by at least one unit per non-saturating push.

Finally, the total increase of Φ is at most $2n^2 + 2n^2m$. Each non-saturating push decreases Φ by at least one unit and at the end Φ is zero. Consequently, the algorithm can perform $2n^2+2n^2m = 2n^2(m+1)$ non-saturating pushes, proving the lemma.

Lemma 2 and 3 implies that the total pushes either saturating or non-saturating is bounded by $nm + 2n^2 + 2n^2m$. Supposing that all these pushes are successful, we now estimate the total number of non-successful pushes. A push can be refused only when the receiver lifts (but the sender is out of date). As there are at most $3n^2/2 - 5n/2$ lifts, so at most $3n2/2 - 5n/2$ non-successful pushes. A non-successful push needs a non-successful message. This implies that total number of messages being exchanged over all pushes, is at most $(3n^2/2-5n/2+nm+2n^2+2n^2m) = 2n^2m+7n^2/2+nm-5n/2$. These messages are PUSH-REQUESTs and PUSHREQUEST- ANS(NOK)s.

To summarize, the total number of messages used is bounded by $2mn + 4mn +2n^2m+7n^2/2+nm-5n/2 = 2n^2m+7nm+7n^2/2-5n/2$ that is correspondent to $O(n^2m)$.

4.2 Timing Cost

For the notion of time, we assume that all message delay times are bounded and equal. The distributed asynchronous algorithm is analyzed using the virtual notion of pulses of the algorithm. A pulse may actually be considered as the equivalent of a (global) clock pulse, or simultaneous clocks' ticks in a synchronous distributed system. During each pulse of the algorithm, nodes receive messages, perform local computation, and send messages destined to be received at the beginning of the next pulse.

Lemma 4. *The maximum number of pulses is at most* $n+2n^2$

Proof: Number of pulses for the last init message propagated from sinks to sources is at most equal to the longest path from sources to sinks. So the number of pulse in this phase of algorithm execution is less than n.

Now we consider number of pulses in second phase of algorithm. Consider a value of flow pushed from source to sink: if it is not trapped at any node, it is transmitted straight toward sink. And the number of pulses for this is the length of path on which flow is transmitted across. This number is less than n. If that value of flow is trapped at a node then this make node lift. So the number of pulses that assures a value of flow either pushed to sink or returned to source, is at most equal to the total number of lifts of all nodes on the longest path from source to sink hence is less than $2n^2$, proving the lemma.

The time complexity of algorithm is measured with at most the maximum number of pulses during execution of algorithm, that is $O(n^2)$.

5 Conclusion and Future Works

The estimate of message complexity can be still reduced. An amortized analysis on the numbers of pushes and on the number of lifts should give a better bound. And the algorithm can be still improved by *heuristics* in lifting a node.

We think that it is not possible to obtain a bound less than $O(n^2m)$ with $n = |V|$ for this kind of distributed maximum flow algorithm, but is possible to obtain improvements on the coefficients and other terms.

In the future we will improve this algorithm in order to adapt to the real-time flow problem [15].

References

1. Andrew V. Goldberg: Recent Developments in Maximum Flow Algorithms. Technical Report, April 1998
2. Andrew V. Goldberg and Robert E. Tarjan: A New Approach to the Maximum Flow Problem, Journal of ACM, 35(4):921-940, 1988
3. Harold N. Gabow: Scaling Algorithms for Network Problems. Journal of Computer and System Sciences, 31(2):148-168, 1985
4. Andrew V. Goldberg and Satish Rao: Beyond the Flow Decomposition Barrier. Journal of ACM, 45(5):783-797, 1998
5. Lester R. Ford and Delbert R. Fulkerson: Flows in networks. Princeton University Press, Princeton, 1962
6. Ravindra K. Ahuja, Thomas L. Magnanti and James B. Orlin: Network Flows – Theory, Algorithms and Applications. Prentice-Hall, Inc. USA, 1993
7. Jack Edmonds and Richard M. Karp: Theoretical Improvements in Algorithmic Efficiency for Network Flow Problems. Journal of ACM, 19(2):248-264, 1972
8. Dinic: Algorithm for Solution of a Problem in Networks with Power Estimation. Journal of ACM 19:248-264, 1972
9. Karzanov: Determining the Maximum Flow in a Network by the Method of Preflows. Soviet Mathematics Doklady, 15:434-437, 1974
10. J. Cheriyan and K. Mehlhorn: An analysis of the highest-level selection rule in the pre-flow-push max-flow algorithm. Information Processing Letters 69:239-242, 1999
11. Boris V. Cherkassky and Andrew V. Goldberg: On Implementing Push-Relabel Method for the Maximum Flow Problem. Algorithmica, Vol. 19, pages 390–410, 1997
12. Richard J. Anderson and Joáo C. Setubal: On the Parallel Implementation of Goldberg's Maximum Flow Algorithm. Proc. of the 4th Annual ACM Symp. on Parallel Algorithms and Architectures, pp. 168–177, 1992
13. Valmir C. Barbosa: An introduction to distributed algorithms. The MIT Press, Chapter 7, p200–216, 1996
14. Tuomo Takkula: A preflow-push algorithm that handles online max flow problems in a static asynchronous network (Revision 1.18). Chalmers University of Technology, Gothenbourg, Sweden, 2001
15. Naya Nagy and Selim G. Akl: The Maximum Flow Problem: A Real-Time Approach. Technical Report, Dept. of Computing and Information Sciences Queen's Univ., Canada, 2001
16. R. Ahlswede, N. Cai, S.-Y. R. Li and R. W. Yeung: Network information flow. IEEE Trans. on Information Theory, 46:1204-1216, 2000

Author Index